Curiosity's Cats

CURIOSITY'S CATS

Writers on Research

EDITED BY

BRUCE JOSHUA MILLER

MINNESOTA
HISTORICAL
SOCIETY PRESS

www.mhspress.org
The Minnesota Historical Society Press is a member of the Association of American University Presses.

Manufactured in [the United States of America/Canada]

10 9 8 7 6 5 4 3 2 1

∞ The paper used in this publication meets the minimum requirements of the American National Standard for Information Sciences—Permanence for Printed Library Materials, ANSI Z39.48–1984.

International Standard Book Number
ISBN: 978-0-87351-922-9 (paper)
ISBN: 978-0-87351-933-5 (e-book)

Library of Congress Cataloging-in-Publication Data
Curiosity's cats : writers on research / edited by Bruce Joshua Miller.
    pages cm
  Includes bibliographical references.
  ISBN 978-0-87351-922-9 (paper : alkaline paper) —
  ISBN 978-0-87351-933-5 (ebook)
  1. Learning and scholarship. 2. Research. 3. Authorship. 4. Historiography. 5. Scholars—Biography. 6. Authors—Biography. 7. Historians—Biography. I. Miller, Bruce Joshua.
  AZ186.C87 2014
  001.2—dc23
                                            2014005369
This and other Minnesota Historical Society Press books are available from popular e-book vendors.

For my wife, Julia,

for Pam McClanahan,

for my parents, Jordan and Anita Miller,

and my brothers, Eric and Mark,

and for independent booksellers everywhere

CURIOSITY'S CATS

- 3 -
Bruce Joshua Miller
INTRODUCTION

- 9 -
Ali Selim
STAY HERE AS LONG AS YOU LIKE

- 33 -
Steve Yates
TO UNDERSTAND YOU MUST BREAK IN

- 48 -
Alberto A. Martínez
DATING ALBERT EINSTEIN

- 73 -
Katherine Hall Page
RESEARCH CAN BE MURDER

- 87 -
Margot Livesey
HE LIKED CUSTARD

- 95 -
Theodore Kornweibel, Jr.
PROSPECTING THE PAST

- 120 -
Bruce White
A GOOD TURN EVERY DAY: A BOY IN DULUTH IN 1926

- 149 -
Annette Kolodny
CURIOUS ENCOUNTERS IN MY SEARCH FOR VINLAND

- 171 -
Jan Reid
COMANCHES, COWBOYS,
AND A POLITICAL ROCK STAR

- 202 -
Bruce Joshua Miller
THE MAD BOMBER GUY

- 245 -
Philip J. Anderson
PILGRIM VOICES:
PURITANS, IMMIGRANTS, AND HISTORICAL RESEARCH

- 267 -
Ned Stuckey-French
AN ESSAYIST'S GUIDE TO RESEARCH AND FAMILY LIFE

- 285 -
Marilyn Stasio
YOUR RESEARCH—OR YOUR LIFE!

CURIOSITY'S CATS

Bruce Joshua Miller

INTRODUCTION

This remarkable collection of thirteen original essays presents an engaging mix of writers—novelists, historians of science and literature, journalists, and a filmmaker—who explore, in a personal and informal way, the excitement or disappointment of scrutinizing books, periodicals, photographs, and other documents in libraries, conducting face-to-face interviews, or wandering obscure and lonely patches of geography in the course of their nondigital research projects. In addition to accounts of research done in support of published books or a completed film, _Curiosity's Cats_ includes essays about research heretofore unsung, done in a spirit of pure inquiry or for reasons only the essayist can explain.

In "To Understand You Must Break In," fiction writer Steve Yates remembers the boyhood summer day he accidentally destroyed his family's "prized Curtis Mathes television set." From that moment on he was free to explore the world around him, "the miracle of the public library and the vigorous society of a neighborhood full of children," a season of adventures that led him toward fiction writing.

Such a message would be anathema to the digital acolytes of our present era, when students at all levels (not to mention many parents) find screens of various dimensions commanding much of their attention. Students sleep with their smartphones, text during classes, and research term papers by clicking in the search field of our One True Church of Inquiry. In his 2013 presidential address at the annual meeting of the American Historical Association, William Cronon shared observations on his students' approaches to research and their reading habits:

> One of my deepest fears about this brave new digital world has to do with reading itself . . . It seems to me that the book-length monograph on which our discipline has long relied is very much at risk as texts

migrate from paper to screens . . . My deeper fear comes from watching my own students, many of whom no longer read books for pleasure. If they have any prior experience doing research, almost all of it is online. If a piece of information cannot be Googled, it effectively does not exist for them . . .

In a manically multitasking world where even e-mail takes too long to read, where texts and tweets and Facebook postings have become dominant forms of communication, reading itself is more at risk than many of us realize. Or, to be more precise, long-form reading is at risk: the ability to concentrate and sustain one's attention on arguments and narratives for many hours and many thousands of words.

As three-year-olds fix their vulnerable eyes on iPads and children shun the creativity of outdoor play for online games, the *cats* of this volume provide a healthy corrective to the presumptions of the wired world.

One of these presumptions is that everything an educator or student or scholar needs is available through the Internet, an opinion apparently shared by Department of Education secretary Arne Duncan and many school superintendents as they champion reliance on computer technology for classroom teaching. Such digital advocacy carries the smug certainty that anyone raising objections to the unbridled growth of technology is a Luddite, an ignoramus, a fool, or a fuddy-duddy. Despite the unqualified embrace of the digital revolution by many people in positions of authority, legitimate concerns of all sorts have been raised about the physical and psychological effects of the unrestricted use of wireless devices, particularly by children.

My point is that one cannot discuss the convenience and benefits of the digital access many of us enjoy without including the social, political, and environmental consequences of our device-centered world. The reliance on coal and nuclear power by major online services, the proliferation of toxic waste in the form of discarded cell phones and computer equipment, and the withdrawal from society fostered by technology that Sherry Turkle has written about ("The Flight from Conversation," *New York Times,* April 22, 2012) are just a few examples of the unhappy reality behind the sleek edifice of our ubiquitous screens.

My purpose in this introduction is not to frame a lengthy indictment of our misplaced technophilia (and I do not speak for the writers included in this volume) but, in part, to draw attention to an oppositional dimension residing within this book. Nonetheless, many of the essays discuss the invaluable resources offered online. Fact checking my own essay, "The Mad Bomber Guy," based on research I began more than twenty years ago, I found myself reflexively looking things up on a search engine. While I was occasionally surprised at what I found, I was more often surprised by what I found no trace of.

The esteemed textual scholar G. Thomas Tanselle has written, in "Texts and Artifacts in the Electronic Era," that convenience of textual access comes "at the price of removing them [texts] from their original contexts." I believe this was a prescient remark, as the more easily accessed a text becomes, the less likely delivery will include its context. Take for instance the immensely valuable *New York Times* digital archives. Unlike the microform text, which has its own drawbacks, digital access cuts, as with a scissors, an article out of its page, yielding a portable document format, an isolated electronic image without a view of articles or advertisements on that same page or the facing page.

What is the provenance of the article? How did it get there? Writers doing hands-on research surely want to know. *Curiosity's Cats: Writers on Research* is a book about contexts, primary sources, and the indispensable value of libraries and archives as repositories of original books, documents, manuscripts, newspapers, periodicals, photographs, and tracts. The destruction and dumping of printed artifacts such as books and newspapers by major libraries has been chronicled by Nicholson Baker in his book *Double Fold: Libraries and the Assault on Paper*. As I write, controversy rages around the misguided "renovation" plan that would transfer a large portion of the New York Public Library's research collection on Fifth Avenue to storage in New Jersey and would sell off the Mid-Manhattan branch across the street.

Tanselle's brilliant essay (easily found at a site on Columbia University's web page) explains how misguided is the idea "that [research library] book stacks can gradually be abandoned as texts are incorporated into machine-readable databases." The printed book is not simply a disposable wrapper of words but a tangible record of printing, publishing, textual, and cultural history inseparable from its life as a physical object. "The misconception that texts are easily extractable from books," writes Tanselle, "has contributed to policy decisions—all the more shocking for being deliberate—that will mark the present as an age of destruction on a scale beyond even that of the book burnings of the past."

While not every essay presented here was born of visits to a research library, all of them required examination of paper records or interviews and concomitant action beyond computer searches.

In "Dating Albert Einstein," a tour de force of convincing logic and skillful research, Alberto Martínez recounts his efforts to determine the exact date of Albert Einstein's "flash of insight" that brought to fruition the theory of special relativity. Martínez traveled to Switzerland, examining rare books, newspapers, and manuscripts. Writing his essay required an understanding of philosophy, history, Einstein's biography, and the layout of the city of Bern, where Einstein lived.

"I'd heard, too often, the old admonition: write what you know," says the novelist Margot Livesey in her essay "He Liked Custard." "I was slow to understand that research could allow me to know more. Slower still to understand that research has its own dangerous siren song." She adds that although the Internet has made research easier, "for me there remains no substitute for the living encounter, the way a woman's face changes as she tries to tell you what it's like to lose her memory."

We learn from reading "Stay Here as Long as You Like" by filmmaker Ali Selim that he spent "nineteen years of my life creating and distributing a film" based on the short story "A Gravestone Made of Wheat" by Will Weaver. The research for the script of what became the movie *Sweet Land* was no simple matter. A turning point in his struggle to breathe life into his characters came when he discovered a cache of historical farm photographs at the Minnesota History Center library.

Like Selim, other *cats* in this collection measure their research experience not in terms of weeks or months but years. "The research and writing of the novel [*Comanche Sundown*] consumed twenty-five years," Jan Reid explains in his essay, in which he describes the difference between researching a novel and his recent biography of Ann Richards, *Let the People In.*

Literary critic and scholar Annette Kolodny spent untold years researching her book *In Search of First Contact: The Vikings of Vinland, the Peoples of the Dawnland, and the Anglo-American Anxiety of Discovery.* "Altogether, over the years," she tells us in her essay about interviews she conducted in New England, "this research took me to Norway, Denmark, the Archives of the Indies at the University of Seville in Spain, the Canadian Maritime Provinces, Maritime Quebec, the tip of New-foundland, and all across northern New England."

Historian Theodore Kornweibel, Jr., has spent a lifetime break-ing new ground in the field of African American history. "I wouldn't choose to be a heart surgeon or a rock star. Too prosaic," he writes. "Amazonian explorer or astronaut? Not exciting enough. For real thrills give me history, raw history, unexplored history, history you have to dig out, dirt-under-your-fingernails history. The zenith of *my* prospecting has been to uncover the black railroad heritage in all its forgotten complexity and unrecognized drama, published as *Railroads in the African American Experience: A Photographic Journey*."

In "An Essayist's Guide to Research and Family Life," Ned Stuckey-French says "at our house it's all research all the time." As an essayist and literary historian married to novelist Elizabeth Stuckey-French, he knows whereof he speaks. For most of the contributors to this book his words might stand as a motto.

I think of this book as a house with adjoining rooms where our curious cats, like musicians, practice their art. While reading Alber-to Martínez, try listening to Mozart, Antonin Dvořák, or Beethoven. Theodore Kornweibel might go best with jazz, maybe bebop. While reading Marilyn Stasio's suspenseful "Your Research—or Your Life!" start with "I Heard It Through the Grapevine" and end with "A Whiter Shade of Pale."

All playfulness aside, I believe the music and substance of each es-sayist's voice requires no accompaniment. A poetic essay such as Bruce White's "A Good Turn Every Day: A Boy in Duluth in 1926" begins in delight and ends in wisdom, and this alone makes the price of admis-sion to this house of cats worthwhile.

Chicago, Illinois
January 2014

ACKNOWLEDGMENTS

First, thanks to all my cats: you were a pleasure to herd! It has been a wonderful experience to work with and publish you.

This book was born as a result of a conversation I had with Pamela McClanahan, director of the Minnesota Historical Society Press, during a mild Chicago winter where we talked about library reading rooms and the pleasures of research. Pam's immediate endorsement of the idea of a book of essays set things in motion: my heartfelt thanks to Pam for her confidence in me.

I am grateful to Shannon Pennefeather for her patience and for making this a better book than it would have been had she not taken it in hand.

Design and production manager Dan Leary worked his magic to produce a cover that many an author might envy and some mystery authors kill for.

Thanks to Marilyn Stasio for her advice and encouragement and her willingness early in the project to assume the guise of a feline. Thanks also to Margot Livesey. And special thanks to Ali Selim for his enthusiasm and help.

I also offer special thanks to Steve Yates, whose alacrity in becoming the first of curiosity's cats to provide a manuscript advanced this project immeasurably.

Thanks to my wife, Julia Anderson-Miller, for slogging through an early draft of my essay, "The Mad Bomber Guy."

Many others made helpful suggestions about the book, including Lisa Baudoin, Andrew Chapman, Franklin Dennis, Ed Devereaux, Pat Frovarp, Paul Ingram, Alex Holzman, Gianna LaMorte, Mark Crispin Miller, Lynn Mooney, and Clair Willcox.

Stay Here as Long as You Like

One Sunday morning in the fall of 1990, I read a story in *Picture Magazine*, a supplement to the *Minneapolis Star Tribune*. I was drawn to the story because on the contributors' page there was a photo with the caption "Minnesota Author Will Weaver." He was bearded and windblown, clearly standing on the plains somewhere looking upward to the place where good, intelligent people gain answers or strength. Or so I thought then. Now, after years of photographing people, I know we have the subjects look up because it tightens portions of their skin, giving them a smooth, youthful elegance. Anyway, I knew I wanted to be a writer, to have people one day refer to me as a "Minnesota Author," and this alone drew me to read Will's story, "A Gravestone Made of Wheat." It was a fateful decision that would define my life for nearly the next two decades.

I was deeply moved by the story. It is about a Norwegian immigrant farmer living in Minnesota named Olaf Torvik whose wife, Inge Altenberg, has recently died. The local sheriff arrives after the funeral to remind the family that, though traditional in these farming communities, home burials were no longer legal. The family would have to take Inge's casket to town, to the cemetery.

This causes Olaf to think back to the time Inge first came to Minnesota. His parents, who continued to live in Norway, were sending a German girl—who had survived the horrors of World War I by hiding in their village—to Minnesota as a mail-order bride for their bachelor son. In the United States, following the war, there were laws that forbade the migration of "enemies" and "undesirables" and, in fact, Germans.

Inge remains in Minnesota. She and Olaf build a life, a family, and a vast farm together in spite of being ostracized from the community. Now, in the present time, it doesn't seem right to Olaf to bury his beloved Inge in town alongside the very people who rejected her some fifty years ago. His clear memories of the two of them and their life together on this land bring him to a decision: a surreptitious burial deep in the wheat field, far away from the sheriff's curiosity.

The story concludes with this paragraph:

> The furrows rolled up shining in the night light. Olaf knew this earth. It was heavy soil, had never failed him. He knew also that next year, and nearly forever after, there would be one spot in the middle of the field where the wheat grew greener, taller, and more golden than all the rest. It would be the gravestone made of wheat.

I cried when I read that, not only because it is a specific and powerful moment in Olaf's life, and a very fine and surprising ending to a lovely story, but also because those words made the emotional context of the story more immediate and personal for me. Those four words—"and nearly forever after"—were inclusive of me, and my generation. They took a story that was ostensibly about our great-grandparents and thrust it through subsequent generations, through our grandparents and parents down into me and beyond, to generations not yet conceived. In that story was the greatest history lesson I had ever experienced and the strongest connection I had ever felt to my heritage. What had been *over there* was suddenly transported *right here*.

I read it again. And I cried again.

I thought if those words moved me, they would surely move others. In those four words lay my decision to spend the next nineteen years of my life creating and distributing a film inspired by that short story. I procured the rights from the author, Will Weaver, for a stated period of time—three years, I believe. Somewhere along the way he realized that this process takes a lot longer than anyone could imagine, and he somehow—inexplicably, for I had not done anything yet to earn his faith—believed I would see it through. He sent me a supportive note in which he wrote, "you have rented an unused room in my house, rearranged the furniture to suit your needs, yet much to my liking. As long as you find the room useful, you can stay here as long as you like."

In Will's poetic way he was saying, "take your time in making the movie."

And I did.

Clearly I wouldn't have signed up for nineteen years, nor would have Will. I was new to the process. I had no idea I would spend fifteen years writing the script and procuring financing, and that the film, which was released in 2006, would live on in our house (and in our garage, storage space, and bedroom closet and on our dining room table) forever as my wife and I managed international distribution. In the beginning, I truly believed that I would present the short story, with all of its scope, history, and themes, inclusive of those four words, to any Hollywood producer and he or she would buckle, cry as I did, and finance a sizeable budget.

I tried. They didn't.

I can pooh-pooh their shortsightedness, their narrow-mindedness, Hollywood's seemingly idiotic, formulaic, greedy blockbuster mentality, but in reality what I was envisioning from Will's story wasn't a big, commercial film—I just didn't know it yet. I would learn that *Sweet Land* was a small and personal film. Hollywood's rejection gave me the time to mature, to research and discover, in a very authentic way, what the industry means when it says "small and personal." Ultimately, understanding this scope, scale, and tone was at the core of what made *Sweet Land* successful.

The emotional truths of the story resonated with me when I read it. I am a romantic by trade and temperament; I had been in love from as early as that sort of thing is allowed, so I knew the feeling. I was in love at the time I read the story and remain in that particular love. I met my wife when I was working at Grand Performance Cycles in St. Paul, Minnesota. She arrived one day to buy a racing bike. Thirty years later we still ride together. By the time the story was published that Sunday morning in 1991, we had two of our three children and I was well on my way to exploring the themes of family and fatherhood. I assumed I would be able to write about all of these themes from experience, however embryonic my knowledge may have been at the time.

But the story was about so much more.

There were themes I couldn't begin to grasp until I went back to the source material to understand the scope of its history. Will forces the reader to do the math, not my strong suit. He tells us that Olaf's parents wrote a letter "in June of 1918" saying they were sending a girl for him to marry. I assumed letters traveled by boat, and that it would have taken around two years for several to go back and forth as they made plans, which would have brought Inge to Minnesota around 1920.

And when she arrived, she lacked proper documentation to be legally married, and so another round of letters went back and forth, putting us in 1921 or 1922. While they waited for these letters, Olaf slept in the barn loft and Inge stayed in the house. In the eyes of the community they were living in sin and were shunned. But they fell in love, and no documented evidence or community disapproval could take that away, and so one night Inge left the house and climbed to the loft, where she and Olaf consummated their love.

In the final part of the equation, Will Weaver tells the reader, "That night she came to him in the loft was 45 years past." So, Inge's burial, depending on the international postal service's efficiency back in the 1920s, I was proud to have calculated, would have taken place in 1967, maybe 1966.

I didn't have to go to the library to realize that Inge, a German and an illegal immigrant, lived in Minnesota through some very explosive and interesting times: World War II, in which her eldest would most likely have served; the unrest of the 1960s; the volatility of the farm economy throughout the century; Hubert Humphrey's contributions to national politics; and the arrival in Minnesota of the Vikings and the Twins.

But I needed more *information* about what it meant to live through these times. Thinking back to what the word meant then, when I began this project, versus what it means now makes me realize that "information," the definition of information, the use of information has changed so drastically with the Internet, I probably could not make the same film today that I set out to make twenty-two years ago.

My daughter is seventeen and has held a smartphone in her hands or pressed into the back pocket of her skinny jeans for as long as I can remember. The paperless bills tell me she sends and receives, on average, nearly twenty thousand texts per month. If I really want to know something about her—how she is feeling, how she did on the math test, what her dreams are for her future—I can ask her, looking into her eyes in a way that we used to call "personal" (now they call it "analog"), and she'll probably say, "I don't know." But if I text her one of these questions, I'll get a meaningful and oftentimes revealing answer.

Her smartphone plan also gives her 2 GB of data per month to access the Internet, which is, if you believe the commercials, all the information in the world available anywhere, anytime, at your fingertips.

No libraries. No encyclopedias. No analog connection with other human beings.

Once, I saw a cartoon in the *New Yorker* entitled "Before the Internet." Three people sit in a restaurant booth. The first asks, "Who played the superintendent on that TV show from the early seventies? The one with the three veterinarians?" The second person calmly says, "I don't know." But the third, in a hair-raising panic, screams, "Oh, my God! We may never know."

AI, or "after the Internet," is the only world my daughter has ever known. She is the last in a line of three children and, as a result and much to her chagrin, gets a lot of quality adult time with her two delightful parents and their entertaining friends. No matter how compelling she may find the new show at the Los Angeles County Museum of Art, or conversations at dinner with writers and artists, or the natural beauty of standing on the summit of Mount Baldy, she always has her smartphone in hand. A friend is texting her. She is texting a friend. Multitasking, she simultaneously listens to our conversations and, if one of the adults so much as quietly wonders, "Who played the super on that TV show from the early seventies?" my daughter, within seconds—nay, by the time the last aspiration of the question mark has left our lips—is reciting the name of an obscure actor that has no meaning in or impact on her seventeen-year-old life, and yet she reads to us all of his credits, then links to who wrote that particular show and all of his credits, which takes her to another link about the Emmy Awards. And then, with her phone's GPS and yet another link, she can show us a Google Map 360-degree street view of the actor's star on the Hollywood Walk of Fame. She'll add, "Oh, I know where that is. It's right by Tender Greens, see? Remember that great salad we had there?" At which point all of the adults have long forgotten the original query.

Information has changed. What is it, exactly? Is the actor's name really information? I mean, of course it is information, but is it really? In the old days, up until the time I was about thirty-five, information was protected in specific places. We would do research to find information, and then we would use it, store it, connect it, relate it, and interpret it in an attempt to form opinions and gain knowledge. Some of it was here, some of it was there, but information didn't float in space, through the ether: you had to go find it in bricks and mortar.

When I was young, my parents constantly and dutifully updated their set of *World Book Encyclopedias,* and our living room bookshelf was usually my first, most lazy stop for information. Remember the twelve-page glossy supplement the publisher would send when, for example, the Vietnam war ended, or when *those who know best* decided conclusively that the world was round, or homosexuality was not a mental disorder, and you would peel off a wax-paper ribbon that covered an adhesive strip so you could permanently affix these conclusions and corrections into your main source of information? I loved doing that. It was what we would today call "interactive." And it gave the information contained therein a feeling of being current and complete. If for some reason our *World Book* or its supplements didn't answer my questions, I went next door.

Our neighbors in the big red brick house were historians, archivists, and, to a certain degree, hoarders. They owned, cataloged in chronological order and cross-referenced, a complete set of *National Geographic* magazines from their first subscription in 1921. This family was so knowledgeable and efficient that if we called in advance to request a specific issue, it would be waiting on an old library table in their basement by the time we arrived five minutes later. If I had a broad topic, but no specific issue referenced, they would have multiple magazines waiting with the pages opened to articles they thought applied. They moved in mysterious ways. I think all of this information was part of their being. They had the type of brain that will no longer exist by the time members of the Internet generation are in their fifties or sixties.

But not all information existed in *National Geographic,* either. If what I needed for a term paper wasn't available next door, one of the neighbors would contact the Minneapolis downtown library and ask for some books to be pulled on my behalf. When I arrived the next day, the books would be waiting on a rolling cart behind the head librarian's desk.

Visiting the library, whether a branch or the majestic and all-encompassing downtown library-with-planetarium, was a field trip filled with excitement and a sense that "anything could happen." It felt like a place where information *should* reside. People cared about this information, knew where it was stored and how to access it; they respected it and shepherded it in a way we don't with Internet information. The library was filled with readers, people looking outside of their head for knowledge, not blogging for personal validation or fishing for like-minded conspiracy theorists. When you went to the alphabetically organized stacks in search of books by Norman Mailer, which may have been all checked out, you might for the first time encounter Naguib Mahfouz, read *The Palace Walk,* and thereby expand your universe beautifully. Today, if you Google "Mailer," you'll get twenty-nine thousand results about envelopes and postage scales but nothing ever, no way, no how about Naguib Mahfouz, or Curzio Malaparte, for that matter. I love the Internet and Google, or "the Google," as George W. called it, and I use it constantly when I write, but I don't consider twenty-nine thousand comparisons and definitions of envelopes to be useful information, nor do I feel that any combination of these results will expand my universe, inform my horizons, or improve my writing in any way. It just doesn't feel like research, not in the way I was taught research should feel—like a journey, rather than an accident.

Aside from alphabetical connections, I made human connections during my library visits. Perhaps a librarian was interested in why I was looking for soil conditions from 1910 to 1923 in the Red River Valley, and revealed she had grown up on a farm there. Or, wandering the stacks, I struck up a conversation with a man who had read *Minnesota Farm Economy: The Sugar Beet, Boom or Bust* and knew of a book better suited to my needs. He walked me over to its Dewey decimal–mandated position on the shelves, and we talked the entire way. Sadly, that has all changed. Transmitting an SMS text with poor punctuation and acronyms like "LOL" or "@TEOTD" is not a human connection forged.

To find out more about the characters' lives in Will Weaver's story, I went to the library. I read books on the wars, on twentieth-century politics, and on farming. I read academic treatises on the wheat boom of 1913, which I surmised Olaf would have somehow experienced. And, before I knew it, I was churning out drafts of the script that contained numbers-based, archaic historical minutiae, like election result percentages from the Woodrow Wilson versus Charles E. Hughes presidential run; 1920 Chicago grain exchange rates; or Northern Pacific Railway schedules in and out of St. Paul.

I was never a historian. My history professor in high school, Sylvester Turbes—clear, passionate, and inspiring—mesmerized me, but since he never uttered the words, as Will Weaver had—"and nearly forever after"—I never understood what, for example, the landing at Kips Bay, or the building of a macadam road in Colonial Virginia had to do with me. So, I was very proud of the research I had done and of the drafts I was producing. I could hardly wait for Professor Turbes to see the film and reconsider the average grade he put on my report card.

It took me a while—perhaps a long while, thus the nineteen years—to realize I had forgotten to include the human truths, the authentic emotional core that make a story a story and not a documentary. I am told *Sweet Land* is "about" a great many things: religion, community, xenophobia, history, relationships, agriculture, generations, heritage, commerce, and a host of other themes of which I was unaware but about which I was invited to speak to various enthusiastic groups in the aftermath of *Sweet Land*'s success.

What it is really "about," what audiences connect with more than anything else, I believe, is love, pure and simple. *Sweet Land* is about a man and a woman who do not speak the same intellectual language but who share an energy that they each find vital to their lives. Honestly, I don't know many men and women who do speak the same language, and so *Sweet Land* is, in a way, about all of us.

My job as a storyteller is to create authentic characters and put them in a three-dimensional world where they can duke it out, much to our delight. In many ways, the men and women of 2005 are hungry, lonely, cold, desirous, fulfilled, or satiated in very much the same manner people were in 1920 or 1530. Some of the details of daily life are different, for sure, but the foundations of humanity remain the same.

During this time, I taught myself to write. I first had to understand my failure in the initial drafts, to be able to read them and say, "*this* is right, and *that* is unnecessary." It took longer than one would think. Then I had to seek out ways of discerning the difference between historical backgrounds versus emotional authenticity, of understanding what foundations of the human condition were the same in 2005 and what details were different from 1920. It makes sense, but creating a three-dimensional world from a time you never witnessed while keeping it emotionally authentic and relevant for today is . . . well, for me it was a knock-down, drag-out challenge.

I had the idea that maybe the Minnesota Historical Society would have more information that directly related to my quest: papers, memoirs, letters—hell, maybe even love letters that were filed in a box somewhere, untouched by academic hands and interpretation. I imagined discovering a diary from a farmer who lived in Minnesota around 1920 detailing all of his deepest thoughts and emotions that was then found under the mattress by his family when he died and subsequently donated to the historical society for preservation. Hey, a guy can dream, can't he?

The library at the Minnesota Historical Society was new, brand new. The building and the librarians had a sense of pride. It was windowless but warmed by the perfect selection of lights. Whereas other libraries felt like they presented an opportunity to ferret out information, this one made me feel I could gain knowledge just by being inside its four walls.

They had stuff: boxes of documents, letters—mostly official—and newspapers. The librarian found a diary, a farmer's diary from 1916. My heart raced for a moment, but then I found pages of entries such as, "August 23—fixed fence"—pages and pages of days with a single, three-word entry justifying how he spent the valuable hours in a day rather than revealing his feelings, emotions, or desires.

I read everything I could and hired a research assistant to read more, hopefully to offer a perspective that my brain could not access. Still, I ended up with drafts and drafts of my script consisting of historical detail and very little emotional revelation. I am not sure why, but I lamented this to one of the librarians at the Minnesota Historical Society. If only I could access it, whatever "it" was, I was certain I could write it. The librarian—and I wish I had recorded her name because she would still be receiving punctual birthday and holiday cards from me—offered, "How about photographs?"

Simple idea. Such a clear thought. It had never occurred to me.

The next day I returned. She had pulled nearly twenty file boxes of photographs. They were sitting on a dolly cart and took up an imposing 120 square feet of space. Most of the photographs contained in these boxes were journalistic rather than emotional and artistic—an archivist's desire to preserve a building, or a harness, or a pair of boots. They would be interesting for art direction and props in my movie, but that would come later. I had to write the script first.

Those twenty boxes held probably ten thousand photos. From those ten thousand, I culled maybe a hundred, mostly formal images. You have to understand that cameras back in the 1920s were huge and cumbersome and photos were rare, costly, and exclusive. There were no snapshots. People posed—dressed in their Sunday best, having prepared for days—and brought expressions to the photo shoot that were a mix of fear, awkwardness, uncertainty, and a sense of expectation that this is how one should look in a photograph. Yet in spite of all that rigidity there was the occasional photograph that benefited from the skills an expert photographer, or perhaps a rank amateur, or a moment of cloud cover over the piercing sun, or possibly a barn animal's grunt that seemed to disarm the subjects for a brief moment and softened their eyes, their expression, or their hands, and within that softening I could access them, their feelings, that elusive "it." Inspired by the eyes and hands and body language of the subjects in these photos, entire life stories flooded into my imagination. I uncovered a photo of a man and his horse (a comedic version of which ended up in the film). The look in the man's eyes, whether it was warmth, soul, or abject fear at the thought of having his photo taken, was so revealing to me; it provided access to his true personality. And his hands, large and rugged from probably having cleared his 160 acres of fieldstone and bramble years before, were now gently caressing the nose of his horse, appreciating the creature's existence and loyalty but also, I imagined, comforting the horse, saying, "If you're half as frightened by this camera as I am, I don't know how we are going to get through this, but we'll get through it together."

I had those one hundred photographs copied. I taped them to the walls near my computer. In them I found conflicts and resolutions, sadness and joy. This is where inner secrets lie, where humanity is revealed, and where I found the story I needed to write. Mostly. But I still felt like I wanted more than a man, his horse, and my imagination imposing a reality on them.

I went back to my friend at the library with some abstract and impossible task like, "Do you have any more photos? Photos of people, like, in love?" I thought, wrongly, I would find something in the way they were holding hands or looking at one another. But I knew better, really. I knew there were no such photographs taken at a time when formality undermined spontaneity.

Again, a simple idea from my librarian—the one who should be receiving birthday and holiday wishes from me—in the form of, "Why don't you try talking to people who lived then? Some of them, if you hurry, would still be alive."

My maternal grandparents, born in 1894 and 1896, had passed away in 1989 and 1991. I had listened to them tell stories all my life. From a young age, I had an appreciation for heritage, personal histories, and artifacts in their home. This probably explained, at least in part, my deep interest in and response to Will's story. But I'd never spoken to my grandparents specifically about life on the farm in 1920. I felt woefully stuck again but, taking the advice that I should hurry, set out to ask friends about their grandparents, check with nursing homes, and consult a couple of history professors whom I knew were interested in Minnesota of that era.

I explained to a handful of elderly Scandinavian folks in nursing homes that I was writing a movie and wanted to talk to them about life on the farm around World War I. The movie part threw them for a loop. It probably made no sense or seemed like a lie. Most of them assumed a posture like the subjects from the 1920 photographs, as in, "This is how you talk to movie people." They said obvious things, like "it was cold" and "it was difficult," that sounded as though they had recently watched a PBS documentary and figured that's what I wanted to hear. One Norwegian woman said, "Oh, why don't you talk to Siiri. She's from Finland. She'd probably like to have her picture taken in your movie. I don't."

One night, as my wife and two boys slept upstairs and I sat alone downstairs in the dark living room, wide awake, visited once again by the insomnia whose genesis was probably this project, it occurred to me in that *what-would-my-librarian-do?* sort of way that my mother, though born in 1926, had lived with her parents on the farm and witnessed their connection, their behavior, and their lives.

When I was a kid, my maternal grandfather was my buddy. I loved him. He was strong and big and had an ease my academic, college professor father lacked. Gramps was fun.

But the stories my mother remembered were that of a terrible drunk, a failure who lost the farm—twice—and a mean, bitter man who abused his wife, his children, and his animals. There were no memories of community or love, the stories I felt I so desperately needed. So, I made a trip with my mom down to her childhood farm for a visit that would hopefully nudge some other, more productive memories from her mind.

Ownership of the farm bounced around over the decades but always within her extended family. It was very easy to trace from cousin to cousin-once-removed and locate a telephone number. The farm was about two and a half hours away from the Twin Cities, down in the southern reaches of Blue Earth County outside the town of Granada. We called in advance but could not reach the current owners. We drove down anyway, figuring we could just look at the fields, smell the earth, and feel the sunshine or the rain, whatever we would be blessed with that day.

When we arrived it was quiet. There was no car in the yard. No animals in the barn. There was a new house, a rambler that had clearly been built in the 1960s and replaced the old farmhouse where my mom had eaten, read, slept, and dreamt. Why? We had no idea. I decided to knock on the door to announce our presence. I left my mom in the car temporarily in the event this turned out to be *The Shining* and not a *Sweet Land* research trip. There were a couple of doors on the front of the house that faced the road, and at first I couldn't figure out where to knock. I tried both, back and forth, smiling and waving to my mom, who was most likely listening to MPR on the car radio. Finally, after several knocks, I saw a curtain pull back and an old man, crotchety and frightening, scowl out at me. I smiled, waved, and made one of those meaningless international gestures that say, "Let's talk." He opened the door.

I asked if he was Martin, Martin Henke. He was. I told him I was Evelyn Niemeier's son, William and Sophie's grandson, and that my mom and I were hoping to pay a visit to her childhood home.

"It burned down," he said. "This is not that house."

"But this is the farm, right?"

He looked at me long and hard in that Stephen King sort of way, then he looked out at the car, which was probably an eighth of a mile away and hit by a glare that prohibited him from seeing through the windshield.

"Is she here?" I nodded. "Good. I've got something I've been meaning to ask her."

I knew for a fact that my mom had not set foot on this farm since 1967. I wondered how long Martin had been holding on to his question.

He came out wearing his plaid mackinaw jacket and a mismatched hunting cap with knitted earflaps. Inexplicably—because we were half a mile from the nearest home and over ten miles from town—he locked the door behind him, then motioned for my mother and me to follow. We did. He stopped at a shed, also locked. He fiddled with the padlock, stuck the key in backwards a couple of times before unleashing it. It was a normal farm shed. But on the workbench, laid out on a chamois-cum-shop-rag, he had displayed several hand tools, museum style. Screwdrivers. Blades. Pliers. He went through each one, told us where he had found it out in the field and why he surmised it was my grandfather's tool because of where it was left, what crop had grown over it, how old he thought it was, etc.

He gave all the tools to my mom, returning what, in his mind, rightfully belonged to the Niemeiers, abandoned or forgotten somewhere between 1924 and 1963.

Then he took us out behind the barn. With his big hands and strong arms, he raised up a cast-iron cylinder the size of a fifty-five-gallon drum. It creaked. On the top was a trap door with an intricate hinge system that allowed it to spin and/or lift open. He swung that lid around a few times in all directions to make sure we could witness and appreciate its impressive design. Then he looked at my mom.

"Yes?" she inquired sheepishly, wondering how he wanted her to respond.

"What is it?" Martin asked. He genuinely didn't know.

At this time, my mom was in the early stages of Alzheimer's disease. She was still sharp and alive, but what she remembered and what she had already forgotten or was confused by always fascinated me.

"Did you find it underground?" she asked.

"Three feet down, right by the grove. Twenty years ago. The Blue Earth Historical Society wants it, but I told them I had to make sure the Niemeiers didn't want it first. So, what is it?"

Twenty years ago, when this guy was in his seventies, he finds something made of cast iron that weighs well over one hundred pounds buried several feet in the ground. He digs it up by hand, cleans it off, understands it has some historical significance, can't figure out what, exactly, but then hangs on to it for years, operating under the assumption that my mother or one of her siblings will show up to identify and claim it. That's a different rhythm than we city folk with Internet access live by.

"It's my dad's meat smoker," my mom said, and a light bulb went off in Martin's head.

"Of course," he said, suddenly understanding all the moving parts and racks and compartments. "You'd probably put the wood here, let this part heat up, keep the smoke held in with this lid, and set the meat like this. Of course! You want it back?"

My mom looked at him like he was nuts. She chuckled and said, "No, I don't. I'm a vegetarian," as if everyone knew this fact and we were talking about the requirements of a meatless kitchen rather than a family heirloom.

Martin was thrilled to keep it. So thrilled, in fact, that his entire being relaxed and he asked what had brought us down to the farm. I told him I was interested in my heritage, leaving out the confusing movie part. He liked that a younger man would be drawn to the simple and personal aspects of history. He gave us a tour of the farm and the fields. Explained how the barn was built in 1910. Why the particular wood was chosen. How many locals from the community it took to raise the barn. He was proud of his farm and had probably researched its historical details from locals, previous owners, and maybe even my grandfather.

My mom climbed up the ladder to the loft to show me where her parents had held barn dances on Saturdays—the kind of rabble-rousing, beer-soaked events that ultimately got them thrown out of the local Lutheran church. I watched Martin's hands relive his life experiences on the farm. His giant hands came together gently as he explained how he birthed a calf in an emergency. They squeezed together in a fist as he remembered holding nails, fence posts, or a scythe. He rubbed his palms and tightly ground them together to create friction to show me how he would check the wheat or corn for moisture content before harvest.

I touched the banisters my grandmother had held. I sat on the milking stool that Martin swore had been there since the beginning of time. And I felt another aspect of my script come to life, researched in this human way, so far from the knowledge of the library, but right here in the world where information is being created, where it is too new, too ethereal to yet be considered *information;* it was the revelation that I was searching for, not just what the characters felt or thought but also what they did, how work in the fields made them sweat, how mud accumulated on their boots, and how they touched one another with calloused, dirty hands.

On the drive home, the idea of living research, connecting with it physically, ingesting it tactically and emotionally rather than intellectually, made sense to me. It felt more visceral than all the facts I had accumulated along the way. It was a type of information, just different and, for me, more valid. Or, maybe *vivid* is the word. I realized that I was not just in love, but I was in love like Olaf. As my mom talked in the car on the way home, it occurred to me in a strangely enlightening way that she had married an immigrant, just as Olaf had, a dark-skinned immigrant from an exotic land who spoke a mysterious language. I know it sounds curious, but I had always thought of my father as my father, or the Professor, or an Egyptian, but never as an immigrant, until this moment on this road trip with my mother. I asked her how two such diverse people had fallen in love, and she said, "We both had big eyes, so I guess that was it." She recognized common ground in the smallest of things, like big eyes, but I wondered: had my father been, for a time, ostracized from my mother's family and her community because of their differences? I asked her this and, after thinking about it for a minute, she said, "Oh, you know, they thought he was ... different." I wondered about the story behind that statement, but it was never revealed.

In this trip to the farm, my grandfather's farm, watching my mom and Martin interact with history, the idea of research suddenly felt so immediate and real and, for the first time for me, emotional. So I sat down to write. By this time, it was probably the hundredth draft of my script, but also, really, the first. I can tell you in hindsight that what hit the page was unique, and ultimately very strange and unexpected.

A script is made up of two things: dialogue and behavior—a character's words and his or her actions. A script cannot be internal, cannot be about feelings, because you can't see feelings. If you can't see it, you can't film it, and if you can't film it, you shouldn't write it in a script. True, you can *see* manifestations of feelings, but that qualifies as behavior.

The Scandinavians I know from Minnesota, and the ones we all know from Lake Wobegon, are taciturn and reserved. They move like trout, intelligently and with a minimum of disruption and exposure. They'll look at one another, but not touch. They'll breathe at the same time, so as not to annoy others with an expulsion of carbon dioxide. They won't say they are in love, but they will commit simple yet incredibly powerful acts of love, like cooking a meal or drawing water from the well—acts of love that far outweigh any combination of words available to even the most loquacious poet.

Simple actions. Silent interludes. That's tough to communicate on film, tougher even to write in screenplay form. When I began this process with the reading of Will's short story, I saw charging horses, community harvests, and vistas filled with stormy weather. I had no idea how quiet and abstract this film would need to become before it was made.

Many writers talk about the courage it takes to leave all that raw, painful truth on the page. I lacked that courage. Without it, I found myself coming right up to the moments where something real and powerful—like love—passed between Olaf and Inge. I would stop writing and leave the moment short, wondering what exactly is the energy of love? And if I could identify it, how would it look? Meaning, how would I possibly film it?

I wrote a script that was very sparse, filled with the simple actions and silent interludes favored by Scandinavians. For some readers it was confounding. For others it was delicate and slender, but oddly effective. For me it was a much more clear vision than my facts-and-figures drafts, but perhaps also the result of my lack of writer's courage.

I'll show you what I mean in a page from *Sweet Land*, but perhaps it's best to give you a comparison from a typical action movie so you can see what producers expect versus what they received from me.

* * *

SOLDIER OF PUNISHMENT

EXT. BAKU STATE RESIDENCE—NIGHT
A military GUARD scans the grounds of the large estate. Limos rest quietly in the driveway. Lights are out for the night. He peers through US–made night vision goggles but carries a Soviet-made firearm. All is not quiet, as he will soon learn.

A red laser dot appears briefly on his forehead, and then his head explodes. The Guard collapses dead. High above the transom, a silent and deadly SNIPER refocuses his red laser. Two more GUARDS are dropped with single, silenced shots. The Sniper signals with a gesture.

Below, a NAVY SEAL receives the signal and goes to work dismantling the alarm system housed in the large junction box.

The Sniper employs infrared binoculars to watch his ASSAULT TROOPS take positions as he whisper-shouts orders into a hidden headset microphone.

SNIPER
ECHO CHARLIE! IN THE HOLE!
The Assault Troops swarm the grounds like a hatch of mayflies, but with incredible order. They quickly detonate the door to the residence and enter.

INT. BAKU STATE RESIDENCE—NIGHT

Camera charges in behind the Assault Troops as they rush a stairway in assemblage. With disregard, they knock over a WOMAN, maybe a maid, who in turn screeches an alarming scream.

SWEET LAND

INT. BARN—DAY

Olaf looks at Inge.

Inge looks at Olaf.

He breathes.

She breathes.

Olaf, awkwardly—

OLAF
I have work.

Olaf exits.

Inge watches him walk to his field.

In a situation like Olaf and Inge's—falling in love without a common language to label one's feelings—all that occurs genuinely, honestly, and meaningfully are very tiny, subtle actions. You look. She looks. Your heart pounds (but you can't film that), and you take a deep, calming breath. I thought I'd nailed the emotional core of the story, so I sent the script out to producers, all of whom said, "What the hell happens in this movie? Anything? Or is it just pages of breathing and looking and nothing?"

Actors, on the other hand, saw something entirely different in those moments. For Tim Guinee and Alan Cumming, they told me later, it was a chance to explore humanity and not be chased by aliens, to connect with and portray the real emotions of real people. Elizabeth Reaser said she was drawn to the opportunity *to listen* instead of *to talk*. That's the reverse of why actors are usually hired—to talk. These actors were drawn to the silence rather than the noise. But that's still a tough film to make—"*Alan Cumming, star of stage and screen, in a quiet movie. Not a silent movie, like the Oscar-winning* The Artist, *but a quiet movie.*"

Producers weren't buying it.

But, with these actors attached and with the help of friends and family, I was able to put together the financing for the unlikely feat of making a quiet movie. Thus began a whole new round of research related to the difference between *writing* a quiet movie and actually *filming* a quiet movie.

I knew from my Minnesota Historical Society library visits, through both reading and looking at photos, that most of these farmers in 1920 lived in Sears kit homes. And rural electrification was not in full swing until the New Deal era, so I couldn't see power lines in the compositions of the film and, with our limited budget, I couldn't afford to paint them out digitally. For this, my research now extended beyond the library, to county property tax record offices and local power companies. I asked them where I could find traditional Sears kit homes, still standing on a beautiful landscape, uninterrupted by modern implements and structures like sheet metal silos, AND—wait, I'm not finished yet—with no above-ground power lines visible for miles.

They laughed at me. Farms had been electrified for nearly half a century, and most of my contacts didn't really know what a Sears kit home was or didn't refer to it by that name.

So I went back to the farmers themselves. I drove concentric circles around the Twin Cities looking for old homes with either no power lines or ones that could be easily framed out of the shot. All the old homes had been replaced with contemporary suburban monstrosities or, as with my mom's childhood farm, rambler-style homes designed by the same architect in 1965. I tried to explain the style of architecture the film required, but my detailed descriptions puzzled most people, and they would ask, "You mean an old house?"

Well, yes, I did mean an old house, but not just any old house. There was no way, I was convinced through my research, that Olaf would have bought a farm with an 1890s home. Instead, he homesteads his 160 acres, clears the field himself, and is the first farmer to live there. He builds a lavish barn for his beloved animals and a sod house for himself because, in Norwegian culture, anything more would be showy and arrogant. But when the postal service delivers the letter saying that his parents are sending the girl, he goes to the Sears catalog, picks out a floor plan, and plunks down $623 in cash. Two weeks later a pile of lumber, all nails and hardware included, arrives by rail at the train depot in town. Olaf carts it to his land and erects a home in a couple of weeks. So, an old house, yes, but specifically a simple one built in 1920. Like a Sears kit home, of which no one really seemed to have a clear vision. I used my hands to explain the scope and shape and straight lines. I asked if anyone had ever been to the Mac-Groveland neighborhood of St. Paul, which I knew to contain several Sears kit homes, now referred to as "bungalows." Three weeks into this research all I had was, "No, not around here." Maybe, as we had done in Mac-Groveland, the farmers referred to these homes by another name.

I went back to my mom. She knew what I was looking for. She is an artist, a proud graduate of the Minneapolis College of Art and Design, and worked as an illustrator for the great Minnesota department store Dayton's, back in the 1950s. She offered to draw a picture for me. But before she got to work on the image, she saw a documentary on PBS—maybe even as coincidentally as that night—based on William Gabler's photo essay *Death of the Dream: Farmhouses in the Heartland*. It documented the last of these homes still standing before time and the elements took hold and they were destroyed or fell to the ground. She bought Gabler's book for me, and I took it around on my research trips.

I showed farmers black and white images of the type of home I was in search of, but still most would say, "No, not around here."

One day, on a farm outside Lindström, a good Scandinavian town in Minnesota, I stopped an old farmer, maybe eighty years of age, on his tractor. He obliged me, climbed down, and took a cursory look through the book. "No," he said. "But maybe you want to check with my mother."

"Your mother? How old is she?"

He told me she was 104, born in Sweden in 1900, the same year I imagined Inge would have been born. He told me she was sitting up on his porch that very moment.

His mother was a beautiful woman, sharp and clear. She understood everything I told her about making a movie and looking for a location with historical accuracy. She took the book out of my hands and carefully and rigorously paged through it like a dutiful Scandinavian, driven by a now-forgotten type of work ethic. She stopped on every page, examined every image, and gave each ample time to show me she cared and would answer thoroughly.

When she finished, she closed the book, handed it back to me, and said, "Why don't you go to the place where they took those pictures?"

"Sorry?"

"Why don't you go to the place where they took those pictures?"

Oh, I hadn't thought of that. "I wonder where—?"

She turned the book over in my hand and pointed to a credit on the back that said most of the homes were in Lac qui Parle and Chippewa counties on the South Dakota border. Within hours, the records office in Montevideo had identified several of these homes still in existence. I also learned that, while most farms are a quarter section, 160 acres, many of the farms in Chippewa County were larger, a full section of nominally one square mile or 640 acres, because in modern times farms needed to be bigger to be economically viable and, over the transition period of the past fifty years, one man would have bought up his uncle's quarter section, and then his cousin's, and so on, until he owned the entire section. In many cases, an uncle's old Sears kit home stood on a far corner and the new home, and the power lines, sat opposite. This was a dream come true for us, not the death of a dream at all.

We quickly selected three farms with the most potential. The houses would require less work, the power lines weren't visible, and the yards were generally free of modern structures. We met with Jim Robertson, the owner of the farm we liked best (and ultimately used), and outlined our crazy idea of making a movie, plowing up his modern, hybrid soybeans in the middle of July, replacing them with an heirloom variety of an older crop like wheat or winter barley, and slapping a couple of coats of paint onto his grandparents' house, which he'd only used for seed storage since the 1980s.

He shook his head, unconvinced. We spent a couple of weeks of just visiting, breaking the ice, walking his fields with him, awed by their cleanliness and efficiency, which we commented on liberally.

His fields were clean, meaning he had found a way to keep corn from contaminating the soybean field and wheat from contaminating the corn. It made harvest and storage easier and offered higher, more pure yields per bushel. He made us either wipe our feet or remove our shoes altogether when we entered a field, as you would do when entering someone's home that recently had canary yellow wall-to-wall carpeting installed.

On one of these walks we came across a mound, a place where the ground rose up, like a berm, and the crop was denser, maybe even a little taller. And could it have been more golden than all the rest?

My knees grew weak and I lost some of the blood flow to my head as I thought about the line from Will's story—

> The furrows rolled up shining in the night light. Olaf knew this earth. It was heavy soil, had never failed him. He knew also that next year, and nearly forever after, there would be one spot in the middle of the field where the wheat grew greener, taller, and more golden than all the rest. It would be the gravestone made of wheat.

I stopped, stood there, and stared at this deeply moving line of fiction come to life before my very eyes. Jim turned and asked, "You alright?"

"Yeah," I stammered, searching for the words, imagining this must be the secret burial place of his grandmother, or maybe his great-great-grandfather, who originally came on the boat across the Atlantic, took the train from New York as far west as he could, and then finished off the journey to his new home by wagon train. He had cleared this field with his bare hands, I imagined, and wanted to be buried here, the most truthful place he had ever known.

"Who—is—buried—?" I couldn't go on as I gently brushed the palm of my right hand over the wheat beard—the bristly material that protects the wheat kernel (see, my library reading did yield some retained knowledge).

Jim looked down. He couldn't really figure out what I was looking at, wondering about, or asking after.

"This?"

"Yes," I said, "What is this?"

"Oh, that." Jim looked around, mentally measured the distance from this special high spot in the field all the way to the road, then from where we stood back to the house. He rubbed his cleanly shaved chin and said, "Probably an old outhouse."

"Sorry?"

"Probably just an old outhouse."

I couldn't tell if I was crushed, humbled, or enlightened, but it was a pivotal point in my life and my understanding of the rhythms of life in general—how we perceive things and how we would like them to be.

I love the Internet. I love sitting at my desk, writing, having facts and figures, names, maps, tidbits at my fingertips. It makes my writing *seem* richer and more detailed, if it is not actually so. And I love the library—especially that librarian at the Minnesota Historical Society who should remind me of her name if she reads this—and the smell of books, especially old, musty ones that have been handled by professors and historians, people far smarter than I who have possibly left something of their own brilliance scrawled in the margins. But the work I do, whether I originally set out to do this or not, seems to be more from the heart and less from the head, more about how I feel than what I think. To access and understand that, I have learned, I need to go find the heart of the matter. It is not in books; not, for the most part, in the library. It's in life. It's in the hands, eyes, and memories of my mom, of Martin Henke, of Jim Robertson, and in all of humanity. That's the kind of authentic information you can get only from the primary source.

As long as I am stuck in that data contract with my cell phone provider, my daughter can search Google all day long for "wheat," "field," "grows a little taller," or "A Gravestone Made of Wheat," and even when she comes up with 99,900 results (which she will), she will never touch the beard of the stalk, never smell the breeze rolling across Chippewa County, and never learn to discern the difference between a sacred family burial plot and a covered up old outhouse, fertilizing deeply in a way commercial fertilizers just can't. Because today information resides inside our smartphones. We research with our thumbs and never connect one discovery to the next. Knowledge is fleeting. We don't retain it because we carry it around in the back pocket of our skinny jeans.

It makes me wonder. A generation from now, will four words like "and nearly forever after" have the same impact?

ALI SELIM is a writer and director of television commercials, documentaries, music videos, and the Independent Spirit Award–winning film *Sweet Land,* named one of the Ten Best Films of 2006 by over a dozen critics. Recently, he has directed episodic television for HBO and CBS. A native Minnesotan, he now resides in Los Angeles and no longer shovels snow.

Steve Yates

To Understand You Must Break In

*I*n the last forty minutes of wakefulness there comes without fail a bitter drift of self-loathing and doubt. Especially in the days before taking my first published novel, *Morkan's Quarry*, back to readers in my home place, Springfield, Missouri, this anxiety crept up from the floor, from around bookshelves, from the grout in bathroom tile. Often it was as fleeting as gray vapor over the darkening water of exhaustion. But sometimes it was as dense and clasping as the deadly miasmas that arose from old quarry waste pools. I am a fraud; all this in my novel I have written is worse than a Punch and Judy puppet show, less than shadows on a cave wall in a lame pantomime of what once was real life. Some nights as the dates to the first book signings approached, I became so overwhelmed with this strangling torpor that I vowed to e-mail my publisher the next morning and tell him all was off, cancel the contract, destroy the copies.

I am not like other fiction writers, who frequently operate with the simultaneous burden and affirmation of teaching writing to others. Instead I work in scholarly publishing, in marketing, in bringing the peer-reviewed content of historians, literary critics, and comics studies experts to its widest possible readership. Though I received an MFA from the esteemed creative writing program at University of Arkansas, and though I regularly published short fiction and excerpts from novels in such magazines as *TriQuarterly, Southwest Review, Ontario Review,* and *Missouri Review,* when one serves authors for twenty years, there is and will always be a feeling of fraudulence, of illegitimacy when my work is published. I serve authors; I am not, cannot be one. There was but one answer to this fear: return to and reread the books that had inspired me to create *Morkan's Quarry*—those being *Inside War: The Guerrilla Conflict in Missouri During the American Civil War, Borderland Rebellion: A History of the Civil War on the Missouri-Arkansas Border, Wilson's Creek: The Second Battle of the Civil War and the Men Who Fought It,* and the two most important to me, *The White River Chronicles of S. C. Turnbo* and *Rude Pursuits and Rugged Peaks: Schoolcraft's Ozark Journal, 1818–1819*. Without this retreading and refitting, I could never have faced my townspeople with a novel made up from their past.

* * *

Possibly the best stroke of intellectual good fortune in my young life came when I fried our prized Curtis Mathes television set. Summer vacation had just started, and I was nine. My father, furious and perhaps financially pinched, did not replace our TV until well into football season. So I spent a summer immersed in books and in the limestone hills of the Missouri Ozarks. Living those golden, television-free months, I discovered all the aptitude and subject matter I would ever require to attempt the study of humankind we call fiction. That summer propelled me to write a novel about people who were nothing like my parents and me, a novel about Irish Catholic owners of a limestone quarry surviving the American Civil War.

I did not intend to destroy the Curtis Mathes. It carried cartoons and brought a bandwidth of the outside world to suburban Springfield. Early on Saturday and Sunday mornings evangelists from Koshkonong weekly declared Armageddon near at hand. They wore extraordinary green and beige, western-styled suits, and they talked of seven-headed dragons, numbers stamped on foreheads, and many other enthralling miseries. Sometimes on the screen, the wickedly appointed aircraft of our empire swooped down to spray bullets or streams of flame into emerald jungles far away where enemies lurked. One evening, the national news reported that a rock band from England declared Her Majesty the Queen was not a human being. Who knew such stuff could be uttered? From its cabinet of stained wood, lovingly constructed by my father, the Curtis Mathes surely made its contributions.

To turn it on, one pulled a silver stalk topped with a wee circular lozenge. In a dawn languor, I eased this knob outward very slowly and discovered that by leaving it in limbo between on and off, a white coruscation rose up from the depths of the dimmed charcoal screen. This was new, and nothing like the whirling, hissing snowfield of static when we lost the broadcast signal. These white curls and ribbons swam all about like phosphorescent creatures merrily surfacing from a dark lagoon. Extraordinary! I had to show my sister. Julie eyed this warily, but agreed to keep watch while I fetched a cola.

When I returned, she was crouched behind a chair, the television set was smoking in a solid, black column, and the friendly white creatures were evolving into orange horns of fire. The Curtis Mathes, a sophisticated and expensive home entertainment device, was done for.

It is cliché to blame television for anything now, let alone for the dumbing and numbing of the American mind. So cliché in fact we have given up on recalling its culpability: its being the first home screen where language was digitized, electrified, scrolled, and flattened, where the original carrier wave for thought and expression, the careful sentence, began a transmogrification into the brute image. This scolding heard too often about television's badness has now become worn and yet remains mortally threatening, not unlike Satan in the Catholic saw about the Devil's greatest trick—convincing mankind that he, the Devil, does not exist even while his sinister allure is omnipresent. Televisions now blare and flicker from garages, Laundromats, kitchens, home and restaurant dining rooms, waiting rooms, saunas, and bathrooms. We can now, if we must, watch television on our desktops, laptops, and phones. We have largely lost our ability to shun television's stupefying influence. That stream of sound and image bears the most pervasive riptides of the psychic tsunami in which contemplation, observation, reason, and expression are overwhelmed and washed to sea by the savage electron. Even when Dad restored a new Curtis Mathes to our family room, I never again trusted it. I had learned it was not a mirror; none of my people, nothing of their lives were reflected there.

Along with its consuming, dumbing flicker, television gave stage to a goal now shared all across our numbed empire: fifteen minutes of fame! (With YouTube, is this now forty-five seconds of fame?) That life's ambition is to be televised at any cost is the reductio ad absurdum of the obnoxious principle of self-expression. How many ways has the supposed value "express yourself" entered into and made relative (if not irrelevant) our teaching, our creating and writing, our evaluating? What is bad or good, styled or sloppy holds no power; there are no standards in an ecosystem where self-expression is the ideal rather than one of many available starting points.

I am convinced that the absence of a television for an entire formative summer taught me that the wonder of the world was for certain not inside me. It was without. Expressing myself would take no time at all and would leave nothing of lasting value. My greatest desire was to comprehend others, to be inside someone else's mind, to share seamlessly that narrative called consciousness. I obsessed on this: How could my sister, my father, my mother think the same thoughts that I did, see the universe in anything near the same hue and yet make such wildly variant choices and engage in such spectacular conflicts? Were their valuations of even simple concepts—such as *quiet* or *dinnertime*—anything like mine? Breaking these barriers, reaching into the hearts and minds of others was an inordinate and as yet unpurposed obsession. And the barriers were profound.

Without a television, the miracle of the public library and the vigorous society of a neighborhood full of children took over my suddenly gridless, unscheduled life. This prompted imagination and sparked curiosity: imagination prompted by books of ghost stories, space aliens, and sea monsters, biographies of presidents, astronomers, sports heroes, World War I aces, histories of the Crusades and far-off lands—Tsarist Russia, Austria-Hungary, Habsburg Spain, and the Holy Roman Empire; curiosity sparked by the strangeness of my suburban peers and even more by the myriad differences in their parents and in the professions they pursued, in their parents' capabilities and quirks, and in the ways in which their parents managed their homes and money and their life's desires.

Reading alone does not make the spinning of a fictional universe possible. That softest of sciences, the observation of humanity is a co-equal part of fashioning the seamless dream. My people, the characters of the Ozarks, are fully discoverable only in the interstices of the historical record, as in between the harried prison reports from Gratiot in St. Louis as described in Louis S. Gerteis's great book *Civil War St. Louis:* eleven prisoners delivered this day from DON'T KNOW WHERE, to be held under charges of DON'T KNOW WHAT, by the authority of DON'T KNOW WHO, AS NO PAPERS CAME WITH THESE MEN. There is no fiction without imagination's invention from the crude and glorious research materials of observed humankind.

Mr. Nichols drove an ancient Kaiser-Frazer motor car that smelled like a rusty boat dock. He always wore gray hats and matching three-piece suits, and he could name the make, model, and year of any unusual car he spotted. Mr. Price dismantled every engine he purchased and let his son Greg keep iguanas, geckoes, and chameleons. Their home smelled like metal filings. Mr. Arbeitman regularly survived stupendous accidents at his "steel company." The pole to a basketball goal fell across his back; an iron pipe speared his bicep; a girder knocked him senseless. To the smug urban and academic condemnation of the American suburb and its ticky-tacky homogeneity, a raspberry. They all look the same because you do not see.

Beyond the public library, I discovered my parents' home library, books I rarely understood but read and reread because my father and mother had them in their minds. St. Augustine's *City of God*, Plato's *Republic*, Karl Marx's *Das Capital, Njal's Saga*. But most important and most readable was the history book by my father's favorite professor, 836 pages long, Duane G. Meyer's *The Heritage of Missouri*. Herein were stories no other book seemed to tell, peering back into an unwritten age of natives, the Osage and Delaware, then illuminating Spanish and French explorers, and onward through Bleeding Kansas and finally to President Harry S Truman and the Japanese surrender on the battle-ship USS *Missouri*. Unlike other books about Missouri, in which Jefferson City, Kansas City, and St. Louis seemed the only worthy and civilized settlements, Springfield, my Springfield and its surrounding keep, the Ozarks, bore equal mention. In several stretches of the narrative we even achieved an importance. That battered, green hardcover textbook with shining, slick but graying pages told me there was a story here. Tramping the hills with my chums, I heard armies with German accents marching in the dawn and arrows whistling in the woods.

But where else other than in that green, decaying book were our stories told? When I spoke with my pals about the blood vengeance and cracked crowns of guerrilla warfare or of the exploits of Brigadier General Nathaniel Lyon at nearby Wilson's Creek, the rousing portions they could tolerate. But that their homes, their lives, these hills needed stories told? The notion met with blank stares, and eventually there came the sarcastic comment that I attended a private, "laboratory" school and not reasonable Pershing Elementary. I was daffy, the daydreamer, the mutant. Shoot . . . they didn't even know who General John J. Pershing was!

My mother's grief over the loss of a child, a premature baby dead when I was four, lasted many years. Often with me in tow and later with me and my sister, she traveled through old Galloway Village just west of Southern Hills subdivision, past the rattling, smoking lime quarry and kilns and the row of "ghost houses" mostly derelict and shrouded in lime, to the cemetery where she buried her first daughter, my sister Debbie. I came to associate the limestone, the tombstones, the lost village with the whole Stygian act of traveling to where the dead rested, to remembrance of all things past, to where the stories waited, to where a grief, one that I could not yet absorb or share but certainly could follow, was told and retold. The limestone, the act of mining it—my curiosity sent me to geology books. I learned that the stone came from shards, skeletons, chitin, the leavings of the dead from a great, shallow sea that once covered the land. The calcium carbonate was corollary to our bones, just as seawater was saline kin to our blood. Limestone began its slow accretion as the powerful, governing metaphor to the story of the Ozarks and my hometown.

As a young man, when my life seemed frayed and out of control, I would drive to Sequiota Park, then an abandoned and polluted hatchery across from the quarry, and there I would center myself. I knew from watching the crusted silos and kilns and their crawling, white-caked dump trucks, the foreboding lights and bilious steam at all hours of the night, something behind barbed wire and wrought iron awaited me there, something of the untold story of how buildings arose, and how roadways and railways stretched out into our hilly wilderness. Alongside me, reflected in the age-sloped glass windows of old storefronts abandoned, the moonlike glow of the quarry beckoned, its image an invitation, a portal, and a barrier. Back of those windows and that reflection waited interiors I longed to know.

You never know where or when the seed will be planted. Dr. Katherine Lederer at Missouri State told me this, and said it was paraphrased from a Civil Rights crusader. In 1989, in her African American literature class, I was a bleary-eyed, sleep-deprived junior, worn out not for the usual reasons of too much booze and fraternity. No. At sixteen I was hired by a forward-thinking sports editor at the Springfield *News-Leader,* and I miraculously kept the thirty- to forty-hour-a-week job as a sports writer and agate clerk all through college. Near the end of a semester of Ralph Ellison, Richard Wright, and Toni Morrison, Dr. Lederer told us the story of the 1906 Easter lynching of three black men in downtown Springfield by a mob of two thousand whites, and of the aftermath, of the exodus of 20 percent of my town's population, of blacks fleeing terrified that the burning of the black quarter that happened in Pierce City in 1904 would happen once more.

I am white. Springfield, in the twenty-one years I lived there, never recorded at census more than a six percent black population. In my high school—I transferred my junior year to a large public school—we graduated 365 students in 1986. No one in my senior class was black. Yet my parents were civically and historically minded people, educated citizens, both with post-baccalaureate degrees. No book in our home, nothing they shared spoke of this harsh chapter. If it was in Duane G. Meyer's great book, I missed it, too enthralled elsewhere. My father especially was filled with pride about Springfield. He served on the airport board, was president of the chamber of commerce for a stint, and later became our district's state highway commissioner. We were Springfield, Queen City of the Ozarks through and through. A lynching, three innocent black men torn from the city jail, hanged from a steel tower topped with a replica of the Statue of Liberty, then burned before a howling mob of two thousand whites. For all I once knew of us, I now had to ask again, who were we? Who are we?

Though it was only a small portion of Dr. Lederer's account, I latched on to and could not let go of this: among the many blacks she interviewed to create her book, *Many Thousand Gone*, a lore persisted. Subject after subject claimed that a local quarry manager (some said owner, but this was inexact) took a stand in the aftermath of the lynching when another mob seemed ready to form and burn out Happy Hollow, home to most of Springfield's black population. In the wake of that awful tide gathering, the quarry manager had given his black powder monkeys dynamite or at the least the keys to Marblehead Quarry's boom shack and instructed them to mine or threaten the mining of Springfield's most affluent, white streets. The terrifying calculus was simple and brutally clear to white elites—protect Happy Hollow from destruction, or we blow your castles sky high. I knew enough history and had learned enough about racial conflict in Dr. Lederer's class to recognize that no white man could lay down that fuse or even the threat of it and walk away. Every summer our newspaper ran a brief about some quarryman or excavator losing his blaster's license and being banned from state contracts for letting the least trickle of dynamite out into the world. Usually he was busted after stunning fish in a lake somewhere. But wildlife is not the concern here. You see, quarry owners and managers are those rarest of citizens, trusted with explosives which, in the hands of some criminal or anarchist or revolutionary, could pose effective, destructive, mortal opposition to the will of government. Even the threat of dynamite used this way was professional suicide, but in a racially charged climate it was personal, social immolation as well, a martyrdom. And to me it was hope, courage, and even violent reasoning amid the fires of Gehenna. One of my townspeople witnessed the grossest hate and said, Stop. No more.

The quarry owner's story would not leave me. He roiled at the base of my brain stem all through graduate school in the writing program at the University of Arkansas in Fayetteville. There came another stroke of good fortune, brought on again by stupidity and curiosity. Denied the chance to teach English my first summer there, I needed cash, and so I hired on with the Arkansas Highway and Transportation Department. I applied thinking that the position (whatever its brief, amorphous, official description was) would involve construction labor, shoveling, chatting in parking areas, mowing maybe. Good physical work outdoors. AHTD told me Friday I was to be on a survey crew come Monday. I spent that weekend with books from the U of A library on surveying basics and how to read blueprints, then faked my way through all of June holding rods level and brandishing blaze-orange flags at traffic. AHTD granted me three summers, nine blaring months of ever increasing responsibility, measuring behind theodolites and survey guns, circuiting tremendous cuts through limestone mountains, studying bridges flung dizzily above bayous and valleys, inspecting earth-moving and concrete pours to box culverts, observing blasting, and monitoring the outgoing mixes at concrete plants. For a full month, we surveyed an abandoned quarry that was to be blasted, taking readings on unstable cliffs that loomed like castle walls. Each day we found ways at the crumbling edge to court death. I learned physically and emotionally something of the gloom, oppressive danger, and fatigue pervading work in a mine. It took little to imagine the ghosts of fallen quarrymen sulking in the heat shudders along the stone. I arrived home exhausted, crusted to the knees in lime and concrete, red clay dust in my ears, hair, eyes, and pores. I loved and absorbed every grueling minute of those three summers.

In graduate workshop, in a short story set in contemporary suburban Springfield, he surfaced—the 1906 quarry owner. Owner . . . I was ready to allow history, memory, and forgetting and all the transformations of collective memory to work their will with the material. He arrived as the ancestor of a depraved, suburbanite narrator. But there was no meshing the two stories. James Whitehead, mentor and workshop director that semester, told me plainly to strip the quarry owner and the lynching out and start my first novel using that separated material.

By that time, I was twenty-five and profoundly trusted libraries and knew what could be gained in them. After all, books on surveying and blueprint reading secured me financially during three summers of graduate school in a wholly unanticipated labor. The University of Arkansas library still used card catalogs in 1993, those long wooden drawers of recipe card–sized book abstracts sporting Dewey decimal information in their upper left-hand corners. Three of these proved invaluable to the writing of my first novel, *Morkan's Quarry,* published by Moon City Press in 2010. The card catalog described two copies of Halbert Powers Gillette's *Handbook of Rock Excavation: Methods and Cost* published in 1904 and one copy revised and published in 1916. Here was a book created when engineers could still write like Henry David Thoreau and think like James B. Eads. Gillette covered rock work and quarrying methods from ancient hand drills through steam's dominance in mining to just before the advent of gas-powered drills. So complete and revealing of quarry practice was the 1904 edition, I did the unthinkable. The copy I checked out again and again had not been in circulation since 1936. There was a second copy of the 1904 edition on the shelves too. This one was staying home. It cost me $189.00, and I was threatened with denial of my MFA degree unless I relinquished the book or paid. Poor as red dirt, I nonetheless wrote the check. Holding the book in its crumbling cover now, I know its worth, know I have paid, and yet I still feel like a thief.

Gillette's *Handbook* fit in one's hand and pocket, was flexibly bound—a publisher and author superbly matching content and format to an end user's needs in the field. It is filled with tables and narrative examples of harrowing conditions, with critiques of ill-conceived but all-too-common bad practices, with curiosities and triumphs of working in shale and schist, granite, garnet, and limestone. Better than any memoir or diary, it was the unalloyed valence of a quarryman's thoughts.

From the Missouri Bureau of Geology and Mines came yet another remarkable book. I discovered it in a list tipped into either the *Missouri Historical Review* or *Ozarks Watch,* I don't recall which. Hardcover, published in 1907 at $4.00 plus shipping, *Lime and Cement Resources* was a 255-page report commissioned by the governor of Missouri. In the introduction, the geologist authors claimed that because of the "phenomenal growth of the Portland cement industry . . . there is at the present time a constant inquiry from the general public for information concerning the nature of the materials used in the manufacture of Portland cement and the distribution of such materials throughout the state." Clearly I was on to a hot property, at least red hot in 1907. In the very first illustration, Plate 1, was Marblehead Lime Company, Springfield, Missouri, photographed with a landscape lens and printed in a foldout thirty-six inches long. The photograph was not dated, but if the book appeared in 1907, one can assume the photo was taken near the date when John Kelso, the quarry manager Dr. Lederer referred to, had charge. The long rails, the locomotive docked beside the seven kilns, the piles of crushed stone, the vast maw of the hole diving beneath what would become National Avenue, what a find this cheap book! He had walked this picture, my quarryman. "The plant now has an output of 850 barrels per 24 hours . . . The quarry, near where the kilns are located, consists of a regular sunken pit 425 feet long, 325 feet wide and 60 feet deep. This is the only sunken quarry in the state which is operated for the manufacture of lime." Sunken Quarry. An inescapably moral phrase.

Despite coming from if not privilege at least comfort, I was well aware of the cruel economic realities of the mining industry. The main characters of this saga I was creating would face a raft of very unappealing moral compromises and dodges if they were to be believably rendered. Marblehead Lime did not employ Springfield's blacks out of any enlightened sense of benevolence or desire to promote racial harmony. The quarry employed them because they didn't ask a high wage and wouldn't ask one any time soon. From working with the AHTD, I learned plenty about difficult, dangerous physical and mental labor out of doors. Interviewing limestone quarrymen from the Indiana Limestone Institute of America, I learned what Sonny Curtis (and later the Clash) meant about breaking rocks in the hot sun. Prison labor commonly supplied the quarryman's need for stone breakers, as in the famous, lost painting *The Stone Breakers* by Gustave Courbet. Kilns required broken stone, and in 1906 and before there were few ways around hiring or forcing a squad of prisoners or ultra-low-wage stone breakers with sledgehammers to sweat at this work. And if the labor were not cost-free prisoners, quarry owners devised the company store and the company town, so ably described in Gregg Andrews's *City of Dust: A Cement Company Town in the Land of Tom Sawyer*. Workers really could end up in indebted servitude owing their souls to the company store. Add to these seemingly inescapable evils the loudness of such operations, the destructive and disruptive blasting, the white, annihilating lime dust, and very soon a quarry becomes an acutely unpopular neighbor. If all your china shakes, if your pipes sing and moan, if your cows won't give milk and your chickens won't lay, the night blasts at your friendly, neighborhood limestone quarry may not hold much charm. In fact the "constant inquiry from the general public" cited by the Missouri Bureau of Geology and Mines may not always have been a product of entrepreneurial curiosity and civic pride. I had to discover how my quarryman navigated and made his peace in Springfield, how my townspeople accepted or denied, welcomed or fought him under usual and later violently unusual circumstances. Otherwise his breach with them in the aftermath of the lynching would seem inevitable and be without impact.

Understanding a whole town, now that's an arrogant assumption and a seemingly massive barrier. To take the collective memory of my hometown and perform on it that magical disentanglement that Maurice Halbwachs performed on the Holy Land, to isolate the original present tense twine of emotion and event, could it even be done? The newspapers of 1906 tout faith cures for cancer, magnetism for healing, reduction potions for obesity, New York's fashions for Easter. Editorials blame nervousness, distraction, and melancholy on a society moving too rapidly. This past does not sound too far removed from our present, the century so recently turned. From Dr. Lederer's collection of photographs, I jotted the store names and building advertisements downtown—Globe Clothing, Inc., Springfield Cigar, National Exchange Bank, Widbin & Fox Retail, a banner for Evertz stoves, made by my mother's people. Fashion was certainly different, as were conveyances and equipage, but the faces, the eyes, not different at all when they looked toward the camera.

One night during graduate school, I took a friend of mine from Virginia, a fellow writer in the Arkansas program, home to Springfield. After listening to Miller Williams read poems and answer questions at

Drury College, we hit the nightspots I knew from my university days. It was one of those magical spring nights. Dozens of old friends and people I knew before I moved were out enjoying it—Billy, owner of Billy's Chili, and Councilwoman Owen, mother of an old grade school friend; Fitzwater (best man at my wedding and a local troubadour) and Gilkerson and Bender. A party erupted at an old band mate's house, and before we left, my Virginia friend exclaimed, "This is incredible. You know everyone in town!" It was the one moment in my life that I might have agreed, might have been exuberant and lit enough to believe I could know my whole town.

Not wanting the night to end, my friend asked to see more haunts. We were near enough Galloway, I figured: why not? He's a writer. He'll understand. I had just started writing *Morkan's Quarry* and its sequel, but research, a lifetime of it, was about to come to a breakthrough. We slowed the car—a black Chevy Blazer I adored—when the oaks and sycamores of Lone Pine Road narrowed in after crossing Battlefield Road. The quarry, smoking and lit in the night, like a stretch of the moon grafted upon the earth, impressed him. The headlights of the Blazer played across the mostly abandoned village, the old "ghost houses" as my sister and I called them on trips with our mother to the cemetery. "What was in them?" he asked. Anything a village needed. I told him of the picnic tradition, how the well-to-do in Springfield would take carriages out here to have weekend lunches in "the country." Our headlights revealed empty Sequiota Park and the shimmering, vacant, polluted, square pool of the old hatchery, a Gothic and mysterious setting.

I do not know which of us had the idea, staring at a two-story, empty storefront with wood so dried and twisted it looked as if the structure had been built from old pallets of deal wood. We were parked; I was sharing lore. I do not know which of us said, "Let's see if we can get in." Our adventures had so far been too filled with good fortune and zany encounters, a perfect halo of a night. I kept a handheld spotlight in the Blazer; he had a penlight on his key chain. We were out of the car and headed to the back of the derelict store in no time. Only at the back door to the ghost house did some sobriety return. When the cool porcelain knob turned and the door opened with hardly a sound, we fell hushed. Inside the ghost house, that heavy soil and metal smell of old toolsheds clasped our faces as if a moist hand covered with dirt and cold grease reached out of the inky dark. Our flashlights snapped on and carved cones of yellow in a dusty murk. Old tools, sawhorses, fresh lumber, salvaged and broken wood, a stove. Outside I could see the Blazer sitting alone in the gravel lot, highlighted beneath the glow of a streetlamp and the aurora of the quarry. And there it came over me, on the carrier wave of adrenaline. Looking out on the quarry, its lime clouds, its skeletal white, its dim but sure lights like ancient eyes on the watch, I felt what the local must have felt, my townsman looking out on any quarry, whether here in Galloway or in downtown Spring-field. Over there was money, power, explosives, a poison, a threat, even if it meant commerce, a white shroud that baptized all of smell and taste and vitality. Death—and it was owned by the ones I wished to write about. There was what the townspeople felt—fear—and it took the breath from me. It was so still in the ghost house, and neither of us had spoken in a long while, and we had both, without comment, switched off our torches. The lonely, vulnerable Blazer sat out there, and it was well past midnight. Fear, I knew it fully now. That would be how my townsmen felt staring out at that scar of a quarry.

There is more, of course: not just fear of arrest, or fear of power, or fleeting, imagined emotional identification with souls passed. Just as there is a defining line between great books of history and mere-ly workmanlike carriers trudging a timeline of details, fiction has no lifeblood without one further immersion. And I will not be the first to say that research of the heart must go straight to the wound. There is the surety of experience that transforms research into something that transcends fear and, through its recombination of the observed and the read and the lived, fashions what would otherwise be fraudulent pantomime into living flesh on the page.

I see the hallway. Elongated, darkened, the beige-patterned, papered walls looming over me—I am small again, and there are no sentences for this. Only raw flashes from the amber of memory, that inescap-able dream. At the end of the hall is the closed door to my parents' bedroom, and from it a searing, yellow light at its base. And a wailing, unrestrained, in a voice I know is my mother's, but keening in a tenor I have never heard. Why am I without? What has happened that they would shut me away? I must get to her.

Long the hall, cold the brass knob and the slick, shining, wood-stained door itself, shining from the light at its base or is it from some

Steve Yates in a cemetery in Rodney, Mississippi. Photograph by Hunter McKelva Cole

other jaundiced, tremulous light? Forbidden. Not to be opened. My parents' door. But her cries are too much.

Open the door, and there is mother, facedown upon the bed in only her bra and panties, pounding the bed sheets with closed fists, kicking the mattress with her lean, lovely feet, and there is no restraint to her cries, no moderation to her grief. Daddy, face streaming, strokes her back, but his wet, shining eyes stare into the middle of a hole of nowhere as his wife wails. Both sets of my grandparents are there, an unheard-of rarity, standing apart from the bed, holding one another close. I had never seen and never saw again my mother's parents, the Evertzes, clutch or comfort one another. But today they do so, gasping. The look on my paternal grandparents Mary's and Roma's faces—so clearly they wish to embrace and console their son. But my mother's cries fill the room, and I recognize the child like me in her, the full-throated fit in her pounding on the bed. That cry I will never forget, that moment when the greatest love turns to heartbreak and the soul looses unchecked agony. Debbie is dead, someone whispers to me. Debbie is dead, little sister has died. She won't be coming home. I am in the presence of the loving human heart absolutely broken. Is there any truth more plain and devastating? I will hear this sound again from my sister Julie's throat when Roma dies; I will hear it unmistakably from my own wife in hospital one day—the loving heart given over wholly to its grief. There is no human sound like it, so clearly individual and at the same time so profoundly universal in its bitter tenor of abandonment and dismay.

Our social order, our numb, depraved, televised "normalities" want that door to remain forbidden and shut. Fiction, the study of humankind, wants it torn open and, no matter how painful, wants to stand first the writer, then the reader in the holy presence of that sorrowful passion: emotional truth. Her cries. I tremble to put them to the page. To understand you must break in.

STEVE YATES is the author of *Morkan's Quarry* (Moon City Press, 2010). The *Missouri Review* has thrice featured excerpts from that novel and its sequel, *The Teeth of the Souls,* forthcoming in 2015 from Moon City Press. Pieces of both novels have also appeared in *Ontario Review, South Carolina Review, Kansas Quarterly/Arkansas Review,* and *Elder Mountain: A Journal of Ozarks Studies.* Yates is the winner of the 2012 Juniper Prize in Fiction, and the University of Massachusetts Press published his collection *Some Kinds of Love: Stories* in 2013. Richard Russo and the editors of *Best American Short Stories* distinguished one of his pieces among the Notable Stories of 2009. Yates is assistant director/ marketing director at University Press of Mississippi and lives in Flowood with his wife, Tammy.

Alberto A. Martínez

DATING ALBERT EINSTEIN

*B*ait and switch—no I won't talk about Einstein's secret girl-friends or the brazen socialites who visited the married man to briefly say hello to his German wife, his cousin, gifting her some chocolates or pastries, only to then leave her there and take the celebrity away on a sailboat. Bummer.[1]

By *dating*, I mean instead the research process of figuring out when exactly something happened. Memorizing dates is not an important part of history. Still, sometimes when you're trying to figure out when exactly something happened you discover that it didn't even happen at all. The Internet is flooded with false quotations allegedly by Einstein, some even with false dates. This mythmaking process is formidable, but it leaves us asking: what really happened and when?

In 1905, Einstein published the theory of relativity, which convinced physicists to change their ideas about the nature of time. Against the brilliant Isaac Newton and common sense, Einstein said that time is not independent of everything, but that it varies, for example, for a man sitting on a speeding train instead of standing on the ground. Back then, Einstein was not the gray-maned legendary genius. Instead, he was a plain underachiever. He had a four-year degree from a technical school to teach physics and math, but he failed to get a job as a schoolteacher. He had written to many professors, hoping to land a job as an assistant, but all either rejected or ignored him. He had lived alone in poverty while his family's business collapsed in Italy. He had been rejected by the Swiss military service for having varicose veins and flat, sweaty feet. So a friend's father helped Albert get an unassuming job: he became a lowest-rank employee at the Swiss patent office in Bern. He was a compulsive smoker and coffee drinker. Out of wedlock, he had a baby daughter whom apparently he never met. We know of her existence from letters, but she disappeared: we don't know what happened to her. When his Serbian girlfriend moved to Bern, without their daughter, they married without a ceremony. In his spare time, he worked on physics as an amateur, and he called himself "a heretic," what some nowadays might call "a crank." He and his wife had another baby, a son, in 1904. Somehow, that government bureaucrat in a cheap suit revolutionized physics.

A hundred years later, another theoretical physicist, Michio Kaku, claimed to explain how Einstein did it. In a popular book, Kaku said that in 1905 Einstein had been riding a streetcar in Bern, looking back at a famous clock tower, which led him to imagine that if the streetcar raced away from the tower at the speed of light, then the clock on the tower would seem to have stopped, while a clock on the streetcar would still tick at the same rate. Allegedly, this led Einstein to the relativity of time. But actually, Kaku's account is mistaken: there is no evidence that Einstein ever thought about a streetcar racing away from a clock tower at the speed of light.[2]

Looking west on Kramgasse Street in Bern, 1900. When Einstein conceived the relativity of time, in 1905, he lived on this street, on the left side in a building beyond the edge of this photograph. Some writers speculate that he was inspired by clock towers, trolley cars, and the train station.

In 2003, a professor of the history of science at Harvard University had published a different explanation. He said that in May 1905, Einstein and his good friend Michele Besso were standing on a hill northeast of downtown Bern when Einstein excitedly explained that he could define a new concept of time by exchanging signals between two clock towers. But this story too is just fiction: there is no evidence that Einstein and Besso ever stood on any hill discussing anything about clock towers. And checking a Swiss map for that hill I noticed that there exists no such hill northeast of downtown Bern: instead, it's to the south.[3]

And looking at Wikipedia right now—and who knows what it will say a year from now—it says about Einstein that "Much of his work at the patent office related to questions about transmission of electric signals and electrical-mechanical synchronization of time, two technical problems that show up conspicuously in the thought experiments that eventually led Einstein to his radical conclusions about the nature of light and the fundamental connection between space and time." But really, there exists no evidence that Einstein ever analyzed even one patent application that dealt with the synchronization of clocks. Writers just imagine the connection.[4]

For decades, writers have speculated about the origins of Einstein's relativity. They think that it's a mystery, that there's not much evidence of how he did it. So they speculate: maybe he was influenced by modern art, or a belief in God, or his father's electrical business, or maybe by Swiss clock towers, or maybe his quiet Serbian wife helped him. But Einstein didn't mention any of that at all, when people actually *asked* him, for over fifty years, until he died. In letters, and in an autobiography that he called "my obituary," Einstein instead said that he had been greatly influenced by the Scottish philosopher David Hume. So there! Against our guesswork that his success was triggered *by whatever interests us*, if only we trust the ink on some pages, more than the blank empty spaces between printed words, then we should well accept that young Einstein, the physicist, was actually inspired by philosophy. And it's not a bad lesson.[5]

But when? I was curious about this question because for ten years, from 1895 to 1905, Einstein struggled to solve problems that led to his theory of relativity. So Hume helped him, *but when?* I want to share the addictive process by which researchers try to figure things out, sifting through old bits of evidence, squinting at ambiguous accounts, to try to get a clear picture of the forgotten past. First I'll explain how I found out when Einstein read Hume, and then we'll bait a bigger fish: when exactly did Einstein have the flash of insight that made relativity?

In a letter of 1915, Einstein recalled that he had been greatly influenced by "Hume, whose treatise on understanding I studied with fervor and admiration shortly before figuring out the theory of relativity. It is very possible that without these philosophical studies I would not have arrived at the solution." Shortly before, but when? A few years? Months? I knew of one interesting clue. From 1902 to 1905, Einstein participated in a reading and discussion group in Bern with two friends, Moritz Solovine and Conrad Habicht, and at some point they read Hume. Decades later, Solovine wrote about their meetings, and he mentioned that one day he skipped their scheduled reading of Hume to attend a musical concert, and he gave some details, my clue: it happened in Bern, the performers were a "widely acclaimed Czech Quartet," and they played selections from Beethoven, Antonin Dvořák, and Bedřich Smetana.[6]

If only I could find a trace of that concert, I would then know when exactly Einstein read Hume. So I wrote to a librarian at the Swiss National Library in Bern, Andreas Berz, asking where I might find records of old concerts, perhaps in newspapers? He promptly replied: looking in issues of the newspa-

Ad in a Bern newspaper of March 11, 1905, announcing a concert by "the famous Bohemian String-Quartet" scheduled for March 17, 1905.

Gesellschaftshaus Museum
BERN

Samstag, den 19. März
abends 8 Uhr

☞ **Konzert** ☜
des
Böhmischen Streich - Quartettes

Programm

1. **Jos. Haydn,** Streichquartett D-dur, op. 64.
2. **B. Smetana,** Streichquartett E-moll
   (Aus meinem Leben).
3. **L. v. Beethoven,** Streichquartett F-dur, op. 135.

Preise der Plätze

Saal Fr. 5.—, Balkon Fr. 5.—, 3.—, Galerie numeriert
Fr. 4.—, unnumeriert Fr. 2.—.

Vorverkauf der Billette in der Musikalien - Handlung
F. Gilgien, Marktgasse 9.　　　　　, 4849

*Ad in a Bern newspaper of March 17, 1904,
announcing a concert by "the Bohemian String-
Quartet" scheduled for March 19, 1904.*

per *Der Bund,* he found an announcement for a concert at the French Church in Bern in which "the famous Bohemian String-Quartet" would play music by Beethoven, Dvořák, and Mozart. That was quick! (But what about Smetana? Solovine said that they had played Smetana.) The date of that event was March 17, 1905.

One hundred years later, in March 2005, I flew from Los Angeles to Switzerland to track down various things, including historical dates. In Bern, I walked from Einstein's old apartments to the Swiss National Library, on the south side of the winding Aar River. The very helpful librarian was on vacation, but an attendant took me to the newspaper collections. I soon found the issue with the concert announcement in question, and other ads for that same event. But what if, maybe, the Bohemian String-Quartet had played in Bern not just in March 1905, but at some other dates? I had to check. So I looked at every single issue of local newspapers from 1902 to 1905, the years when Solovine and Einstein were both in Bern. Finally, I did find another announcement: on Thursday, March 17, 1904, *Der Bund* advertised another concert by the Bohemian String-Quartet that would take place on the following Saturday. Other ads in that newspaper and in the *Berner Tagblatt* also announced this event, including its musical program: Haydn, Smetana, and Beethoven. Such bad luck! Solovine had mentioned three composers: *Beethoven, Dvořák, Smetana,* but the March 1904 concert ads did not mention Dvořák, while the March 1905 concert ads did not mention Smetana![7]

So which one was it? *Der Bund* sometimes included reviews of concerts, and sometimes musicians played additional pieces that were not in the advertised programs. I therefore found and translated such reviews for both concerts, but no luck: the 1904 one did not mention Dvořák, and the 1905 review did not mention Smetana. This suggests that either such pieces were played but not cited, or maybe that Solovine's recollection was mistaken—after all, he was *eighty* years old when in 1955 or 1956 he described an event that happened fifty years before.[8]

But which concert was it? To figure it out, I wondered: were Einstein, Solovine, and Habicht all in Bern on the two dates in question? Habicht lived in Schaffhausen, a hundred miles away, and later in Schiers, even farther away, but he sometimes visited Bern, as is clear from letters. Their reading of Hume, Solovine said, happened in Solovine's own apartment. It occurred to me that I might be able to pinpoint the right recital if only I could find any evidence that Solovine was *not* in Bern on one of the plausible dates. In a history book by Ann Hentschel, I found that Solovine left Bern in early March 1904. To check that information, I contacted the state archives of the city of Bern. An archivist consulted the Registry of Foreign Residents (Solovine was Romanian) and confirmed that on March 2, Solovine ended his room rental in Bern and moved to Strasbourg, France. He visited Lyon in August, and finally moved back to Bern on October 18. So he was not in Bern in mid-March 1904, or, more importantly, he did not then have an apartment in Bern.[9]

So there it was: Einstein and his friends read Hume in March 1905. I should say that this is not merely an interpretation. The point is that instead of guessing plausible answers to a definite historical puzzle, we can collect multiple pieces of evidence, however small they might seem, put them together, and then the more bits of evidence we find, the more they jointly press and constrain one another, forbidding certain interpretations and leading to definite answers, information that is not in any one bit of evidence by itself.

On March 6, 1905, Einstein sent two postcards to his friend Habicht, begging him to visit Bern. More than a week later, Habicht did visit, and along with Solovine they all planned to discuss Hume. Where would they meet? An archivist at the State Archive of Bern informed me that Solovine then lived at 16 Gerechtigkeitsgasse, an apartment just west of Einstein's flat on Kramgasse, really the same street with a different name. Einstein and Solovine were then close neighbors. But

Solovine saw posters for the Bohemian String-Quartet, as he later recalled. He told Einstein that they should attend. Einstein himself loved to play the violin, he loved Mozart above all other composers, and the concert ads of March 1905 promised Mozart's String Quartet in D Minor, an intense and dramatic piece. But at that time, Einstein was absorbed in Hume, so he insisted to Solovine that it would be much better to read and discuss. The three friends agreed to meet at Solovine's rented room on Friday, March 17. But when the day arrived, suddenly Solovine could not resist but attend the concert on his own. He left the door to his place open, along with four boiled eggs and a note, so that Einstein and Habicht could meet there nevertheless. Einstein and the mischievous Habicht were outraged. They ate the eggs but decided to smoke tobacco in the room, "like men possessed," because Solovine hated smoking. So they shut his window and smoked at length, Einstein a pipe, Habicht some big cigars, to saturate the place with the

Conrad Habicht with a cigar, Moritz Solovine, and the not yet famous Albert Einstein. Writers usually say that this photograph is from 1903. Actually, it is from the crucial year 1905, as specified in a letter from Solovine to Carl Seelig on April 14, 1952: "Regarding photographs of our times in Bern, I only have the one in which we were photographed all three of us before we separated in 1905." So this was Einstein when he formulated the theory of relativity. Photographed by Emil Vollenweider at his studio on Postgasse 68.

stink that Solovine despised. Then they smeared the ashes and cigar butts on Solovine's table, chairs, plates, forks, teacups, teapot, sugar bowl, and even on his bed! Finally they left. Solovine returned and "when I opened the door to my room I was enveloped by the pestilent smoke of tobacco and I thought I would suffocate." The stench was even on his sheets and pillows, so for hours he could not shut his eyes or sleep. The next day Einstein chastised him: "You awful man, how! You skip an academic meeting to hear a few violinists! You Barbarian, you Beotian! If you ever again allow yourself such an infidelity, you will be expelled with shame and disgrace from the Academy!" That Saturday night their discussion of Hume extended late, until one hour before sunrise of March 19, 1905.[10]

They read Hume's *Treatise of Human Nature* of 1739, "in a very good German edition." Reportedly, "What Einstein liked most about Hume was the unsurpassable clarity of his presentation and his avoidance of any ambiguities intended to give an impression of profundity." Einstein recalled that, above all other subjects, they busied themselves with discussions of Hume. And Solovine recalled: "we discussed for weeks David Hume's singularly incisive critique of the notions of substance and causality." About causality, Hume argued that although certain happenings seem to regularly follow one another, we can never know whether they are really causally connected. We don't know if one event is really the cause of its successor. Thus the notion of cause and effect is a human concept; it's not justified by scientific knowledge. Einstein remarked, "Hume's clear message seemed crushing": human sensations are the only source of knowledge, they're linked only by expectations and habit, and they cannot lead to real laws of nature.[11]

Einstein became convinced that "All concepts, even those which are closest to experience, are from the point of view of logic freely chosen conventions, just as is the case with the concept of causality." While most scientists believed (and still do) that the principles of physics are experimental facts, Einstein the heretic thought that such principles are abstractions, inventions. He later emphasized: "one does not easily become aware of the free choice of such concepts, which, through verification and long usage, appear to be immediately connected with the empirical material." Just a few weeks later, in May 1905, after having struggled for years to solve puzzles about light and moving bodies, Einstein suddenly realized that the traditional notion of time in physics was just a convention, and that he could well replace it with new, freely stipulated ideas.[12]

But when?

* * *

A biographer once asked old Einstein about the "hour of birth" of relativity. He replied that it would be incorrect to speak about it as having a birthday, because "for years the arguments and building blocks were being prepared, though without bringing forth the final decision." Still, when did that "final decision" happen? Decades later he called it *the step,* according to his later colleague Abraham Pais: "When I talked to him about those times of transition, he expressed himself in a curiously impersonal way. He would refer to the birth of special relativity as 'den Schritt,' the step." It happened at some point in early 1905, when he was twenty-six years old—but when?[13]

In the history of physics, some key moments are marked clearly in time. Wilhelm Conrad Röntgen discovered X rays on the evening of Friday, November 8, 1895. Max Planck ascertained the quantum law of blackbody radiation between teatime and suppertime on Sunday, October 7, 1900. Meanwhile, young Albert Einstein slowly pondered questions about light and motion before he abruptly formulated his special theory of relativity in 1905. He characterized his long struggle as having been solved "suddenly," once he realized that the usual notions of time were just concepts that could be changed. But when? Imagine: if physicists only knew when, then they might well have an annual place of pilgrimage to celebrate their hero. To figure this out, I examined published and unpublished letters, books, journal articles, authorized and unauthorized biographies by close acquaintances, interviews, an impromptu speech that Einstein gave in German in 1922 but which was rendered only in Japanese, Swiss residence records, old city newspapers, calendars, and even weather records.

Einstein was helped by Michele Angelo Besso, a good friend who was shorter and older, a bearded engineer who was a bit of a scatterbrain. Here's one anecdote about him, as told by Einstein:

> Michele is an awful schlemiel . . . Again, Michele has nothing to do. His boss sent him to the Casale station to inspect and test the newly installed power lines. Our hero decided to go in the evening, to save valuable time of course, but unfortunately he missed the train. The next day he remembered his assignment too late. On the third day he catches

the train on time, but realized to his horror that he had forgotten what
he is supposed to do; so immediately he writes a card to the office saying that the instructions should be sent by telegraph!! I think this guy
is not normal.

Despite such absent-mindedness, Albert enjoyed talking science with
Michele, who was also versatile and thoughtful. After ten years of pon-
dering the behavior of light, Einstein wanted to review the whole, un-
wieldy problem with his friend.[14]

Looking back, in a talk given in Japan in 1922, Einstein recalled the
turning point. "But by chance, a friend of mine in Bern helped me out.
It was a beautiful day when I visited him, saying, 'Lately, I have one
problem that I cannot figure out in any way. Today I've brought you
that war.'"[15]

At the time, they worked together at the Swiss patent office. To figure out when he made relativity, we should first know where it happened. Some historians have mistakenly said that Einstein then lived
away from downtown Bern. But actually, Einstein himself once told a
newspaper reporter that "the special relativity theory arose at 49 Kramgasse in Bern." It was a small, third-floor apartment with just two windows, in downtown. At that very place, on the column of an archway
of the building, there is now a stone etching that says, in German, "IN
THIS HOUSE ALBERT EINSTEIN CREATED IN THE YEARS 1903–1905 HIS FUN-
DAMENTAL MEMOIR ON THE RELATIVITY THEORY." But it turns out that
the etching is inaccurate. Einstein did not quite write the relativity paper there, but maybe just a few sketchy pages, as we'll see. The individuals who commissioned that plaque simply assumed that Einstein
worked on his relativity paper during the entire period when he lived
at Kramgasse, which illustrates the difficulty of knowing what really
happened where.[16]

With Besso, Einstein discussed his "war," but where?

The editor of Michele Besso's letters claimed that Besso often accompanied Einstein to his domicile on 49 Kramgasse. But that editor
gave no evidence for this claim. It seems to conflate two facts: that Einstein lived on Kramgasse and that in letters Einstein alluded to "daily" walking home with Besso. It almost sounds as if Besso needlessly
followed Einstein home every day before heading back to his own wife
and son. But that editor apparently did not know that in 1905 Einstein
lived in two different apartments and Besso lived in three different

apartments, and by June 1905 Einstein and Besso were neighbors, just three blocks apart, as was shown in later research by Ann Hentschel in Bern. So trying to figure out just when Einstein and Besso walked home together, I realized that Einstein once referred to their "conversations on the mutual way home," which shows that Besso was not just following Einstein: they both had to walk in the same direction to get to their homes, west of the patent office.[17]

Since the evidence does not state that Besso daily followed Einstein to Kramgasse, I still had to figure out where they had their conversation. Again, Einstein said that "It was a beautiful day when I visited him." Apparently the conversation happened at Besso's home. Why would Einstein visit Besso on a workday, if he could just talk to him during the lunch break, from 12:00 until 2:00, or right after work, at 6:00 PM? Thus, Einstein's account of having visited Besso on a "beautiful day" suggests that they didn't go to work that day. And Einstein's work schedule left him free only on Sundays.[18]

Einstein "admitted that he had run up against a complete mental block." So he shared many aspects of the problem: "And I tried various discussions with him." Years later, Besso used the following analogy: "Einstein, the eagle, took me, the sparrow, under his wings into the heights, and then there I fluttered yet a little farther above." Einstein recalled, "By that, suddenly I came up with a clear idea." During so many years, Einstein had pursued and "abandoned many fruitless attempts, 'until at last it came to me that time was suspect!'"[19]

In 1916, the psychologist Max Wertheimer interviewed Einstein at length about the thoughts that led to the solution. Einstein had realized that phenomena of light, magnets, electricity, and moving bodies necessarily involve tacit measurements of time. Reportedly, he asked himself: "Do I see clearly, the relation, the inner connection between the two, between the measurement of time and that of movement? Is it clear to me how the measurement of time works in such a situation?" More specifically, the concept of simultaneity emerged as having crucial importance. Wertheimer reported "characteristic remarks" of Einstein: "the discovery that the crucial point, the solution, lay in the concept of time, more particularly in that of simultaneity . . . The very moment he saw the gap, and realized the relevance of simultaneity, he knew this to be the crucial point for the solution."[20]

Many writers have claimed that Einstein found the solution right then, talking with Besso. But no: further evidence suggests that what he found right then was not quite the solution, but the essence of the problem, the "key" to its solution. What happened next? One biographer remarked, "all that remains concealed in the darkness of a night in May." But actually, accounts by Einstein himself and by several close acquaintances jointly clarify the picture.[21]

An account of those days was published by Einstein's stepson-in-law, Rudolf Kayser, writing under a pseudonym: Anton Reiser. (The name Anton Reiser was the title of an autobiographical novel by Karl Philipp Moritz, first published in four parts, 1785–90, in which the poor and shy protagonist suffered a turbulent youth as he struggled in a rigid and stratified German society.) Kayser interviewed Einstein, who then read the resulting biography in manuscript and wrote a preface, approvingly noting that "The author of this book is one who knows me rather intimately in my endeavor, thoughts, beliefs—in bedroom slippers" and that "I found the facts of the book duly accurate."

Kayser recounted, "When he held the key, with which he was to open the closed door, in his hand, he despaired, and said to his friend 'I'm going to give it up.'" Likewise, two biographers who in the early 1960s interviewed Einstein's son, Hans Albert, claimed that Einstein then said, "I've decided to give it up," and "'It's no use,' he told Besso. 'I'm on the wrong track.'" Apparently Einstein then left Besso—frustrated, but having found at least the crux of the problem, something about time or motion.[22]

Back in his small, cramped apartment on Kramgasse, Einstein analyzed the problem further. How was the notion of simultaneity connected with experience? As reported by the psychologist Wertheimer, Einstein "said to himself,"

If two events occur in one place, I understand clearly what simultaneity means. For example, I see these two balls hit the identical goal at the same time. But . . . am I really clear about what simultaneity means when it refers to events in two different places? What does it mean to say that this event occurred in my room at the same time as another event in some distant place? Surely I can use the concept of simultaneity for different places in the same way as for one and the same place—but can I? Is it as clear to me in the former as it is in the latter case? . . . It is not!

To me, this passage is neat partly because the words "in my room" suggest that these were Einstein's thoughts back in his apartment. According to Wertheimer, Einstein next analyzed the puzzle as follows. He asked himself: how can one determine whether two lightning bolts strike distant places at the same time? Einstein himself wrote that explanation in 1916, for a book published the following year, in which he "spared myself no pains" in presenting such ideas "on the whole, in the sequence and connection in which they actually originated." By conceiving of a feasible physical procedure, one would be able to ascribe a practical meaning, a definition, for the word *simultaneity*.[23]

Next, one of the biographers in question claimed, "That night when he went to bed, he lay awake tossing and turning." Again, the amazing thing is how the wealth of sources provides snippets of evidence that when pulled together create a detailed picture, like a mosaic. Einstein had two stepdaughters (from his second marriage), both married, and hence a second stepson-in-law, Dimitri Marianoff, who like Kayser also wrote a biography of Einstein, this one unauthorized. And Marianoff recounted that he once asked Einstein how he had reached relativity theory:

> He said that one night he had gone to bed with a discouragement of such black depths that no argument would pierce it. "When one's thought falls into despair, nothing serves him any longer, not his hours of work, not his past successes—nothing. All reassurance is gone. It is finished, I told myself, it is useless. There are no results. I must give it up."

But the pieces of the puzzle were falling into place. According to Marianoff, Einstein's thoughts proceeded "In vision," as the "underlying unity of size, structure, distance, time, space slowly fell piece by piece, like a monolithic picture puzzle, into place."[24]

So finally! When did Einstein have his conceptual breakthrough? It was the next day. In an archive in Zurich, I read a letter by one of Einstein's friends since their days as students at the Zurich Polytechnic. Jakob Ehrat quoted what Einstein once told him: "One morning upon awakening, as I was sitting up in bed, the breakthrough thought came to me": the notion that two events that are simultaneous for one observer are not necessarily simultaneous for another. Many years later, one of Einstein's later collaborators in Princeton, Banesh Hoffmann, likewise recalled in a tape-recorded interview that "Einstein said his basic discovery came on waking up one morning, when he suddenly saw the idea."[25]

It is remarkable that four separate secondhand sources, Kayser, Marianoff, Ehrat, Hoffmann, all of whom separately spoke with Einstein at different times, converge on the conclusion that Einstein did not solve his relativity puzzle right after talking with Besso, or at night, but the next morning. Einstein realized that someone on a moving train might see two lightning bolts in a different sequence than someone on the ground. This was a new concept of simultaneity, a relative concept. So Einstein then rejected the common belief that time is the same everywhere, because this belief seemed impossible to substantiate. Inspired by Hume, he thought that no notion in physics should be presupposed as true independent of experience.[26]

Einstein's breakthrough idea was the relativity of simultaneity. Thus Jakob Ehrat's recollection referred indeed to the very morning after Einstein had his thorough discussion with Besso. Einstein promptly informed his friend and coworker:

> So the next day I went back to him again and approached him, without any greetings: "Thank you. I have completely solved my problem." My solution was about the very concept of time. Thus time is not absolutely defined, and there is an inseparable relation between time and signal speed. That previous extraordinary difficulty was solved completely by that, for the first time.

That's what Einstein said in Kyoto in 1922. It seems that that same "next day" when Einstein saw Besso again, they both went to work at the patent office, as Kayser specified:

> . . . the next day it was in the greatest excitement that he took up his duties at the office. He could apply himself to the dull routine only with effort. Feverishly he whispered to his friend that now at last he was on the right track. He made the revolutionary discovery that the traditional conception of the absolute character of simultaneity was a mere prejudice, and that the velocity of light was independent of the motion of coördinate systems.[27]

In 1924 Einstein recalled that "the solution came to me suddenly with the thought that our concepts and laws of space and time can only claim validity insofar as they stand in a clear relation to our experiences; and that experience could well lead to alteration of these concepts and laws. By a revision of the concept of simultaneity into a more malleable form, I thus arrived at the special theory of relativity." For years, Besso described himself as "a midwife."[28]

Einstein's long manuscript, "On the Electrodynamics of Moving Bodies," reached the editors of the *Annalen der Physik* on June 30, 1905, as the editors noted when it was published. At the end of the paper, Einstein had written only, "Bern, June 1905," though he dated some of his other papers with the actual day of completion as well. Comparing all such written dates with all the dates of reception of his papers at the *Annalen* at the time reveals that mail was relatively quick. It usually took only a couple of days for his submissions from Bern to be received at Berlin. Since the paper arrived on Friday, June 30, then it was mailed that same week.

MAY 1905								JUNE 1905						
Su	Mo	Tu	We	Th	Fr	Sa		Su	Mo	Tu	We	Th	Fr	Sa
	1	2	3	4	5	6						1	2	3
7	8	9	10	11	12	13		4	5	6	7	8	9	10
14	15	16	17	18	19	20		11	12	13	14	15	16	17
21	22	23	24	25	26	27		18	19	20	21	22	23	24
28	29	30	31					25	26	27	28	29	30	

The paper was mailed on or around Tuesday of the week when it was received: June 27. Working backward, we can figure out when Einstein had his breakthrough idea.[29]

In his Kyoto speech, Einstein recalled that following his big idea, "Within five weeks the special theory of relativity was completed." But how long did it take him to write the paper? In 1952, Einstein wrote to his biographer Carl Seelig that "between the conception of the idea for the special theory of relativity and the completion of the relevant publication, five or six weeks elapsed." So the theory was completed in about five weeks, and maybe Einstein finished and mailed the paper a week later. One thirdhand account claims that Einstein's wife, Mileva, read the draft. She too had studied physics and mathematics at the Polytechnic, even though she did not complete her degree. A writer who in 1962 interviewed only their son Hans Albert claimed that once Einstein finished, "Mileva checked the article again and again, then mailed it. 'It's a very beautiful piece of work,' she told her husband."[30]

So, if the paper was mailed around June 27, we may count back to six weeks prior. That takes us to about Tuesday, May 16. At that time, Albert, Mileva, and their baby boy had just moved to a new residence in the southwest side of Bern, at 28 Besenscheuerweg. It seems, however, that Einstein actually began his theory *before* moving to southwest Bern. As I noted above, Einstein himself said that his special theory of relativity arose at his home at 49 Kramgasse. Yet soon, on Saturday, May 13, 1905, the Einsteins officially registered their new address, 28 Besenscheuerweg (nowadays called Tscharnerstraße).[31]

Sunday, May 14, was the first birthday of their son, Hans Albert. Did Einstein take his radical step on that same day? Soon enough, on a Thursday, Einstein wrote to his good friend Conrad Habicht, berating him in friendly banter, as usual:

> So what are you up to, you frozen whale, you smoked, dried canned piece of soul, or whatever else I would like to hurl at your head, filled as I am with 70% anger and 30% pity! You have only the latter 30% to thank for my not having sent you a can full of minced onions and garlic after you so cravenly did not show up on Easter. But why have you not sent me your dissertation? Don't you know that I am one of the 1½ fellows who would read it with interest and pleasure, you wretched man?

Einstein had wanted Habicht to visit on Easter, April 23, but Habicht did not. In that same letter, Einstein said that he wanted to send Habicht a "rough draft" of a paper that modified the theory of space and time, and separately mentioned that they had celebrated the birthday of their baby boy. It seems unlikely that the creative breakthrough happened on the same day as Hans Albert's birthday, while the Einsteins were moving. Because, if so, Einstein would presumably remember that his key breakthrough date for relativity had been the same as his son's birthday. Instead, he did not remember the relative birthday, and he "never remembered" his son's birthday. Summing up, Einstein's breakthrough took place sometime during the prior week, May 7 to 13, while he was still at 49 Kramgasse. All that remains is to pinpoint the day.[32]

When did Einstein solve the problem? His account of 1922 suggests that the day when he and Besso had their fruitful discussion was not a workday. Since they did go to work the very next day, the Sunday to

Monday combination stands out. Trusting the evidence, fitting recollections to one another, leaves one very narrow window of time: Einstein visited Besso on the "beautiful" Sunday, May 7, whereupon he found the key to the problem. Then, early in the morning of Monday, May 8, 1905, he awoke to the relativity of simultaneity.

Now, some historical conjectures can be tested. In particular, in 1905, was the first Sunday of May a "beautiful day" in Bern? I thought we might be able to figure this out by looking for weather reports printed in newspapers. So I wrote to Andreas Berz at the Swiss National Library, and he kindly checked old newspapers and replied that "According to these news the sky over Bern was covered on Sunday 7 May 1905." Overcast, a cloudy day, not a beautiful day at all in any usual meaning of the expression!

Nevertheless, I thought that I should personally check the weather records for those days, as maybe they could still help to solve this dating puzzle. So I visited the Swiss National Library and saw that in the early 1900s the local newspapers *Der Bund* and *Berner Tagblatt* each printed weather reports twice per day, in the early and late editions. I looked for an issue of May 7, but it turned out that neither of these newspapers printed issues on Sundays. So I looked up the issues for Monday, May 8, which indeed reported an overcast sky all day, but then I noticed that it was neither a statement about the present, nor a forecast, nor a report about the Sunday weather, but instead it was a report about the previous print day: Saturday. So was Sunday, May 7, a cloudy day? Newspapers printed weather records for a given day on the next day. However, on Mondays those newspapers reported not the weather from Sunday but from Saturday. It seemed that the Sunday weather was just not reported.

As reported twice each day, that first week of May was generally cloudy, with some rain; on most days the sky was completely gray. The temperature hovered around 10 degrees Celsius, about 50 degrees Fahrenheit. On Saturday, May 6, at 7 AM, the temperature in Bern was 11 degrees and the sky was overcast. The next printed report was for Monday the eighth at 7 AM, when there was also plenty of cloud coverage and it was 10 degrees. I did not then notice that the Sunday weather was reported on Tuesdays!

The librarian, Andreas Berz, had told me that in the early 1900s weather reports in newspapers were very brief, but I might be able to obtain more detailed records from the Swiss national weather service. So I contacted the MeteoSchweiz and asked them about records for May 1905. A staff member promptly replied that the Swiss Meteorological Central Institute published comprehensive annals of records of temperatures and precipitation. A copy of the volume I needed was not available at the National Library in Bern, but it was available at the Library of the Swiss Federal Polytechnic, in Zurich.

So I traveled to Zurich; I had to go there anyhow for other things. The Polytechnic or ETH is the school where young Albert Einstein had earned his four-year degree for teaching physics and mathematics. I walked up the stairs and along the hallways, remembering the words of one of Einstein's college friends: "It was our habit to walk back and forth in the long hall off of the lecture rooms. We carried lively discussions about subjects we were studying and about things in general." At the library, an attendant lent me the 1905 volume of the Annals of the Swiss Meteorological Central Institute.

Another hurdle: the weather tables looked incomprehensible. Cryptic symbols and thousands of decimal numbers in long columns. But a helpful key explained the symbols: dark circles designate rain, three horizontal lines signify fog, arrows mean strong winds, and so forth.

Was Sunday, May 7, a beautiful day? Newspapers obtained their weather data from the Central Institute. Precise observations were made daily from locations all over Switzerland, even on Sundays. These observations were reported in the Annals. For example, those records show that on Sunday, May 14, Hans Albert's first birthday, the sky was completely clouded in Bern; there were no hours of sunshine at all. In fact, for five days, from May 13 until the morning of May 18, there were only 2.7 hours of sunshine, total. Bleak![33]

Likewise, the records confirm the newspaper reports I had seen: that the first week of May was mostly cloudy, with rain and fog. For example, the three days prior to Sunday, May 7, had a total of only 4.7 hours of sunshine. There was a lot of cloudiness, considering that for the first week of May 1905, from sunrise to sunset, there were more than fourteen hours per day in Bern, which for those three days could have added up to forty-two hours of sunlight, had it not been so utterly cloudy. Then on Saturday, May 6, it rained for five hours straight, from 7 PM until midnight.[34]

On Sunday morning there were still many clouds in the sky. But

$\lambda = 7^\circ 26'$, $\beta = 46^\circ 57'$,
$H = 572^m$, $G = 0.05 \, ^m/_m$.

Bern.

Mai 1905.
Tellur. Observatorium.

Tag	Lufttemperatur					Luftdruck			Relative Feuchtigkeit			Windrichtung und Stärke			Bewölkung			Niederschlag	Witterung
	7h	1h	9h	(7+1+9)/3	Abweich. vom Normalst.	7h	1h	9h	7h	1h	9h	7h	1h	9h	7h	1h	9h		
1	12.3	20.0	13.0	15.1	4.8	711.7	710.1	708.8	85	57	100	SE 0	NW 1	NW 0	3	7	2	1.6	a △, K ● 6¼–6¾p
2	12.5	7.0	5.8	8.4	−2.1	709.6	714.0	715.5	90	93	100	SE 0	W 0	SW 0	8	10●	10●	21.5	● 11½a–n
3	6.1	11.0	8.1	8.4	−2.2	716.1	715.9	715.3	100	67	83	SW 0	W 0	N 0	10●	6	4	0.2	●° n–7½a
4	6.4	12.7	8.5	9.2	−1.5	715.1	713.7	712.9	99	66	84	N 0	E 1	NE 1	9≡	10	10	.	a ≡ △
5	7.4	11.7	10.0	9.7	−1.1	711.8	709.4	707.8	91	82	100	SW 0	NE 1	SE 0	10	10	5≡	.	≡ III
6	11.8	13.8	9.8	11.8	0.8	707.5	710.6	711.4	86	67	93	SE 1	SW 1	W 0	8	9	10●	4.0	● 7p–n
7	8.3	14.3	10.0	10.9	−0.2	713.9	713.4	713.7	89	58	83	SW 0	NW 0	N 0	10	7	2	.	●° 2¼–2½p
8	10.5	14.2	10.0	11.6	0.4	713.1	711.6	711.4	83	67	96	NW 0	N 0	NE 0	7	10	10●	2.5	● 8p–n
9	9.2	8.7	6.3	8.1	−3.2	712.6	714.9	717.1	99	96	89	NE 0	NE 0	NE 0	10●	10●	10	4.0	● n–6½p
10	6.2	11.9	7.8	8.6	−2.9	716.8	716.7	716.6	82	57	63	NE 2	ENE 3	NE 1	3	4	1	.	↙
11	7.2	15.2	11.7	11.4	−0.2	715.7	714.6	714.0	72	45	64	NE 0	NE 2	NE 0	0	1	0	.	△ I, ↙ II
12	9.9	18.3	14.3	14.2	2.5	712.9	711.6	711.7	80	52	77	E 0	NE 1	W 0	1	2	7	5.1	●° 7½p
13	7.4	6.8	4.9	6.4	−5.5	712.1	712.3	711.9	97	86	88	NE 0	NE 1	NE 2	10	10	9	1.9	● 4–6, 7½–9a, 4½–5½p,
14	4.8	7.0	7.8	6.5	−5.5	709.6	710.4	711.1	96	91	96	NE 1	NE 1	NE 0	10	10	10●	0.6	●° III–n [↙ III
15	7.7	8.8	9.2	8.6	−3.5	709.9	709.8	709.4	100	100	100	NE 0	NE 1	NE 1	10●	10●	10●	3.9	●
16	8.0	10.3	10.6	9.6	−2.6	706.6	707.9	709.2	100	96	98	NE 0	NE 0	SW 0	10	10	9	3.3	Ψ III [●° 7¾p–n
17	9.9	15.2	10.4	11.8	−0.6	711.5	711.4	712.8	100	74	100	SW 0	NW 0	SE 0	10	8	10●	32.8	● 4–8½a, ●△° 3¼–5½p,
18	9.6	14.3	10.5	11.5	−1.0	712.8	712.1	712.6	100	69	98	SE 0	SW 0	SE 0	10	9	8	2.8	● 11–11½a, 11–11½p, *)
19	11.3	17.4	11.2	13.3	0.7	711.7	710.0	709.9	98	62	94	S 0	SE 0	SE 0	9	9	9	2.4	K ● 1¼–1¾p, ● 8½–9p
20	11.6	17.8	10.7	13.4	0.7	708.8	708.2	708.5	96	60	96	SW 0	SW 1	SW 0	8	8	10	4.1	
21	10.9	15.3	11.2	12.5	−0.4	707.7	707.2	705.8	100	68	100	S 0	W 0	NE 0	9	9	8	1.1	● n–I, 0¼–0½p
22	10.4	6.4	4.4	7.1	−5.9	704.3	**704.1**	705.8	97	100	100	E 0	NE 1	NE 1	10	10●	10●	17.6	● 7¼a–n
23	**3.5**	6.0	4.0	4.5	−8.6	705.0	706.2	706.0	100	90	100	NE 0	NE 1	NE 1	10	10	3	.	● n–5½a, ●° 7½–8½a
24	4.3	6.1	5.8	5.4	−7.8	704.8	706.8	708.7	90	86	90	NE 2	NE 1	NE 0	9	10	10	.	↙ I, ●° 1¼p
25	7.2	10.8	8.4	8.8	−4.5	710.3	711.4	712.7	86	67	80	NE 1	NE 0	E 0	9	8	1	.	
26	7.8	16.5	11.3	11.9	−1.6	713.3	713.2	714.1	87	51	86	E 0	SW 1	SW 0	3	6	3	.	a △
27	11.9	19.3	13.2	14.8	1.2	716.0	716.2	717.1	80	39	69	SW 0	W 0	SE 0	2	3	3	.	a △
28	12.2	19.6	14.5	15.4	1.7	**717.5**	716.6	716.6	82	46	58	SE 0	NE 1	ENE 0	1	1	1	.	
29	12.6	22.4	14.8	16.6	2.8	717.2	716.0	715.9	78	46	67	NE 0	N 0	NE 0	1	1	1	.	a △
30	13.7	23.2	15.7	17.5	3.5	716.8	715.1	714.3	78	**31**	63	NE 0	N 0	NE 0	0	0	1	.	a △
31	14.9	**24.8**	17.5	19.1	5.0	714.2	713.0	713.4	70	34	79	SE 0	NW 0	NW 0	0	5	5	.	a △
Mittel	9.3	13.8	10.0	11.0	—	711.8	711.8	712.0	90	68	87				6.8	7.2	6.2	Summe 109.4	*) 18. K ●° 1¼–2, 3p

Weather records for the city of Bern in May 1905, Annals of the Swiss Meteorological Central Institute.

then, the cloud coverage broke. There was no fog, and the skies became mostly clear and sunny. At 1:00 PM the temperature rose to 14.3 degrees Celsius, that is, 58 degrees Fahrenheit, higher than the previous five days. At 2:15 in the afternoon, there was a very light drizzle for just fifteen minutes. In total, there were 8.4 hours of sunlight that day, more than on the three previous days combined! Compared to those previous gray days, that Sunday, May 7, was a relatively beautiful day: warmer and sunny. The next two days became very cloudy and rainy again.

I was really surprised—after all, the weather for May 7 did match my previous conjecture from all the other evidence. So finally, I concluded that Einstein had his breakthrough discussion with his friend Besso on the afternoon of Sunday, May 7, 1905. He went to sleep that night with restless thoughts. On workdays, his job started at 8:00 AM. The married man woke up with a clear, surprising idea: events that are simultaneous to one person might not be simultaneous to another.

Albert Einstein awoke to the relativity of time on Monday, May 8, 1905, at about 7:00 AM.

Of course, we can well doubt the evidence. We might imagine instead that Einstein did not conceive the relativity of simultaneity early on a workday morning. And we can choose to imagine that he did not previously have a helpful discussion with Besso, whom he did not visit on a beautiful day. And we might imagine that Einstein needlessly lied when he said that his relativity arose at 49 Kramgasse. But if instead we do take recollections and documentary evidence pretty literally, then it seems that by the end of the first week of May of 1905, Albert Einstein found a key to open a door.

Disagreements are fine: my goal is not necessarily to convince but, more importantly, to show the curious and obsessive process by which researchers meticulously collect, combine, and even strangle little bits of history to get an increasingly clear picture of the past. At first, a past event seems to be utterly lost in time, permanently inaccessible in a blur of forgetfulness. Unlike with other discoveries or inventions, the young Einstein left no handwritten notes about how he struggled to solve conundrums about light, magnets, electricity, and motion. He even threw away the original relativity manuscript, which today would be worth millions of dollars. But by seeking and pulling together many small bits of evidence—recollections, quotations, and so forth—one suddenly feels that the mysteries are solvable: the snippets of evidence become small pieces in a big jigsaw puzzle, and the more pieces we find and bring to the table, the more it seems as if we are getting closer to a picture of the past.[35]

Compare old history books with history books that were published recently, and you'll see this: there is often such an increase in details, such a finer-grain resolution, that I am regularly astonished by the degree to which some past events are thoroughly documented. And figuring out when, where, and how anything happened are parts of that illuminating process.

When I found the interesting dates about the Bohemian String-Quartet and the Swiss weather records, it was March 2005, almost a hundred years after Einstein published his theory of relativity. I did not then publish these findings, but I wanted to do something to commemorate. I was living in Pasadena, California, where Einstein too had briefly lived and worked, and I remembered the famous photo of him riding a bicycle, elsewhere in California. So on the vacant streets of Pasadena, on Sunday, May 8, 2005, I managed to ride my bicycle without using my hands, which I had never done before.

NOTES

1.   Roger Highfield and Paul Carter, *The Private Lives of Albert Einstein* (London: Faber and Faber, 1993), 203–10.

2.   Michio Kaku, *Einstein's Cosmos: How Albert Einstein's Vision Transformed Our Understanding of Space and Time* (New York: W. W. Norton, 2005), 62. Alberto A. Martínez, "Einstein and the Clock Towers of Bern," in Martínez, *Science Secrets: The Truth about Darwin's Finches, Einstein's Wife, and Other Myths* (Pittsburgh: University of Pittsburgh Press, 2011), 206–15. It is well known that the young Einstein did imagine chasing a light wave and catching up to it, to look at it, but writers such as Kaku have added invented details such as the streetcar, the clock, and the tower.

3.   Peter L. Galison, *Einstein's Clocks, Poincaré's Maps: Empires of Time* (New York: W. W. Norton, 2003), 101–5, 122–28, 136, 140.

4.   "Albert Einstein," http://en.wikipedia.org/wiki/Albert_Einstein; accessed June 1, 2013. Alberto A. Martínez, "Material History and Imaginary Clocks: Poincaré, Einstein and Galison on Simultaneity," *Physics in Perspective* 6 (2004): 224–40.

5.   On debunking the stories about Einstein's wife, see Alberto A. Martínez, "Handling Evidence in History: The Case of Einstein's Wife," *School Science Review* 86.316 (March 2005): 49–56, or Alberto A. Martínez, "The Cult of the Quiet Wife," in Martínez, *Science Secrets,* 193–205. Albert Einstein, "Autobiographisches" (1946), in Paul Arthur Schilpp, ed., *Albert Einstein: Philosopher-Scientist* (Evanston, IL: George Banta, 1949), 13. Einstein to Besso, March 6, 1952, in Albert Einstein and Michele Besso, *Correspondance, 1903–1955,* ed. Pierre Speziali (Paris: Hermann, 1972), 464.

6.   Einstein to Moritz Schlick, December 14, 1915, Robert Schulmann, A. J. Kox, Michel Janssen, and József Illy, eds., *The Collected Papers of Albert Einstein,* Vol. 8 *The Berlin Years: Correspondence, 1914–1918,* Part A (Princeton, NJ: Princeton University Press, 1998), 220. Unfortunately, even authoritative reference works sometimes have mistakes: for example, the editors of *The Collected Papers of Albert Einstein* state occasionally that Einstein's discussion group began to meet in 1903: John Stachel, ed., *The Collected Papers of Albert Einstein,* Vol. 1 (Princeton, NJ: Princeton University Press, 1987), 382; Martin Klein, A. J. Kox, and Robert Schulmann, eds., *The Collected Papers of Albert Einstein,* Vol. 5 (Princeton, NJ: Princeton University Press, 1993), "Chronology," 617; A. J. Kox, Tilman Sauer, Diana Kormos Buchwald, Rudy Hirschmann, Osik Moses, Benjamin Aronin, and Jennifer Stolper, eds., *The Collected Papers of Albert Einstein,* Vol. 11 (Princeton, NJ: Princeton University Press, 2009), "Chronology," 182. But that

is a mistake: primary sources, even in the *Collected Papers*, show that Einstein met Solovine in 1902 (e.g., see Einstein to Mileva Marić, after June 27, 1902, in *Collected Papers*, Vol. 5) and they began their discussion group at Easter 1902 (see Solovine, below). Maurice Solovine and Albert Einstein, *Lettres à Maurice Solovine* (Paris: Gauthier Villars, 1956), x–xi.

7.   "Freitag, 17 März, abends punkt 8 Uhr: Konzert gegeben von berühmten Böhmischen Streichquartett," *Der Bund*, Eidgenössisches Zentralblatt 56 Jahrgang, Nr. 119, Saturday, March 11, 1905, 4. "Gesellschaftshaus Museum Bern. Konzert des Böhmischen Streich-Quartettes," *Der Bund*, Second ed., No. 77, Thursday, March 17, 1904, 4. Several advertisements, including: "Gesellschaftshaus Museum Bern. Samstag, den 19 März abends 8 Uhr. Konzert des Böhmischen Streichquartettes," *Berner Tagblatt*, Second ed., No. 128, Wednesday, March 16, 1904, 2; also in No. 131, Friday, March 18, and No. 133, Saturday, March 19.

8.   "Das Böhmische Quartett in Bern," *Der Bund*, Second ed., No. 82, Tuesday, March 22, 1904, 3. "Das böhmische Streichquartett in Bern," *Der Bund*, No. 132, Sunday, March 19, 1905, 5.

9.   Letters from Einstein to Conrad Habicht, October 3 and November 30, 1903, February 20, April 15, and August 1 and 6, 1904, and two postcards on March 6, 1905—all in Klein et al., eds., *Collected Papers*, 5:23–25, 26–27, 28–29, 30. Anne M. Hentschel and Gerd Grasshoff, *Albert Einstein, "Those Happy Bernese Years"* (Bern: Stämpfli, 2005), 27, 30, 176. Moritz Solovine lived at 57 Spitalackerstrasse from May 13, 1902, to October 24, 1903; 64 Militärstrasse from October 24, 1903; and departed to Strasbourg, France, on March 2, 1904; returned to Bern on October 18, 1904, and there registered his residence at 34 Altenbergstrasse until December 2, 1904. Stadtarchiv der Stadt Bern: *Fremdenregister Aufenthalter / Einzelpersonen* E 2.2.1.3., Vol. 108, Register S, Signature Nr. 232, and Vol. 109, Register S, Signature Nr. 211.

10.   Einstein to Habicht, two postcards from March 6, 1905, in Klein, et al., eds., *Collected Papers*, 5:30. Stadtarchiv der Stadt Bern: *Fremdenregister Aufenthalter / Einzelpersonen* E 2.2.1.3., Vol. 109, Register S, Signature Nr. 211. See also Hentschel and Grasshoff, *Albert Einstein*, 30, 62–63. Solovine's book was published also in German, and in that edition some words and the punctuation differ from his French version. Since Einstein spoke German, I here translate his quotation using the German edition: Solovine, *Briefe an Maurice Solovine* (Düsseldorf: Johann Fladung, 1956), [xi].

11.   Einstein to Besso, March 6, 1952, *Correspondance*, 464. Philipp Frank, *Einstein: His Life and Times* (New York: Knopf, 1948), 67. Frank was a colleague and friend of Einstein; this biography was authorized but not proofread by Einstein. Albert Einstein, "Remarks on Bertrand Russell's Theory of Knowledge," in *The Philosophy of Bertrand Russell*, ed. Paul Arthur Schilpp (Evanston and Chicago: Northwestern University, 1944); reprinted in Albert Einstein, *Ideas and Opinions* (New York: Crown Publishers, 1954), 22.

12. Einstein, "Autobiographisches," 13, 49.

13. A. Einstein to C. Seelig, March 11, 1952, Albert Einstein Archive, Hebrew University of Jerusalem and the California Institute of Technology, item 39–013. Abraham Pais, *"Subtle Is the Lord . . .": The Science and the Life of Albert Einstein* (New York: Oxford University Press, 1982), 163.

14. Albert Einstein to Mileva Maric, March 27, 1901; Stachel, ed., *Collected Papers*, 1:282–83.

15. Albert Einstein, "Wie ich die Relativitätstheorie entdeckte," lecture delivered at the University of Kyoto, Japan, 1922, transcribed into Japanese by J. Ishiwara, first published in the periodical *Kaizo* (1923); also in J. Ishiwara, *Einstein Kyôzyu-Kôen-roku* (Tokyo: Kabushiki Kaisha, 1971), 80. Present translation into English by Fumihide Kanaya and A. Martínez.

16. For example, Galison, *Einstein's Clocks, Poincaré's Maps*, 253. Einstein, quoted in a Berlin newspaper in the 1920s, as noted in Carl Seelig, *Albert Einstein, Eine Dokumentarische Biographie* (Zurich: Europa Verlag, 1954), 148. I have tried to find that unspecified Berlin newspaper, unsuccessfully. This quotation is credible because Einstein read Seelig's book and systematically wrote minor corrections on its margins, without correcting this claim about Kramgasse. A similar quotation is in Max Flückiger, *Albert Einstein in Bern: Das Ringen um ein neues Weltbild, Eine dokumentarische Darstellung über den Aufstieg eines Genies* (Bern: Paul Haupt, 1974), 95. A letter from Einstein refers to the apartment as being on the "2nd floor": Einstein to Conrad Habicht, April 15, 1904, in Klein, et al., eds., *Collected Papers*, 5:26. However, the "Einsteinhaus" museum is located on the "second floor" only if we do not count the street level (ground floor), where there is a business.

17. Pierre Spezialli, "Introduction," in Einstein and Besso, *Correspondance*, xxiv. When Besso was a little old man with long white hair and a white beard, he daily visited the library of the University of Geneva, whatever the weather, and there he met Professor Pierre Spezialli, who was a Swiss historian of science who looked after the mathematics collection. Sometime after Besso died in 1955, Spezialli approached Besso's son to inquire about Besso's papers, and in 1962 they found a hoard of old letters in a cellar.

Einstein recalled that they "discussed scientific questions daily on the way home from the workplace": see Einstein to Besso, March 6, 1952, *Correspondance*, 464, trans. Martínez. Hentschel and Grasshoff, *Albert Einstein*, 21, 57–58, 173. After Besso died, Einstein wrote to Besso's son and sister: "Later the patent office brought us together. The conversations on the mutual way home had an incomparable charm": see Einstein to Vero Besso and Bice Rusconi, March 21, 1955, *Correspondance*, 464, trans. Martínez. Their conversations on the way home ended in late April 1906 when Einstein moved south of downtown, to 53 Aegertenstrasse, as he told Solovine: "Once again I have moved, this time back to Kirchenfeld (Aegertenstr. 53). Since you departed I associate privately with nobody. Now even the conversations on the way home with Besso have ended." Einstein to Solovine, May 3, 1906, *Lettres à Maurice Solovine*, 6, trans. Martínez. Hentschel reports that Einstein registered his new address on April 27, 1906: see Hentschel and Grasshoff, *Albert Einstein*, 23, 177.

18. Einstein, "Wie ich die Relativitätstheorie entdeckte," 80. Again, the blurriness of the past: I still don't know where Besso lived right then. In early 1905 he lived at 15a Falkenhöheweg, but until when? (He was still there on March 4, 1905, when he listed this address in his registration as a new member of the Naturforschende Gesellschaft Bern; see Hentschel and Grasshoff, 74.) Next, Besso briefly lived at 41 Zeughausgasse in 1905, but when? And next, he moved to 15 Schwarzenburgstrasse, still in 1905. When Besso recorded his new addresses with the state, he did not specify the exact dates. Hentschel explains that "federal civil servants were exempted from reporting to the municipal registrar" (Hentschel and Grasshoff, 58).

19. Peter Michelmore, *Einstein: Profile of the Man* (New York: Dodd, Mead and Co., 1962), 46. As Michelmore noted (vii), Hans Albert Einstein did not check his notes nor edit the book. Einstein, "Wie ich die Relativitätstheorie entdeckte," 80. Besso, quoted in Paul Winteler to C. Seelig, March 6, 1952, 5, ETH Bibliothek Hs 304:1068. A. Einstein, February 4, 1950, in R. S. Shankland, "Conversations with Albert Einstein," *American Journal of Physics* 31 (1963): 48.

20. Max Wertheimer, *Productive Thinking* (1945), enlarged ed. (Westport, CT: Greenwood Press, 1959), 228, 174.

21. For example, Albrecht Fölsing, *Albert Einstein: A Biography*, trans. Ewald Osers (New York: Viking/Penguin, 1997), 176.

22. Anton Reiser [Rudolf Kayser], *Albert Einstein: A Biographical Portrait* (Albert & Charles Boni, 1930), 68. Michelmore, *Einstein*, 45. Michelmore's account is indirect and derivative; it is based partly on two days of interviews with Hans Albert Einstein in 1962, and mainly on many earlier accounts, including Kayser's biography of Einstein. Michelmore's book suffers of many mistakes. One minor peculiarity is that he seems to construe Reiser's metaphorical statement about Einstein holding "the key" literally, as though Einstein "reached the steps to his apartment house, he paused briefly and said . . ." Aylesa Forsee, *Albert Einstein: Theoretical Physicist* (New York: Macmillan, 1963), 28. For this biography, Forsee interviewed Hans Albert Einstein.

23. Einstein, quoted in Wertheimer, *Productive Thinking*, 174, both ellipses in the original. Albert Einstein, *Über die spezielle und die allgemeine Relativitätstheorie* (Braunschweig, Friedr. Vieweg und Sohn, 1917), iii, 14.

24. Forsee, *Albert Einstein*, 28. Dimitri Marianoff, with Palma Wayne, *Einstein: An Intimate Study of a Great Man* (Garden City, NY: Doubleday, Doran and Co., 1944), 68.

25. Jakob Ehrat to C. Seelig, April 20, 1952, Einstein Archive, Item 71–212. Banesh Hoffmann, tape-recorded interview by Denis Brian, October 29, 1982; quoted in D. Brian, *Einstein: A Life* (New York: John Wiley & Sons, 1996), 61.

26. Albert Einstein to Moritz Solovine, April 24, 1920, *Lettres à Maurice Solovine*, 18.

27. Reiser [Kayser], *Albert Einstein* (1930), 68.

28. Einstein, "Wie ich die Relativitätstheorie entdeckte," 80. A. Einstein, discographic recording of February 6, 1924, transcribed in Friedrich Herneck, "Zwei Tondokumente Einsteins zur Relativitätstheorie," *Forschungen und Fortschritte* 40 (1966): 133–35; translation from J. Stachel, ed., *Collected Papers*, Vol. 2 (Princeton, NJ: Princeton University Press, 1989), 264. Albert Einstein to the Swiss Federal Office of Intellectual Property, December 21, 1926, in Einstein and Besso, *Correspondance*, 546.

29. Albert Einstein, "Zur Elektrodynamik bewegter Körper," *Annalen der Physik* 17 (1905): 921.

30. Einstein, "Wie ich die Relativitätstheorie entdeckte," 80. Einstein to Seelig, March 11, 1952, Einstein Archive, item 39-013. Michelmore, *Einstein*, 46. As Michelmore noted (vii), Hans Albert Einstein did not check his notes nor edit the book.

31. According to the Einwohnerregister Berner und Schweizer; see Martin Klein, et al., eds., *Collected Papers*, 5:34.

32. Einstein to Habicht, Thursday, May [18 or 25] 1905, in *Collected Papers*, 5:31–32. Hans Albert Einstein, interviewed by Bernard Mayes in 1966; published in G. J. Whitrow, ed., *Einstein: The Man and His Achievement* (London: British Broadcasting Corporation, 1967), 20–21.

33. *Annalen der Schweizerischen Meteorologischen Central-Anstalt* (Zürich: Zürcher & Furrer; Comission von Fäsi & Beer, 1905); Anhang No. 4: Ergebnisse der Registrierungen der Sonnenscheinautographen im Jahre 1905, 4.

34. "Sunrise and Sunset in Bern," TimeandDate.com, available: http://www.timeanddate.com/worldclock/astronomy.html?month=5&year=1905&obj=sun&afl=-11&day=1&n=270. *Annalen der Schweizerischen Meteorologischen Central-Anstalt* (Bern: Tägliche Beobachtungen, Mai 1905), 25.

35. As Einstein informed Julian Boyd, librarian of the Princeton University Library; see Pais, *"Subtle is the Lord,"* 147. Einstein's declaration of having discarded the original manuscript appears in Flükiger, *Albert Einstein in Bern*, 103.

ALBERTO A. MARTÍNEZ is the author of four books, including *Science Secrets: The Truth about Darwin's Finches, Einstein's Wife, and Other Myths* (2011). He was born and raised in Puerto Rico. He earned his PhD in history of physics at the University of Minnesota while he lived in Dinkytown and worked at Vescio's Italian restaurant. He now teaches history of science at the University of Texas at Austin. Although he is often sidetracked by interesting things, he prefers to work on important things. He also prefers cats over dogs, because dogs stare and drool. His favorite dogs are pretzel dogs.

Katherine Hall Page

RESEARCH CAN BE MURDER

I have had a lifelong love of research. Possibly it started junior year in high school with the little dark green metal box I meticulously filled with 3x5-inch index cards for a very wordy final paper about the creation and development of the US Foreign Service—each lined card corresponding to my detailed outline with source and page number noted. I recall sitting at my desk at home surrounded by stacks of books checked out from the Livingston, New Jersey, Public Library. Even more memorable were the trips taken to the Newark Public Library—yes the same as the one in Philip Roth's *Goodbye, Columbus*—and using the reference books there. The library was, and is, an architectural gem—a beaux arts design inspired by an Italian palazzo. The interior is filled with mosaics, murals, archways, columns, and an extraordinary stained-glass ceiling covering the atrium. It was an important building, and I had important work to do. It was a library palace, a bibliophilic dream come true. I would have liked to have moved in.

Thinking back to that kind of research—stacks of index cards, outlines on pads of paper, canvas-covered three-ring binders—I'm struck by how tactile it was compared to the way most research is conducted today. The only touch is that of fingers on keys or a screen and perhaps soon not even that. Siri will do everything for us.

I write mystery novels now, having graduated from term papers—although writing to contract is quite a bit like always having a paper due. The metal boxes have been replaced with notebooks—the French ones with graph paper in an attempt to keep my handwriting legible—but for me the basic research process has remained the same, even in this Googlepedia Age.

My amateur sleuth, Faith Sibley Fairchild, is married with children. Ms. Fairchild is also a caterer (whodunit often irrevocably linked to whoateit). She grew up in Manhattan, fell in love with a New England minister, and finds herself much too far from the Big Apple in Aleford, a fictitious small town west of Boston. The attributes that make up my protagonist, plus the fact that I alternate locales for each book between Aleford and someplace else (Norway, Maine, Vermont, Italy, to name a few) mean all sorts of opportunities—necessities, in fact—to do research. These opportunities have usually been so much fun that it has been hard to stop and write the book itself.

Once I know where Faith Fairchild will find the latest body, I start to amass books, not printouts, about the place—nonfiction and fiction. I also turn to other sources—what is called "B-roll" in film (all that footage that supplements the main event, adding intriguing information). Since food plays a major part in the books, my research takes me to restaurants, markets, and other culinary venues. Throughout these initial preparations, I talk to people. If you want to be a writer, I tell school groups I visit, you have to like to be indoors and alone a lot. Talking to people gets me away from my desk. Upon occasion I travel many miles.

I have never been able to write about a place I haven't been—even Aleford is a compilation of places I have lived in or know near Boston. Some authors are able to employ the virtual world, typing in the requirements for a specific setting and transcribing what pops up on the monitor into convincing prose. I need to not only see the spot but feel it. The first few lines of *The Body in the Piazza* (2013) are

> Faith Fairchild was drunk. Soused, sloshed, schnockered, pickled, potted, and looped—without a single sip of alcohol having crossed her lips. She was drunk on Rome. Intoxicating, inebriating Rome.

I would not have been able to write that without having been there. This is not to say that other forces aren't playing a role. My favorite quotation about writing comes from Madeleine L'Engle, who described the process as "taking dictation from my imagination." This is very different from having one's characters "speak" to one—whenever I'm on a panel and hear a writer say this, I am deeply envious and wish I were not left alone to do the heavy lifting. However, dictation from imagination is hearing a voice in one's mind—one's own—and it keeps on speaking, just before sleep, in the shower, and too often while driving. For a mystery writer, and other writers as well, it's a continuous "what if?"

What if Faith and her husband, Tom, took an anniversary trip to one of those culinary retreats that have become popular in recent years—make pesto and drink vino under the Tuscan sun? I'd been to Italy, but not for many years, and never to Rome. The floor in my study soon became stacked with books, nonfiction and fiction, as I developed a loose synopsis. I read and made notes on them, the titles ranging from Elizabeth David's classic *Italian Food* to E. V. Lucas's *A Wanderer in Florence* and the recent *Rome* by Robert Hughes. I asked friends for recommendations from trips they'd taken to Italy, specifically Rome and Tuscany. What had they enjoyed seeing; what were they dreaming of eating again? I took an Italian conversation class. My five years of high school Latin felt as far back as Romulus and Remus. While "Gallia est omnis divisa in partes tres" and parts of *The Aeneid* still lingered, I wanted a few more current phrases and a sense of the sound of the language on the streets of Italy in the present day.

All the while, I was chary of too much preparation—doing research can easily become like eating peanuts. The line from Elizabeth Hardwick's *Sleepless Nights,* "When you travel your first discovery is that you do not exist," was my goal, and it became a kind of mantra. Time enough to immerse myself in all things Italian upon my return while writing the book. There is a special joy to traveling without a guidebook—I only looked at two. In *The Body in the Piazza* I give Faith an entrancing new acquaintance, met at the start of the trip, Freddy Ives, who tells her to "emancipate herself from her Baedeker" or modern-day equivalent. Adding,

> "You already have everything you need in order to ascertain the true nature of things." Her new friend, for she instantly hoped he would become one, pointed to his eyes, ears, mouth, and head.

In addition, I knew we would get lost—I have a particular talent for it—and that would provide much unexpected material. This type of wandering was a distinct joy in Rome, where we began our trip and where I knew I wanted the book to start. I had the rough outline, like a chalk one, but few details. Scouring the city for the scene of the crime added a dimension to our visit few tourists achieve. I settled on the Piazza Farnese, with its distinctive "bathtub" fountains (originally located in the Baths of Caracalla). I needed a place where the Fairchilds would be the only witnesses. With its relative isolation, the Piazza was perfetto.

We met people. A wonderful cab driver told us the city was a "historic lasagna," and about what we were passing he was not only erudite but passionate. Romans love their city. The most moving conversation we had was one with Fiorella Kostoris, a professor at the University of Rome, a friend of a friend who invited us to dinner and told us the history of the Jewish section of the city, the Ghetto, where she lives, as did her ancestors. Returning to the area for the best meals we had in Rome, we were haunted by her painful stories. In the book, I re-created this feeling for the Fairchilds. We had discovered a great restaurant, Hostaria Giggetto, steps away from the remains of Augustus Caesar's temple of Apollo and the portico he named for his sister Octavia. It is another memorial now. A plaque reads

> On October sixteenth, nineteen forty-three, here began the merciless rout of the Jews. The few who escaped murder and many others, in solidarity, pray for love and peace from mankind and pardon and hope from God.

The Fairchilds enjoy their meal, but this painful reminder is so close they can almost touch it from their outdoor table. It is a scene typical of Rome's layers, some so much darker than others. I might have missed this one had it not been for Dr. Kostoris.

We watched people. Outside a church near the Forum on a blazing-hot Saturday, a bride arrived with her father, got out of the car, took his arm, smiled at the world, walked into the church—and immediately walked out again! She got back into the car. Her dress flowed onto the pavement. Her father paced back and forth talking on his phone. No groom? We stayed put. The bride got out. She paced too. And then suddenly a young woman in turquoise tulle and stiletto heels, clutching a small bouquet, came flying down the steep street so close to us we could smell the cloud of perfume with which she had doused herself. The bride called out in what sounded like exasperation. Then they hugged. All smiles again and the three marched sedately into the church. The small crowd that had gathered to watch the drama unfold nodded to one another. Roman time! Or maybe, sisters!

We traveled north into Umbria and Tuscany, having much the same kinds of experiences as the Fairchilds do in the book—without the corpses. We did not attend an actual cooking school, but I have taken some classes at the Institute of Culinary Education in Manhattan both

Katherine Hall Page and actor/director Gianni Di Gregorio—a chance meeting outside Pane e Vino, one of the great restaurants in Rome discovered while researching The Body in the Piazza.

for pleasure and to research how real chefs—as opposed to reality TV ones—wield knives, stir pots. It wasn't hard to dream up one of these places, especially after spending time in Florence's Mercato Centrale and the city's trattorias and later getting to know the southern Tuscan medieval/Renaissance hill town Montepulciano, home of the justly famous Vino Nobile. When we found ourselves far underground below one of the tasting rooms in the maze of tunnels that connects the town's palazzos, an entire subplot sprang to life from an even earlier time. Discovering that there were also grottoes off some of the tunnels, carved from tufa—a soft limestone—and thought to be Etruscan tombs, was the icing on the biscotti.

I keep a journal when I travel, and it became as essential once I was back home as the photos I took. I relived the trip through both before I started Chapter One—before figuratively putting pen to paper.

However, this process made what I had experienced so vivid that as I became engrossed in writing the book I seldom had to consult either.

The Body in the Piazza is the twenty-first book in the series, and the ones set in other countries follow a similar pattern from the first notion of place to printed page. There have been some interesting footnotes to research on all the books. But first, an important digression.

* * *

It is a truth universally acknowledged, that a mystery writer must know how to kill people.

Despite the fact that I write a traditional mystery series in the spirit of Agatha Christie—not a police procedural, professional detective, legal thriller or one necessitating a knowledge of *CSI* (although I could certainly research all this)—I have to commit murder in an accurate and convincing manner. Simplest, of course, is good old-fashioned bludgeoning, the blunt instrument then conveniently disposed of in a nearby body of water or, better yet, snatched from the woodpile next to the conveniently roaring fire in the hearth. Unfortunately, the same method cannot be used in every book, as surely boredom, and irritation, would result for both the reader and writer. Hence research. My brother, a Conan Doyle fan from an early age, recognized this potentiality after my first book, *The Body in the Belfry,* was published in 1990 (although the murder weapon was a knife, another good standby) and presented me with what has proved an invaluable tool: *The Book of Poisons* by Gustav Schenk, published in 1956 by Weidenfeld and Nicolson (UK). The author gives a thorough account of poisons—devoting a chapter to "The Vegetable Poisons All Around Us," as well as to "The Deadly Plant Poisons of the World," "Animal Poisons," and one of my favorites: "Strange Secrets of Poisons." He covers industrial poisons, caffeine, alcohol, tobacco and betel, hashish, opium, cocaine—each in its own chapter—ending the book with "Poisons as Weapons of War." The last two sentences of his introduction provide an indication of his unique style of writing—page-turner is an understatement:

> It is always a good thing to face the facts without delay. But we need first to steel our nerves, for the facts we are about to contemplate will place quite a strain on them.

Faith Fairchild is a caterer, and food plays a major role in the books. I began to include recipes at the end of each book after many readers requested those mentioned in the text. I put them at the end so as not to interrupt the narrative, i.e., a badly battered body followed by a brownie recipe. The recipes are the most difficult part of the book to write, as they must be original, also relatively simple and without costly ingredients—plus tasty. I try to re-create dishes and ask friends for family favorites. The story that may accompany a treasured cake or soup recipe makes this research all the more meaningful. Repeating a dish, as I must to get accurate measurements, is not a hardship for my own family, especially when it is something like mussels and pasta or a dessert.

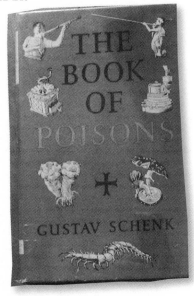

One of the recipes in *The Body in the Cast* (1993) is for "Unadulterated Black Bean Soup." Using Schenk as a guide, the adulterated version produces a deadly result early in the book. Ms. Fairchild's catering business would suffer a swift demise if I used food poisoning too often, but food and crime do go together so well.

I also came across two books, *Armed and Dangerous: A Writer's Guide to Weapons* by Michael Newton and *Deadly Doses: A Writer's Guide to Poisons* by Serita Deborah Stevens with Anne Klarner. They were published as part of the Writer's Digest Howdunit Series and have proved very useful, especially during those first years.

As do many mystery writers, I rely on a physician friend for medical information. My source is an internist and psychiatrist with experience in forensic psychiatry. He currently serves in the office of the surgeon general and is the person sent to head the teams that arrive in the wake of horrific events like 9/11 and Banda Aceh. I admire him enormously.

I was also fortunate early on to make a law enforcement connection with a retired Boston homicide detective who had taken a position with MIT's campus police. His stories were so wonderful (and gruesome as well) that I almost switched my subgenre to make him the main character.

All fiction writers are story gatherers in my experience—and usually expert eavesdroppers. This kind of research is ongoing and can occur in the most unlikely places. Many of the clues in my second book,

The Body in the Kelp (1991), involved a sampler quilt. Sampler quilts are made up of different squares, each with its own name. The same quilt square design can also have different names in different regions of the country (much hinges on this in the book). Quilters loved the book, and I found myself at modern-day equivalents of quilting bees as well as large quilt conventions. Whitney Otto's *How to Make an American Quilt* came out at the same time, and my publisher was both pleased and slightly bemused by all the quilt-related speaking requests. It was after a panel at a national gathering in San Diego that I noticed a woman who had already had her book signed, lingering. She was the quintessential grandmother with silver hair, twinkling bright eyes behind her spectacles, a flowered shirtwaist dress, and—it turned out—a way to kill someone that was undetectable. She had waited until everyone else was finished to tell me in private. It was a doozy involving water in which lilies of the valley had been sitting and tiny quilt needles (I used it many books later). The victim had to be a quilter, but not hard to fit into a plot. Impatient with finger guards, most quilters suffer the occasional pricking of the thumbs, or rather another finger. All the murderer had to do was mark time. The simple plant poison would do its job.

This sidling up to divulge a foolproof method has happened a surprising number of times since then. I'll be sipping a martini at a cocktail party, wondering if I should go for a pig in a blanket, when someone approaches with "that look." It's different from the one on the face of the person who plans to write a book someday when he or she has the time. Also different from the person who wants to know where I get my ideas. I recognize it immediately and am eager to hear what it is—while at the same time wondering whether I should get a name and address to anonymously alert the near and dear.

A totally unexpected suggestion (again I used it, dear reader) came when I was gathering information on ski resorts for *The Body in the Snowdrift* (2005). I needed to get the snowmaking details right and find out how the chair lifts operated. At a ski lodge near Burlington, Vermont, I found a chatty maintenance man. He was proud of the resort's setup and invited me to see the equipment in the pump house, then dropped the bomb while I was standing next to the reservoir of water in the floor that supplied the snow guns: "Get behind someone and push him into this sucker, and before long you'll have the slopes covered in red. Heard about this a few years ago when some fool out in Colorado got drunk and dove in before his buddies could stop him. Guns were on. That's why we keep our pump house locked." The perfect crime—handed to me on a platter.

Whatever the modus operandi, it must be plausible. Just as the killer must be. The method requires research; the killer requires playing fair with the reader—no evil twin on page four hundred or someone who has not heretofore appeared in the book.

*   *   *

Now a few footnotes to the research I have done lo these many years, much of which never appears as such in the book but rather informs it. For example, in *The Body in the Cast* (1993), Faith Fairchild is catering a movie shoot in Aleford. I came up with what I thought was a completely ludicrous idea—a modern remake of *The Scarlet Letter* with Hester in the nude (in a reverse of art imitating life, the movie I pictured in my mind came out with Demi Moore in the altogether two years later). I was creating the kind of director I thought would shoot such a film and had a terrific time reading all sorts of books about various directors—biographies, autobiographies, accounts of shoots like Katharine Hepburn's *The Making of* The African Queen, *or: How I Went to Africa with Bogart, Bacall and Huston and Almost Lost My Mind,* and fun books like *You'll Never Eat Lunch in This Town Again* by Julia Phillips. I read books about the mechanics of movie making and learned what all those people in the credits like the Best Boy do. In my library's Boston-area Yellow Pages I located Media Gourmet, which solely catered TV and film shoots. The day I spent with them was one long dish—the gossip kind—and would that I could have used real names! The star who demanded not just bottled water—of course—but twelve different kinds. The star with the munchies, and so on.

I have written four books that take place almost completely in the past, and historical research may be my favorite. *The Body in the Big Apple* is the tenth by publication date in the series—1999—but it is a prequel and becomes the first in the series chronologically. Faith is an unmarried single woman living in Manhattan in 1989. Going over back issues of the *New York Times* in the library (ah, the sweet, squeaky sound of those microfilm reels!) was fascinating. The most popular big-ticket item for holiday giving that December was a phone you could walk around with—a scientific breakthrough! It was the size of Maxwell

Smart's shoe phone and weighed so much the owner could get in a little resistance training while talking.

Part of the plot involved creating a sixties radical on the FBI's most-wanted list who was hiding in plain sight. Going back through that archival material—the Panthers, Weathermen, and all those acronyms—was time consuming but yielded wonderful information.

My twentieth book, *The Body in the Boudoir* (2012), picked up where *The Body in the Big Apple* left off—January 1990. Again, stepping into the time machine this sort of research involves was a pleasure. Marilyn Stasio's review in the *New York Times Book Review* makes mention of "the retro fun of perusing a vintage wedding menu, shopping at Bergdorf's bridal salon and having tea at the Palm Court in the Plaza Hotel." In a similar manner in *The Body in the Gazebo* (2011), I explored Boston, particularly Beacon Hill, and Martha's Vineyard for scenes that started in the summer of 1929, continuing through the early years of the Depression. I alternated chapters describing the recollections of an old woman, Ursula Lyman Rowe, with my sleuth's attempts, in the present, to solve the long-ago crime. Using Ursula's memories of growing up in Boston—the result of many hours of my research—I hope I was able to convey a sense of life at that time. Here is part of one of her conversations with Faith Fairchild:

> My father was in business and we lived on Mt. Vernon Street on the South Slope of Beacon Hill—the only side according to Grandmother Lyman. Sundays we walked up and over the Hill, past the State House with its big golden dome to church at King's Chapel. Boston has changed enormously since I was a girl, but not that walk, I fancy. The rest of the town is barely recognizable to me today. In my early years, there was no skyline. Just one skyscraper—the Customs House Tower. You can barely make it out now, so many buildings have risen up around it and we certainly never imagined that anything as tall as the new John Hancock building could exist except in the imagination. Father's office was down the street from the Customs House. Peregrine falcons nested in the tower—and still do. I imagine they find it more aesthetic than some of the other buildings nearby. Father always grumbled about the clock on the tower—it never kept accurate time. This was the sort of thing that mattered to him, and his associates, I dare say. The area was, and is, Boston's financial district, convenient to the wharves. Father would sometimes take me with him to the office when he went in on a Saturday and we'd go down to the harbor after he'd finished whatever it was he had to do.

He used to joke that if the wind was right, we could smell molasses. I'm sure you've heard about the terrible Molasses Flood in 1919. The tank where it was stored exploded and killed more than twenty people. Over two million gallons spilled out in a wave that was over thirty-five feet high. Father always mentioned the statistics. Ten years later—the story I'll get to eventually starts in the summer of 1929—people would still claim some of the downtown alleys got sticky when it was hot and perhaps it was the power of suggestion, but I did think I could smell it on those long ago walks.

You're sitting here so patiently, Faith, and I know you're wondering where I'm going with this, but I promise you, it's going somewhere. Just now I'm trying to give you a sense of what it was like in Boston—for my parents and for me. They grew up in another century and the changes the Twentieth brought were rapid and must have been bewildering to them at times. Especially the changes during the 1920s. I've often thought this was the beginning of the notion of a generation gap. Young people in the Jazz Age were so very different from the kinds of young people their parents had been in what was still the Victorian Age . . .

In *The Body in the Attic* (2004), the Fairchilds house-sit on Brattle Street in Cambridge, Massachusetts, and the children find a diary written in the 1940s by a woman who was living there then. In this case I was able to talk to people in the Cambridge area who remembered the era, in addition to mining information from books. As in *The Body in the Gazebo*, I alternated past and present—first writing the diary as a whole before dividing it into chapters that were spaced throughout the book.

Despite my love of conducting research by turning pages, people have always been my best sources. None more so than the late Paul Sewall, a fisherman in Deer Isle, Maine, without whom I could not have written *The Body in the Lighthouse* (2003). Paul loved to fish, and while telling me everything about catching lobsters—how much money he had to spend for insurance, fuel, bait, traps, a mooring, equipment, maintaining the boat before he even launched her each season—what he conveyed most was his love for the sea. Just as the cab driver in Rome had made his passion for the city palpable, Paul's simple words describing how he felt each day on the water—"There's no place on earth I would rather be"—told me everything. He was a born storyteller, describing the way his grandfather had fished with a compass and a plumb line—"No GPS, no radar"—in the same spot Paul fished, as had his father. I know Deer Isle well—have been spending summers there for over fifty years—but he opened my eyes to a part of island life I did not know and had perhaps been taking for granted. And there was his sense of humor—exactly like the one popularized by Marshall Dodge and Rob Bryan in their *Bert & I* collections—with phrases like "Happy as a clam at high tide" and "Just because a cat has kittens in an oven doesn't make them biscuits." Paul's strong Down East accent—which caused a friend from France to remark with a smile after a visit with Paul, "I did not understand one word he said"—is getting harder and harder to find these days.

My last example is the most personal. I was writing *The Body in the Bookcase* in 1996 when I left my desk to accompany my mother and my aunt on a trip to Norway to see relatives. My grandparents were Norwegian. My grandmother and her sister came to this country around the turn of the twentieth century after their parents died during one of the periodic tuberculosis epidemics that ravaged the country. Their oldest sister told the two teenagers there just wasn't any way for her to support them and the two youngest children. So off the sisters went to America—by sail—not speaking a word of English. At that time you ended up in places where others from your village had preceded you, and in my grandmother's case this meant Brooklyn and the large Norwegian community that was well established there. Shops in the Bay Ridge section still sold Norwegian goods and newspapers in Norwegian during my childhood. My grandmother was lucky to find work with a wealthy family in Manhattan; the lady of the house taught her English. After she met and married my grandfather—homesick for birch trees—she boarded a train going out of the city. When she saw some, she got off, found an agency, and rented a place for her family. It was East Orange, New Jersey. She remained homesick for Norway all her life.

This trip with my mother and my aunt (by air!), which I knew would be my mother's last, is a vivid example of the way a book—*The Body in the Fjord* (1997), in this case—can sometimes come to life virtually fully formed. When I returned home, I put aside the other book and wrote this one instead.

That particular June was when the story of the Lebensborn babies broke—the papers, magazines, and TV were filled with accounts of the children, then in their fifties. This aspect of the Nazi occupation was never mentioned—if people knew, they chose to "forget"—until the silence was broken by a documentary. Here is the description of the Lebensborn homes one of the characters gives in my book:

"The Stalheim Hotel was used in the war for something the Germans called a Lebensborn Home. We had nine of them in Norway. They were breeding places for the world the Germans envisioned after the war. We Norwegian women were especially prized because of what they thought was our pure blood. That all the children we produced with their soldiers would be tall, strong, and blond. After the occupation, German soldiers were encouraged to father children with Norwegian women. It was their duty to the Reich. When they got pregnant, some of the women went to Germany. Some stayed where they were and had them, yet that was very hard. You have to understand I make no judgments of them, but others did, often their own parents, and it was terrible for them. Most went to have the babies in these homes."

"But what would happen to all these babies? Who would raise them?" Pix asked.

"They were sent to Germany or in some cases adopted by parents here, who were sympathetic to the Germans. We were all not in the Resistance, remember. Quisling had his supporters.

"After the war, the children who remained in the homes were claimed by their mothers or adopted by Norwegian families. Some of the children who had been sent to Germany were traced by refugee organizations and brought back here for adoption if the mother did not want them, which was usually the case. The fathers were, of course, known only to the mothers and mostly their names were not recorded. The children were given two names at birth, a Norwegian one and a German one. They used to have mass christenings, twenty-five babies at a time. The babies were well looked after, but it was horrible—the whole idea and raising them like so many prize sheep. There is a story that one of the women soldiers assigned to Stalheim refused to be there and ended up at the bottom of the canyon."

"Nobody mentioned these children . . ."

An estimated eight to twelve thousand children were born in the homes in Norway alone. There were other homes in Germany, Poland, and elsewhere. I knew the Germans had a concentration camp, Grini, close to Oslo; I was also aware how my Norwegian relatives had suffered during the war. We were still sending them food packages in the early 1950s. Some had been in the Resistance. In one case, the Nazis sent a close friend's mother and fiancée to Grini in retaliation for his activities. His mother died, and his fiancée, later his wife, suffered from the trauma for the rest of her life.

With all this in my background, the horror of this eugenic experiment, these homes to create a perfect race—"Fountain of Life" is the literal translation—hit hard during the trip. I knew I would have to do more research and it would be impossible not to write about it. I have many more examples of the kind of research I do, yet none as poignant. It seems a good place to stop.

* * *

I do not mean to imply in this essay that I do not embrace technology. I am definitely not a Luddite, although I am depressed by the prospect that the Morgan Library and other places will have precious little to display in the future. Looking back at the days of my manual typewriter (an Olympia), carbon paper, Wite-Out, the miraculous invention of Corrasable Bond, the giant leap forward when someone gave me an IBM Selectric with those fonts on interchangeable metal balls—I don't miss any of them. I use my MacBook to write now, and, yes, I Google all sorts of things—fact checks for dates, the correct spelling of a name. What high tech can't ever replace is the joy of doing research by leafing through a book and coming across something new; taking a trip to someplace different; returning to someplace treasured; or—the best— talking with someone in person.

KATHERINE HALL PAGE is the author of twenty-one adult mysteries in the Faith Fairchild series and five for younger readers. She received the Agatha for Best First (*The Body in the Belfry*), Best Novel (*The Body in the Snowdrift*), and Best Short Story (*The Would-Be Widower*). She has been nominated for the Edgar, the Mary Higgins Clark Award, the Macavity, and the Maine Literary Award for Crime Fiction. She has also published a series cookbook, *Have Faith in Your Kitchen,* and *Small Plates,* a collection of short mystery fiction. A native of New Jersey, she lives in Massachusetts and Maine with her husband.

HE LIKED CUSTARD

I drive along the track, past the lake with its many swans, and park at the foot of Mount Helgafell. A narrow sheep path zig-zags up the hillside through the long grass. Despite its name, Mount Helgafell is only a little over three hundred meters high, but it is famous as the home of Gudrun, a heroine of the Sagas. I climb slowly, taking in the ever-expanding view, occasionally startling a small, grub-by sheep. Then, quite suddenly, there is nothing but broken rocks on all sides, and I am in the full blast of the wind that blows continuously over the many volcanoes, extinct and otherwise, of Iceland. Near the summit, I see the ruins of a small hut which my guidebooks various-ly describe as having belonged to a shepherd, a hermit, or some early Christian saint. I stand in its shelter to take photographs of the village of Stykkishólmur a few kilometers away, and the bay beyond. No one knows I am here, save the sheep and the ravens that circle overhead. I picture my heroine, Gemma Hardy, standing in just this place, hearing in the cry of the ravens the voice of her lost fiancé.

As a young writer, I was slow to realize that doing research is one of the deep pleasures of writing fiction. My early stories suffered from a surfeit of imagination and a paucity of accurate detail. To my youthful ears the very word *research* suggested dusty books, indexes, and crabbed notes. If I'd wanted to spend my days in the stacks of a library, I'd have stayed at university rather than becoming a waitress. Writing short sto-ries, where often all that was needed was a glimpse of a combustion engine or one brief fact about breeding Pekingese dogs, allowed me to maintain my prejudices. I'd heard, too often, the old admonition: write what you know. I was slow to understand that research could allow me to know more. Slower still to understand that research has its own dangerous siren song.

But, after some years of working on stories and writing a novel set in contemporary Edinburgh, I decided to write a pair of novels based on the lives of my dead parents. The book about my mother, Eva Barbara Malcolm McEwen, who died when I was two and a half, would be largely imagined. I knew almost nothing about her, but I was fascinated by the stories people told me about her relationship with the supernatural. Former patients complained that the hospital wards where she worked as a nurse were regularly visited by poltergeists; she saw "people" who were not visible to most other people. The book about my father, John Kenneth Livesey, who died when I was twenty-two, was an even more inchoate undertaking. He was fifty when I was born, and his early life was, like my mother's, shrouded in mystery. Still, I had read a number of wonderful biographies about people who had been dead for much longer than him. Someone knew what Sartre was wearing when he visited Delphi; someone knew what Katherine Mansfield said to Virginia Woolf at tea. Surely I could find out about my father's boyhood and young adulthood, and surely something in the stories I discovered would suggest a novel?

My father had been dead for fifteen years when I decided to write about him, and for ten years before that we had not been on good terms. He was disappointed in me. That is the word I remember from the letters he wrote to me, letters which he carried into the room where I did my homework and set down on the table. I wish I had kept them—there were only three or four—but I read them hastily, at arm's length, and tore them up. I never mentioned them; neither did he. I stayed up late doing my homework, desperate to leave home, to study, to travel. I never outwardly disobeyed my parents, but my father felt—how could he not?—that I was bitterly at odds with my stepmother. He had long ago chosen her over me, and he continued to do so at every turn. Night after night when the three of us sat down to supper in our remote farmhouse, I ate as quickly as possible and spoke little.

My father during these difficult years, and for as long as I can remember, had emphysema and smoked heavily. His false teeth were yellow, as were the fingers of his right hand. His clothes were threadbare to the point of embarrassment. Need I add that I was young and had no mercy? His last letter to me, written shortly before he had his fatal heart attack, detailed how disappointed he was that I was wasting my degree, that I didn't seem to want either marriage or a career. Of course I didn't answer but a few days later left to stay with friends. I have no memory of my last glimpse of him, or of our last words. The next time I saw him was at Perth crematorium.

I did not expect writing a novel about him to make me like my father, but I did hope to recover that part of him that had been largely eclipsed by my stepmother. (And I should say that I now believe he was right to choose her; only she could give him the care and companionship he so sorely needed.) He was born soon after the death of Queen Victoria and grew up in the Lake District, where his father was the minister of a small parish. As a boy he had climbed the hills looking for peregrine falcons, but at fourteen he was sent off to school. A grateful parishioner, whose son had been killed in France, paid for him to attend Shrewsbury School, a famous public school along the lines of Eton. He went on to Clare College, Cambridge, where he did a BA and failed to get his golf blue. After graduation, he taught in several of the boys' private prep schools that flourished in Britain at that time. In his early thirties he moved north to Scotland, where he spent most of his teaching life at Trinity College, Glenalmond, a school founded by William Gladstone in 1847 and still going strong.

I seldom asked him about his early life, but the various all-male institutions he'd been part of kept excellent records. I sent letters—this was before e-mail and the Internet—to Shrewsbury School, to Clare College, to the surviving prep schools, and to my grandfather's church, asking anyone who remembered my father to get in touch.

I received a heartening number of responses, and over the course of two years I visited as many of these elderly men, and one elderly woman, as time permitted. These visits almost invariably involved a journey of several hours on the train from London to some small town, where I would make my way to the home of my interviewee. Tea would be served. The weather and my journey would be discussed. Then I would turn on my tape recorder and ask eagerly about my father.

"You knew John Kenneth Livesey. Do you remember how you met? What your first impression of him was?"

I hoped for stories, detailed, vivid, scandalous, that would bring my young father to life.

"Well, I remember him," my interviewee would say.

"What did you do together?"

"He smoked. I remember he offered me a cigarette."

"Was he a rebel? Did he have a girlfriend?"

"Have you tried the shortbread? My daughter made it."

What I gradually learned was that these elderly men, who had kindly responded to my requests for information, remembered my father but did not remember anything about him. I finally, piercingly, understood this when I went to talk to Godfrey, who had shared a study with him at Shrewsbury School in 1916. By the time I met him, in the 1980s, Godfrey lived in a small flat in a leafy suburb of south London. I was struck, when he opened the door, by his beautiful long face and by his frailty. He seemed barely to exist inside his suit. We shook hands and he ushered me into a small sitting room before excusing himself to make tea. I sat poised with my notebook and tape recorder. This man had lived with my father for two years.

Godfrey returned carrying a tray, the teacups rattling in his grasp. No wonder his handwriting had trembled on the page. He asked me to pour the tea and talked about the swallows nesting in the eaves of his house, and the local train service.

"So you shared a study with my father," I said.

"Yes. I dug out some photographs to show you."

He produced two large black-and-white photographs, showing rows of boys in dark uniforms against a dark building. "So here I am," he said, pointing to a plump, awkward-looking boy.

"And is my father here?"

After some searching Godfrey pointed to a pretty, fair-haired boy standing at the end of a row.

"So what was he like?" I said. "Was he studious? Did he play sports? Did you stay up late at night talking? Did he believe in God? Did you talk about the war and whether you'd fight when you were old enough?"

There was a long pause. Then Godfrey said one sentence about my father. "He liked custard."

While he went on to describe how awful the food at the school had been during the war, I wrote down the sentence. Like most of my interviewees, Godfrey began to talk about what really interested him: himself, his memories, his life. And I, as I had with the other elderly men, asked questions and took notes. If I couldn't find out more about my father, I could at least learn about his peers—that generation who had the dubious blessing of being too young for the First World War and too old for the Second.

He liked custard. It is not a lot to build a novel around, but in my dozens of interviews it was the most specific thing I learned about my father. At the same time as I was interviewing octogenarians, I was also reading widely, both in the library at the Imperial War Museum and elsewhere. Although this was before Pat Barker published the *Regeneration* trilogy, before Sebastian Faulks's *Birdsong* and Michael Morpurgo's *War Horse,* there were many nonfiction accounts of the savage waste and heroism of what was then called the Great War. I plunged rapturously into John Keegan's *The Face of Battle* and Martin Middlebrook's *The First Day on the Somme.*

The novel I hoped to write sank beneath hundreds of pages of notes. I still know a good deal about the First World War, and I am still eager to talk to octogenarians. But I was never able to turn all the wonderful details about life in the first three decades of the twentieth century into fiction. My father remained shadowy, my plot vestigial, the psychological arc sketchy.

As for the novel about my mother, that too had a perilous voyage. It began on an autumn day in 1987 when a family friend told me about seeing, in Eva's presence, a very ordinary-looking woman walk through a locked door. In my notebook I wrote down the title, *Eva Moves the Furniture,* and resolved to write a novel about a woman who is accompanied by otherworldly companions. When the book was finally published, those four words were the only part of the original that survived the many years, and the many drafts. My problems with Eva's book had, I think, the opposite source from those with John Kenneth's. In the case of my father, I thought I could meld research into a novel. In the case of my mother, I thought the subject matter was so interesting—my dead mother! her relationship with the supernatural!—that it did not require research. Of course I had hoped to learn more about Eva herself, but when I couldn't, when my letters went unanswered or came back unopened, I didn't turn to exploring the Second World War, even though Eva had worked as a nurse throughout those years. I had sworn off wars. They didn't help me write novels.

While I tried and failed and tried again to write about Eva, I was writing other novels, which required research, but I had learned my lesson. I no longer embarked on massive expeditions to understand the Battle of the Somme. Instead I wrote the novel as best I could and then went looking for what I needed to know. On my way to teach one evening at Emerson College in Boston, I decided to write a novel about a banker who finds a baby at a bus station. Before I started class I wrote down, "Banker, baby, bus station." A few weeks later I had a residency at the MacDowell artists' colony with my friend Andrea Barrett. While she wrote her wonderful collection *Ship Fever,* I worked on *Criminals.* Trying to avoid some of the mistakes I'd made in the most recent version of *Eva Moves the Furniture,* I decided that this novel would take place in a short period of time and have a vigorous plot. As I typed, I kept a list of things I needed to learn more about:

> Insider trading
> Being a recent immigrant to a small Scottish town
> Living on the dole
> Betting shops
> Psychosis

When I left the colony three weeks later, I had, with Andrea's help, most of a first draft. I plunged happily into the necessary research without worrying about being overwhelmed.

As I waited for *Criminals* to be published, I turned back to *Eva.* I had another idea as to how I might make the novel work. I no longer remember what it was, but I do recall that six months later I knew that it too had been a snare and delusion. The novel still had, albeit in a slightly different form, all the problems that had made people reject it. I turned instead to writing a novel about a woman who loses three years of her memory and, in doing so, falls prey to her former boyfriend. I soon realized that in this case I couldn't simply make a list of all that I didn't know and keep writing. Even to draft certain scenes, I needed to learn more about how memory works. But despite the lure of memory palaces and Oliver Sacks's case histories, I managed to remain focused on my three main characters and their relationships. The bad boyfriend became a beekeeper, which was a wonderful excuse for talking to some of London's many beekeepers and visiting their hives. Another character became a roofer, which led me up several ladders.

Shortly after *The Missing World* was published, I had the now-familiar thought that I could make *Eva Moves the Furniture* work. I had long given up hope of publishing the novel, but I did want to finish it to my own satisfaction and to be able to recycle the seven drafts that cluttered my study. Walking down the Charing Cross Road in London, I stopped at a secondhand bookshop. I probably looked at several other books, but all I remember is picking up the one with a dark red binding called *Faces from the Fire*. When I opened it, I found an account of the legendary reconstructive surgeon Archie McIndoe, who ran a burns unit at East Grinstead in Kent during the 1940s, where he treated many of the pilots who were burned in the Battle of Britain. I bought the book for a pound and began reading on the way home. The Second World War was the cradle of reconstructive surgery in Britain, and McIndoe was a pioneer of new techniques for dealing with the terrible injuries of the Blitz. Some of his young patients remained, even after fifteen or twenty operations, unrecognizable to their mothers, but at least they could go out in public without people fainting at the sight of them. As I read the vivid account of his work, I thought I had found the perfect metaphor for the complicated relationship Eva has with her supernatural companions. In retrospect it seems almost unbelievable, but, after a decade of work on the novel, I understood for the first time that Eva, like every other child born in Scotland in 1920, was growing up to face the Second World War. I hurried back to the wonderful library at the Imperial War Museum, knowing that research could give me the tools and the material I needed to finish my love song to my mother.

Nowadays I feel that if I didn't write novels I would have to pretend to do so in order to justify the odd, haphazard exploration of the world that I call research. How else could I rationalize visiting Iceland and the Orkney islands, talking to roofers and neurologists, studying beekeeping and acting and Asperger's? Of course computers and the Internet have made these explorations easier, but for me there remains no substitute for the living encounter, the way a woman's face changes as she tries to tell you what it's like to lose her memory.

Writing this essay has made me think, once again, about all the time and work I poured into those failed pages about my father. He was a beautiful, charming, witty young man whose life was vitally constrained by two wars, poor health, lack of money, a dominating mother, and a lack of ambition, but it was my vision of his life and not the life itself that failed. Now I wondered if, with the help of Google, I could have shaped the material into a novel. For the first time I typed his name—John Kenneth Livesey—into the search engine. Here is the first entry I found, at the website for British executions.

John Kenneth Livesey.
Age: 23
Sex: Male
Crime: Murder
Date of execution: 17th December, 1952
Place: Wandsworth
Method: Hanging
Executioner: Albert Pierrepoint

A thrill ran through me. My father, my deeply respectable father, was connected with murder, at least in name. Here was something scandalous, something more exciting than custard. Perhaps the name wasn't mere coincidence. My father was an only child, but his father might have had a brother. I could try to find out. Who was murdered and why? And what about the elegantly named executioner? How had he chosen his profession, and did he have a second job? For five minutes, perhaps ten, I took feverish notes. Then a blue jay scolded in the tree outside my window; somewhere an old-fashioned phone rang; I remembered the novel I am currently trying to write, which has nothing to do with my father, nothing to do with murder in the 1950s. I closed the search. But I still have the notes.

MARGOT LIVESEY grew up in Scotland and has taught at several American colleges and universities, including the Iowa Writers' Workshop, the Warren Wilson MFA program, Brandeis University, and Bowdoin College. She is the author of a collection of stories and seven novels, including *Eva Moves the Furniture* and, most recently, *The Flight of Gemma Hardy*. She now lives in Cambridge, Massachusetts, and teaches at Emerson College.

Theodore Kornweibel, Jr.

PROSPECTING THE PAST

I'm a historian, and a prospector. I dig for buried veins and pan for specks of the past which, when patiently collected, yield lasting treasures. If you Walter Mitty me, I wouldn't choose to be a heart surgeon or a rock star. Too prosaic. Amazonian explorer or astronaut? Not exciting enough. For real thrills, give me history, raw history, unexplored history, history you have to dig out, dirt-under-your-fingernails history. The zenith of *my* prospecting has been to uncover the black railroad heritage in all its forgotten complexity and unrecognized drama, published as *Railroads in the African American Experience: A Photographic Journey* (2010). So if you've got your pick honed and pan at the ready, let's see how real gold, not iron pyrites, can be found.

Having stated my case for being a prospector-historian, I readily admit there's no perfect job. Everyone, Bill Gates and Magic Johnson not excepted, has to suffer obnoxious coworkers, going-through-the-motions associates, narcissistic clients (or interns, customers, students—fill in the blank), and just plain ornery people. Everyone has Dilbert experiences. But my profession comes close to perfection. (Close, but no cigar. For thirty-six years, lacking a teaching assistant, I read every essay exam, every research paper, every plagiarized student submission. Professor's purgatory.) I wouldn't trade a day of it for anything else.

But first the back story, starting with a cheap shot by blaming my father. Born in Victorian England at the end of the nineteenth century, he received and passed on to his three sons the virtues of a classical education (Latin was mandatory). He wouldn't directly answer questions that had pedagogical potential. Instead, "Let's look it up." Four titles were essential: a dictionary, atlas, thesaurus, and encyclopedia. In our household, it was the *World Book Encyclopedia*. As a "Leave It to Beaver" family, we spent evenings together in the living room, reading everything from the *Los Angeles Times* to Raymond Chandler to Bruce Catton to encyclopedia entries on cattle ticks and the Caucasus

Mountains. Plus the *Reader's Digest* monthly feature, "How to Increase Your Word Power."

Bruce Catton got me hooked on Civil War history about the age of eight or nine. We lived then in Glendora, a three-block-long main street village exactly 26.21 miles east of Los Angeles on the Pacific Electric Railway, the self-proclaimed "Largest Electric Interurban System in the World." (Only a passion for trains equaled my new passion for the war.) I discovered Catton's popular trilogy, reading backward beginning with *A Stillness at Appomattox* and then every other Civil War book on the single shelf in our one-room public library. But I had to dig deeper. The prospector in me had been conceived. Catton only scratched the surface. Specifically, I needed Douglas Southall Freeman to tell me why General Pickett's Confederate troops charged to such fruitless, bloody deaths at Gettysburg. And Freeman's take on why Union troops failed to simply walk into Richmond when the Petersburg crater exploded.

My first Civil War book purchase was a big one, a used copy of Freeman's three-volume, 825-page *Lee's Lieutenants: A Study in Command*. It was a huge investment for a child on a fixed income. Somehow I found it at a used book store (sadly, no longer in existence) in downtown Los Angeles. I was only barely into my second decade so of course wasn't yet driving, but this shop was only a block or two from Pershing Square, where father parked the Hudson Hornet, and equally close to Clifton's Cafeteria, famous for its façade of fanciful waterfalls and forests where birthday cake was always free. The bookstore was a classic, if not classy, literary emporium. High ceilings made it seem bigger than it was, and it smelled of antiquity and musty books. Compared with our humble public library, this was a child's treasure chest of knowledge. Several months and all three volumes later, I returned to purchase Freeman's four-volume, 1,150-page magisterial *R. E. Lee: A Biography*. These were original editions, the biography bound in red covers, *Lee's Lieutenants* in black. A hefty advance on my allowance was mandated for these purchases. With these acquisitions both a Civil War library and a young historian were birthed. Ironically, I absorbed Freeman's pro-Confederate viewpoint and until my college years was partial to the Lost Cause. Civil War history and the history of slavery moved in silent parallel universes, and I knew nothing of the latter. So for several years I read practically nothing but Civil War history. Preparation for a life's calling had begun. I was beginning to understand what it was to be a historian and to catch my first glimpse of prospecting.

We moved from Glendora to Newport Beach in Orange County, as Republican as California got, between the sixth and seventh grades. As I was still enamored of the Civil War five years later, my eleventh-grade US history teacher offered me a challenge. *The $64,000 Question* was the most popular television quiz show in the mid-1950s. I never saw it because my parents refused to buy a TV until my brothers and I were safely graduated from high school. When a contestant whose expertise was the Civil War appeared on the show, Mr. Newland copied the questions and answers and quizzed me in class the next day. I answered correctly until the $32,000 level, where I flubbed one part of the multi-answer question. Mr. Newland thought my "performance" impressive enough to relieve him of teaching for a while. For two weeks I lectured my peers, who probably thought my pedantry was as boring as waiting for General McClellan to get the Army of the Potomac moving toward Richmond. I knew from that moment that I wanted to teach history. But I needed to prepare to *study* history, *research* history, *dig* for history. In short, I had yet to discover the *craft* of a scholar and prospector.

Fast-forward to 1964 and the beginning of graduate work in history at the University of California campus at Santa Barbara. One of my first research seminars was taught by Professor Wilbur Jacobs, a well-known authority on the American West. Still fascinated by the Civil War, I had discovered the library's Wyles Collection of Civil War and western history, specifically *The War of the Rebellion: A Compilation of the Official Records of the Union and Confederate Armies,* seventy volumes of military dispatches and other documents. Something led me to investigate the war in southern California, and then on Santa Catalina Island (the "island of romance" about which the Four Preps sang in 1958). Professor Jacobs was disdainful: "There's not enough there to make a decent seminar paper." With my pride and (unpracticed) skills hanging in the balance, I persisted and wrote an "A" paper. Traveling to Washington once school was out, I found more sources in the National Archives. The result was my first publication, "The Occupation of Santa Catalina Island During the Civil War," in the *California Historical Society Quarterly.* My fellow graduate students dubbed me "the greatest living authority on Catalina Island in the Civil War" (which I was), although any distinction was dubious. The results of this experience were threefold. I had proven Professor Jacobs mistaken. I reveled in the experience of being the first (and, to this day, only) "scholar" to research that most significant topic. And seeing my name in print made me giddy. Only two more steps and I could legitimately call myself a scholar.

Degree in hand in the summer of 1966, I had to try my wings, see if this teaching aspiration would fly. But colleges weren't interested in an untested MA with only teaching assistant experience. Except one: Prairie View A & M College, in rural Texas. The school's heritage resonated with convictions deep within me. While at UCSB I had become active in CORE, the youth-led civil rights organization, and with Cesar Chavez's United Farm Workers movement. Abandoning my family's *Time* magazine Republicanism, I embraced political and ethical radicalism. (The Vietnam War only furthered these convictions.) Prairie View was a state school, still segregated, all black except for a half dozen faculty members. The job itself wasn't particularly exciting: teaching five sections of a US history survey each semester. But the adventure and self-discovery were priceless. I found a hospitable environment due in part to the fact I was a white man who didn't act or think like whites with whom students were familiar. It didn't hurt that I was only four or five years older than most of my students. They were less than interested, though, in the political, economic, and diplomatic (read: "white") history I was prepared to teach. But they were curious about their own history, which their college rarely offered. I knew next to nothing about black history. My total exposure had been limited to reading Michael Harrington's *The Other America,* James Baldwin's *The Fire Next Time,* and Stanley Elkins's controversial *Slavery: A Problem in American Institutional and Intellectual Life.* (Note to authors: avoid eight-word subtitles.) So I started reading the basics of black history in the library at night—*Up From Slavery, The Souls of Black Folk, The Negro in Our History*—and "teaching" the same the next day. The result was certainly not profound. But a world—black history—began to open before me, a world so uncharted that every topic cried out for prospecting. Precious metals poked out of the earth everywhere. This was the most exciting history I had ever encountered, more exciting even than the Civil War, containing tragedy, heroism, racism, perseverance, faith, and more. I knew then what my life's work would be. Political convictions met intellectual passions. I would be a prospector-historian, mining rich veins of an abused but unvanquished people's past. Prairie View was my inspiration.

Returning to California, I met and courted Catherine in the Haight-Ashbury district of San Francisco during the 1967 "Summer of Love." How could I not fall in love with a long-haired beauty who wore no makeup and looked like Joan Baez? The next year, new wife in tow, I embarked on PhD studies at Yale. Nineteen sixty-eight was also the birth year of the first black studies undergraduate program, at San Francisco State. No PhD program would exist for two decades. So I constructed a curriculum of one-on-one independent studies and directed readings under the umbrella of American Studies. A previously unresearched dissertation topic practically grabbed me, again providing the thrill of being first to stick my pan in an uncharted stream. The resulting thesis (later my first book) focused on the black socialists who defied J. Edgar Hoover and the rest of the government in the World War I and Red Scare years. Writing the umpteenth biography of Marcus Garvey, George Washington Carver, or W. E. B. DuBois held no allure. I wanted to bore new shafts into the bedrock of black history. My business cards could have read, "Prospecting my Specialty." Each of my subsequent books was the first volume on its topic. Certainly not the last word. But someone has to pan or wield pick and shovel in an exploratory effort. I didn't want to mine someone else's claim.

Next stop, Lafayette College, my first post-PhD teaching job. Looking for additional information on the black socialists in the National Archives, I stumbled onto a little-used treasure. In the 1940s the FBI, short of storage, copied all its Progressive Era investigative reports onto 8 mm microfilm and then destroyed the originals. Remarkably, nothing was redacted. The entire set was 955 reels of microfilm, including 110 index reels. The bureau, like other government agencies of the time, identified black individuals, organizations, and periodicals by race with a "(c)" indication.

Nobody had ever written much about the successes and fates of all the black radicals—socialists, communists, nationalists, journalists, draft resisters—of the Progressive Era and the twenties. The FBI collection was simply too massive (unless you're David McCullough, with a stable of research mules). Each index reel contained thousands of 3x5 cards with a single name, organization, or publication on it. One might spool through hundreds of cards before finding one with a (c) designation. I couldn't afford to spend half the summer going through index reels and losing my sanity in the process. But I had discovered that many of the archives' nonprofessional staff were Howard University students. They graciously recruited friends to troll through the index-es. I paid them by the reel, and it was money well spent. There were enough sources for not one but two books. I wrote first on the postwar Red Scare years. Learning that another historian was planning a book on the war years impelled me to finish my own World War I volume quickly. I was the first to mine these FBI files for black history topics, the first prospector-historian to pan this stream.

But the mother lode of mother lodes was yet to be discovered. Ser-endipity came out of nowhere. In 1993 (several years before the FBI books were finished) I received a call from the Railroad Museum of Pennsylvania asking if I could recommend anyone to speak on Afri-can Americans and the railroads. Why ask me? Despite being a railfan since infancy, I had never linked these topics. And to this day I have no idea how they got my name. But I agreed to do a lit search. Aside from a few volumes on the Pullman porters and chapters of other books on the struggles of black labor, there were only bits and pieces. No one had a broad expertise. "But if you're desperate, I could put together a slide show," I said. They were desperate. Armed only with a carou-sel of slides, a sketchy narrative, and a few railroad songs and blues, I suddenly had a hit on my hands. Other museums also wanted any-thing African American in hopes of attracting more black visitors, and I was invited to present my dog and pony show at the North Carolina Transportation Museum, the California State Railroad Museum, that state's department of parks and recreation, and my hometown institu-tion, the Pacific Southwest Railway Museum.

It gradually dawned on me that a book—a big, comprehensive, il-lustrated book—was begging to be written. Pieces from my past jelled into a new passion, uniting vocation (black history) with avocation (railroads). Why I waited so long remains a mystery. Certainly I had no understanding at the beginning of what "comprehensive" encom-passed. Of all my book projects, this one would require the deepest preliminary mapping, the deepest exploratory mining. It was not un-til I was well into the project that I understood the multiple untold narratives of black firemen, brakemen, roundhouse and shop workers, maintenance-of-way laborers, porters, cooks, waiters, car cleaners (including women), redcaps, and more. Not to mention the struggles against white unions or the railroads' complicity in perpetuating racism. I truly didn't know what I was getting into. A presidential biographer may have a new angle, but she knows her book's parameters soon after reading what has preceded her. The same holds true for most fields of history. But not black history, where the mother lode was still largely hidden or, at best, unexplored. I only developed a methodology and research plan gradually, well after leaving the starting blocks.

Where to start? Without an archival GPS and with the Internet still in its infancy, I sent letters to every archive, museum, and research library in the South asking if they had primary sources, including photographs, pertaining to black railroaders. Not unexpectedly, I got a large number of negative responses. Worse, some institutions simply didn't know what they had. Positive responses had to be prioritized. It was during a brief exploratory trip to North Carolina's Research Triangle (Durham, Chapel Hill, and Raleigh), funded by the North Caroliniana Society, that the rudiments of a research plan began to take shape. Duke and the University of North Carolina had lots of antebellum records, but few pertaining to railroads. Studying industrial slavery was going to be much more difficult than exploring agricultural bondage. Did extensive corporate collections exist? Photographs from the Reconstruction period onward became increasingly important, but the search for an authentic image of enslaved railroaders turned up nothing. I needed to define new topical categories if I was to perfect a research strategy. Help—a potentially rich vein—lay in the state archives in Raleigh. The North Carolina Railroad Commission, in the years after the *Plessy v. Ferguson* decision (1896), received aggrieved letters from black travelers containing explicit descriptions of the indignities of segregation. Among these documents was hard rock my prospecting had not previously exposed: courageous individuals unafraid of exposing the lie of "separate but equal." Dr. J. W. Jones, a physician from Winston-Salem, bombarded the commission with multiple complaints concerning too few seats for blacks, old and rickety coaches, a single toilet for both sexes, and the practice of white men smoking and gambling in the Jim Crow car. A chapter on segregation was beginning to take form along with a new type of evidence to seek.

The research trip to North Carolina broke new ground, but little more could be accomplished until funds to relieve me of teaching for

Railroad stations in the South, like this one in Littleton, North Carolina, segregated passengers in waiting rooms, cafés, rest rooms, and entrances. "Separate but equal" wasn't equal, however. Accommodations for whites were almost always bigger and more commodious. North Carolina State Archives photograph, Theodore Kornweibel Collection, California State Railroad Museum

an entire year were assured. I was pretty certain San Diego State University would grant a sabbatical at half pay for 1998–99, but it wasn't until the National Endowment for the Humanities awarded a fellowship to cover the other half that I could make firm plans. About the same time I received three additional short-term stipends. The bulk of my research would have to be accomplished in one concentrated (academic) year. Other hurdles remained. A research path had to be plotted so that I could visit as many repositories as possible without retracing my steps. Ithaca, New York, became my first stop, and I intended to end up a year later in Texas. Renting cars would soon bust my budget, so I decided to buy a used car, avoid costly airport parking by leaving it with friends for quick trips home to California, then return to the same location to resume my itinerary.

It goes without saying that I wasn't free to take only my needs into consideration during this year-long odyssey. My two sons were in their late teens, not an easy age to parent. My wife was patient, resourceful, and wise, but not a saint. She would need periodic R&R. To complicate matters, she decided, just days after I arrived in Philadelphia to begin my first research trip, to take two other teenage boys into our home. Their mother had fled to Mexico to evade drug charges, leaving them homeless. Catherine, a social worker by training, couldn't let them remain that vulnerable and made a unilateral decision. I recognized it was the Christian thing to do, but I wasn't thrilled to learn about it over the phone and have no input into the decision.

I bought a used car in Philadelphia for $6,900, a big, heavy 1991 Buick Regal Limited sedan with leather seats and power everything. It was a battleship, the biggest car I had ever owned, with only 36,000 miles on it. (Little did I know how valuable that dreadnought would be, months later in Savannah.) My first destination was Cornell University's Kheel Center for Labor-Management Documentation and Archives. Here I discovered another bonanza piece to my evolving research methodology puzzle. The Illinois Central Railroad Papers included a "Negro Affairs" category containing correspondence between IC officials and a fearless, in-your-face black brakeman. Thomas Redd not only took up his own cause but advocated for fellow employees less brave than he. Here was the puzzle piece: the story of black railroaders was only half told if I focused on categories of workers, statistics, and policies. The other half had to be personal stories. Some would involve victims of segregation, like North Carolinian Dr. J. W. Jones. Others were railroaders like Redd, a "smart negro" whose persistence was an increasing headache to company officials. Although he was unsuccessful in effecting change, his defiance had to be given prominence in my narrative. Now that I knew what to look for, other heroes began to emerge from obscurity.

The state archives at Harrisburg was next, then on to Strasburg and the state-run Railroad Museum of Pennsylvania, a week at each thanks to a small grant from the Pennsylvania Historical and Museum Commission. In Harrisburg I met a black archivist who instantly recognized the uniqueness of my research, having already begun to earmark

This Illinois Central Railroad shop laborer's portrait, made by an Office of War Information photographer during World War II, is an iconic image displaying the determination of black railroaders not only to do their "bit" to aid the war effort but to uphold the dignity of their race. Library of Congress photograph, Theodore Kornweibel Collection, California State Railroad Museum

photos and documents for a future exhibit. If scholars have unsung heroes, they are archivists. Get on their bad side (e.g., be rude and demanding), and you will likely not see half the treasures in their facility. Thank them, appreciate them, don't ask them to bend the rules for you, and they will be your scholarly BFFs. And not infrequently they *will* bend the rules. (At a certain large research facility the librarian granted me access on days when it was officially closed to the public.)

The Railroad Museum of Pennsylvania has one of the three best photo collections in the country, on which I worked furiously. After tiring of constantly fetching individual files, the largely volunteer staff allowed me to pull them from the closed shelves myself. Making copies of every photo showing a black railroader, I began to compile a census of which lines used black labor. By no means were all in the South. But there was much more than statistics as I learned to "read" photographs for the social history of daily life. Some of my favorite photos focus on human activity, with the railroad as a backdrop. The biggest breakthrough at Strasburg, however, was the "discovery" of unexplored riches in railroad employee magazines. This turned out to be as obvious as picking gold nuggets off the ground. Why had it taken so long for the light bulb to switch on? Southern and non-southern lines alike persisted for decades in identifying black workers by race. Every issue of these

Unlike World War I, when women were barred from filling male railroad occupations that required much muscle, during World War II women performed many manual labor jobs. Black women like this Santa Fe freight trucker wearing layers of men's clothing to ward off the cold were restricted to lower status–lower paid work. Library of Congress photograph, Theodore Kornweibel Collection, California State Railroad Museum

monthlies was illustrated with photographs of black as well as white employees and their families. Once again watching the clock, I photocopied any page that had at least one mention of a black worker, even if only a two-sentence obituary. I could digest all this later, at home. Working through the (combined) Reading Railway and Jersey Central Lines magazine—the roads ran almost entirely in New Jersey and Pennsylvania—I was surprised to find black employees in such a wide variety of occupations, although never as firemen and brakemen, two very common jobs for black men in the South. The use of unskilled black female labor during the world wars, I would find, was not unique. A chapter on women railroaders was starting to take shape.

By now my research strategy had pretty much jelled. As a prospector-historian I was on the hunt for three categories of "gemstones," all precious. Photographs, of course, were a high priority. My book had to be richly illustrated; I would take publishers to the mat on that score. I had already discovered the marvelous collections at the California State Railroad Museum and the Railroad Museum of Pennsylvania. The DeGolyer Collection at Southern Methodist University was likewise essential. (There are also collections focused on a single line, like the Kansas Historical Society's fine Santa Fe Railway photographs.) Work on photos could be tedious. Most railroad photographers are (still) focused on trains, locomotives, and cars. Working railroaders, including blacks, were rarely the centerpiece of a photo. But precisely because photographers were rarely interested in black workers, they tended to capture them unposed. All the richer for me.

A second absolute priority was employee magazines. In fact, they became my most important source. Some large southern lines' magazines had multipage sections featuring "News of Our Colored Employees." The content was far richer than just promotions, retirements, and obituaries. A vibrant communal life of black railroaders and their families was coming into focus. Who was courting whom; who got married; to whom was a child born (often accompanied by the infant's photograph); who had a fruitful garden or a successful hunting trip; who purchased a home or property; who traveled out of town or received guests from afar; whose child graduated from high school or (especially noteworthy) college; who served on the deacon's board or the Dorcas Society at church; who was a member of the company baseball team, what was their record, and what were the highlights of recent games?

For a century, white railroaders barred blacks from membership or meaningful participation in labor unionism. Membership in black unions like the Association of Colored Railway Trainmen was important for building solidarity among black railroaders all over the South. But the association didn't have a seat, much less a voice, at the bargaining table. Theodore Kornweibel Collection, California State Railroad Museum

And much more. The African American railroad experience, I learned, encompassed far more than what individuals did on the job. They built and led communities; found recreation; dodged racism; modeled traditional American virtues; and were a foundation for the black middle class. Remarkably, no one had ever dug into these magazines for the social history of any group of railroaders. Here was I, a prospector-historian, having stumbled upon a streambed of uncounted riches. How could they have been overlooked for so long?

A third vital category of evidence was individual railroads' corporate records. I knew this source would be hit and (mostly) miss because railroads were infamous for discarding personnel files. Most lines had little sense of history other than donating a worn-out steam locomotive for display (and rust) in a city park. Were any extensive corporate collections extant? Miraculously, much of the voluminous records of the Pennsylvania Railroad had survived—so many, in fact, that they required distribution among a number of archives. I focused on the Hagley Museum and Library in Delaware, whose PRR collection included detailed documentation of this northern railroad's employment of "colored" workers. The Pennsy touted itself not only as the world's greatest railroad but also the most benevolent toward blacks. Several charts recorded the exact number of black workers, broken down by gender, occupation, and region. Not surprisingly, there were no black engineers, firemen, conductors, or brakemen. The "Big Four" white railroad brotherhoods—unions—had a racial lock on such jobs in the North, although southern roads employed both African American and white firemen and brakemen. The breadth of manual labor jobs filled by blacks—unskilled, semiskilled, and (only a very few) skilled—was astounding. I finished furious photocopying at the Hagley with a much fuller picture of the roles blacks could (and could not) fill on any line.

Seaboard Air Line Railway black fireman and brakeman. Until the civil rights era, blacks in the South could aspire to be firemen but not engineers, and brakemen but not conductors because the forbidden jobs carried prestige (the "brave engineer") and authority over white men. Theodore Kornweibel Collection, California State Railroad Museum

The Hagley was not far from College Park, Maryland, site of the new National Archives main branch. Again, I feverishly photocopied hundreds of pages detailing the Fair Employment Practice Commission during World War II and the World War I–era Federal Railroad Administration. More good-sized nuggets which revealed the federal government's unwillingness to privilege black railroaders as it did whites. Close by was the University of Maryland, whose library yielded a nearly complete employee magazine set for the Baltimore & Ohio Railroad, a line which straddled both North and South. The Maryland Historical Society in Baltimore, housing much of what remains of the B&O's antebellum records, was disappointingly silent on whether slaves were used in its early construction. I'm convinced they were, but conservative railroad historians reject that hypothesis. The B&O Museum redeemed Baltimore, however, yielding a number of splendid photographs, some of which adorn my book.

Were there other corporate histories waiting to be uncovered? Yes and no. My next stop revealed a particularly significant, if partial, collection, plus 100 percent southern hospitality. The Virginia Historical Society in Richmond, which also awarded me a short-term research grant, had precious jewels I had not previously seen: antebellum records, in this case, of the Richmond, Fredericksburg & Potomac Railroad. As some of the most gracious archivists I would encounter brought out boxes of files, I trained my eyes to look for delicate light-blue sheets of paper about the size of business checks. These were contracts between railroads and individual slaveholders for the "hire" (rent) of slaves. Had I stumbled upon King Solomon's Mines? Almost. All sorts of information were revealed in these documents, including slave prices, occupations, conditions of employment, responsibility for runaways, and, of course, individual slaves' names and ages. These handwritten contracts were as close to knowing a railroad slave, 130-plus years after the fact, as I would get. The society's holdings also included annual reports from a variety of antebellum southern railroads, which typically listed the number of slaves owned or hired, their monetary value, and their job categories. Enslaved black firemen and brakemen were common, skilled blacksmiths less so. These reports represented a new category of documentation. Why hadn't I spotted it earlier? My prospector-historian's instincts weren't infallible. Even as I looked for annual reports at each new research site, I found more of them in the *American Railroad Journal*. Eventually I amassed evidence that slavery was practiced by a large majority of the more than one hundred antebellum southern railroads. A chapter on slavery, which had been only a title in a provisional table of contents, was being written, railroad by railroad. And a controversy over railroad slavery, which would catapult me into the news, was brewing. What had been missing from my historian's radar appeared to me as if, looking for gold, I had stumbled upon a vein of silver.

Before leaving the state, I headed for Virginia Tech in Blacksburg and the Chesapeake & Ohio Railroad Historical Society in Clifton Forge. Both had superb photographs as well as nearly complete runs of two more employee magazines, those of the Norfolk & Western Railway and the C&O. Again, I photocopied up a storm. But southern hospitality had vanished, although to be fair to that honored tradition, Clifton Forge was just a few miles from the West Virginia border, and the mountaineers aren't as well known for gracious manners. I attended church the Sunday before Thanksgiving and introduced myself as an out-of-state visitor with nowhere to go for the holiday. No invitation was forthcoming, which didn't enhance my opinion of Baptists. Not relishing the thought of a festive dinner at the local KFC buffet, I called a friend living near Roanoke and invited myself to dinner. Friendship trumped religion; it was a splendid Thanksgiving.

Done with Virginia, I flew home out of Charlotte for a brief respite. Upon my return, I skipped South Carolina, having learned through correspondence of nothing of significance there. I'm certain I missed some nuggets—they were lying exposed all over the South—but I had to use my time economically. Georgia was my focus, the site of two exciting mines. The Georgia Historical Society, occupying a stately mansion in Savannah's historic district, had the most complete files of any southern railroad I would find. The Central of Georgia Railway ran only within that state, even though as a "bridge" route it handled many luxury passenger trains from the Midwest to Florida. It evaded Interstate Commerce Commission oversight, however, because it owned track only in Georgia. The CofG collection included another rich vein, a "Negro Complaints" file regarding Jim Crow accommodations. Here again I discovered another courageous African American who would not shut up, E. C. McGlockton. The indignities he described, particularly the behavior of a conductor, were without excuse. This lout set up office in the Jim Crow car, put his feet on the table, and spat on the floor. More grist for the segregation chapter.

Either I was working to the point of exhaustion or I was daydreaming on my way to Wendy's for a quick baked potato and cup of chili when I ran a stop sign, rammed broadside into a small car, and flipped it over. To my great relief the driver was pulled out, uninjured. I readily confessed my guilt to the Savannah police, who inexplicably cited me only for running the stop sign. Chastened, and with my big heavy Buick only cosmetically damaged, I slinked out of town and made for Atlanta, where another discovery awaited me.

I'm still mystified why I hadn't recognized such an important topic while finding hints of it much earlier in the North Carolina archives. The Georgia archives contained extensive records of the late-nineteenth-century convict lease system. Slavery hadn't been as systematically barbaric. Prisons were emptied, with convicts—90 percent of them black—leased to railroads and other enterprises. Their average life span was shorter than during slavery. The sexual abuse inherent in women chained to men was the most graphic racism I would encounter in all my research.

I left Atlanta for a stop at home, plotting my last three trips. There were still claims too promising not to explore. Returning after three weeks of R&R for Catherine and my turn to put out teenage brush fires, I headed for St. Louis's Mercantile Library, where a complete run of the Missouri Pacific Railroad employee magazine awaited me. This sojourn was particularly pleasant as I avoided a Motel 6 and instead enjoyed the hospitality of my wife's aunt, a renowned audiologist at Washington University. Scholar-to-scholar, we shared discoveries, plaudits, and "aha" moments, as well as dead ends and misplaced notes and rejected papers. We understood one another so well because, both of us being prospectors, we were happily digging where no one had dug before.

To the northeast lay Chicago, my next destination. The Newberry Library granted me a two weeks' stipend which didn't stretch far in the Windy City. I found modest lodging (with kitchenette) in Downers Grove and, come Monday, joined thousands of businessmen and women aboard a Metra train to Union Station, then headed off to the Newberry by taxi. Its treasure was the Pullman Company collection, including, *mirabile dictu,* personnel records for thousands of porters and maids. Even better, the *Pullman News* revealed a wealth of community life, including the tragic fate of a summer (college student) porter who died in a derailment. His mangled body was identified only by his Phi Beta Kappa key earned at Dartmouth. Many porters were unofficial paramedics, with stories of delivering babies, nursing the sick, and dispensing medicines for everything from menstrual cramps to hemorrhoids. These were evocative specks of gold destined for a chapter on the overworked and underpaid porters. Later, the candid reminiscences of retired porters collected by oral historians proved even more valuable. Their memories were often colorful. Bing Crosby was a generous tipper, bestowing twenty-dollar bills upon being delivered a cocktail or sandwich. Jack Benny was the opposite, a cheapskate in life as in character.

My last major stop this trip was the Louisville & Nashville Railroad archives at the University of Louisville. How lucky could this prospector get? One of the special collections volunteers was a retired L&N executive who led me straight to photographic treasures. A complete run of the railroad's employee magazine was also available, and I again photocopied furiously. But most intriguing were oral histories recording the experiences of black women railroaders who worked like men while enduring white male prejudice during World War II. Well satisfied, I flew home to relieve my wife, who was now approaching sainthood.

My next-to-last trip focused on Mississippi and Alabama. How could the Magnolia State not offer excellent prospecting? Surprisingly, Ole Miss had little to share. But there was interesting material at its younger sister, the University of Southern Mississippi in Hattiesburg. Even better was the University of South Alabama just across the border in Mobile, a pretty campus whose special collections contained company records for the Gulf, Mobile & Ohio Railroad. The "Rebel Route" lived up to its nickname, openly resisting civil rights laws requiring equal opportunity for black secretaries. Reversing direction for Jackson and the Mississippi archives, I unluckily ran into the long Memorial Day weekend. Every public building was shut tight for three days. I indulged a pity party as I checked into the sole remaining downtown motel, seemingly doubling its occupancy when I arrived Friday night.

Saturday morning, I awoke to a beehive of activity. At least seventy-five people—families and singles, blacks and whites—had trans-

During World War II white women flocked to jobs in railroad offices from which black women were barred. Black women were more likely to be assigned dangerous work, like these women cleaning out potash cars for the Santa Fe with no more protection for their lungs than bandana handkerchiefs. Library of Congress photograph, Theodore Kornweibel Collection, California State Railroad Museum formed the motel into party central. Many wore bright orange T-shirts lettered "Pig Out XVI" on the front; on the back were two jolly fat pigs holding beer steins above the legend "Living High on the Hog." I recognized a smoker in the parking lot, but two small steel drums sitting atop propane burners, their contents being stirred with canoe paddles, were unfamiliar. "What's in the kettles?" "Crawdads." Plus sausages, ears of corn, and spices and more spices. "Come back later and have some." Did all Yankees get such instant hospitality? Not sure the invitation was sincere, I said I didn't want to crash a party. "Y'all join us." I played my last card. What was the cost? "Nothin', jes' join the fun." Resistance was futile: I was destined to pig out that day (and much of the next) with folks whom I didn't know from Adam but who were soon good buddies.

The crawdad pots simmered throughout the afternoon, their paddlers seriously attentive. While kids of all ages splashed in the pool on this temperate eighty-degree afternoon, others got down to serious conversation with Bud, Miller, and Coors. Those into the hard stuff drank discreetly. Late in the afternoon, two groups went into action. One pulled the pork, now having smoked twenty-four hours, while others poured the contents of the drums onto two butcher paper–covered picnic tables. Then everyone bellied up and, snapping the heads off the crawdads, sucked out the spicy morsels of meat. Sausages and corn were similarly dispatched. Napkins were useless. My mouth screamed from the spices. I tried anesthetizing it with beer, to no effect. The corn on the cob, having simmered in spices for eight hours, paralyzed my lips. But who could resist such a feed?

The pig that laid down its life to appease our carnal appetites finally arrived around six. Out of coolers came coleslaw, potato and bean salads, homemade barbecue sauces (for those who felt the smoked pork actually needed enhancement), macaroni and cheese, beans, and the ubiquitous white bread. Not French bread or potato bread or whole grain bread, but whiter-than-white Wonder Bread. Barbecue isn't complete without it. Everyone feasted. But the best was yet to come. As the sun set, a gen-u-wine good old boy appeared, opened his guitar case, and dove into a repertoire of classic southern music. There wasn't a hillbilly or honky-tonk song or blues he didn't know. He just needed lubricating to keep going. That man could sing, whether Elvis or Muddy Waters, the Possum or the Singing Brakeman. He sang me to bed, utterly exhausted, not to mention intoxicated. When our musician finally quit, I have no idea. Probably when the booze ran out.

Next morning, while the upright went to church, the hung over hung out as the party continued. Special arrangements must have been made with the motel management, for the parking lot didn't empty till late afternoon. The only thing I paid for was a T-shirt with the fat smiling pigs (which I still have). This party had started sixteen years earlier at someone's farm and moved to Jackson when it overwhelmed the farm's septic tank. I hope it's still going on. Truth be told, this was the absolute highlight of my research year, and it had nothing to do with railroads. I was prospecting unaware. The Hope Diamond was right in front of me: genuine southern hospitality.

Back home for a brief visit, then to New Orleans to begin the last major research trip. Tulane University's library had a complete run of the *Illinois Central Magazine*. This (and the Missouri Pacific's monthly) helped me understand how railroads that served both the South and the Midwest navigated sometimes-dangerous racial waters. Jobs off-limits to blacks in one region were permissible to them elsewhere. After Tulane, I was more than eager to beat the southern heat and get home for good. Only one stop remained, and it was mandatory: the DeGolyer Collection at Southern Methodist University in Dallas. No railroad pilgrim can bypass this hallowed place containing over 15,000 photographs and many more negatives representing 4,000 American railroads. A week there was barely enough, but I found sufficient images to fill at least one book. This well-known seam was still producing high-value ore. Finally, I could head for home on cruise control as my big Buick crossed mountains and deserts to reach San Diego, where I sold the car for only a thousand less than I had paid for it a year and twenty thousand miles earlier. I actually finished research in subsequent brief visits to the California State Railroad Museum in Sacramento and a road trip with Catherine to the Midwest to see the Kansas Historical Society's marvelous Santa Fe Railway photo collection. Topeka itself didn't have much to offer, but I had a pretty female research assistant at my elbow. My photo cup runneth over.

Then, abruptly, my work attracted a national spotlight. I feel sheepish admitting this, but I didn't see it coming. Activists in the slavery reparations movement were filing lawsuits seeking damages from modern corporations for past harm (enslavement) perpetrated by their antebellum corporate ancestors. The chief targets were insurance companies, banks, and railroads. *USA Today* devoted almost an entire issue to examining these contemporary industries' past connections to slavery. The lead reporter heard of my work from an archivist I had met somewhere. I had indeed found valuable ore in the antebellum record. Should I keep my claim a secret? The evidence was too important, too timely, to remain hidden until I published it. The reporter interviewed me, I sent him copies of documents, and the resulting articles anointed me the expert on the topic. Should the case get to trial, I would be an invaluable resource to the plaintiffs. I realized I had to make an important decision: should I keep my personal convictions about reparations private, at least until the trial was over? Simply let the facts speak for themselves? Yes on both accounts. By now I was being quoted in other newspapers, invited to a news conference at the National Press Club, and pursued by agenda-driven talk show hosts. Columbia University sponsored a two-day reparations conference in New York where I spoke but still kept my personal convictions private.

This notoriety—was it Andy Warhol's "fifteen minutes of fame"?—brought several unforeseen consequences. I offered to share my documentation with CSX Corporation and Norfolk Southern Railroad, the two biggest systems still operating on rights-of-way constructed by slaves. If they used that data to refute my conclusions, so be it. I had confidence that my methodology and analysis could withstand scrutiny. But neither railroad accepted. The response of the Union Pacific Railroad, however, was downright hostile. UP had just opened a new museum in Council Bluffs, Iowa. I wanted to look at the Missouri Pacific Railroad archives (the UP absorbed the MoPac in 1982) simply to search for photos of this line which bridged the South and the Midwest. But I was barred from the museum and told that, should I have any business to conduct with the railroad (including visiting the museum), I must address their attorneys. Door slammed shut. And so it remains to this day.

An equally unanticipated effect of my slavery research was to ignite a debate among railroad historians. These include some odd ducks: actual railroaders, trained historians, amateur historians, tourist-line railroaders, and railfans. Each knows a lot about at least a little piece of railroad history (and little about a lot of other things). Everyone is an "expert" on something. Now, with rumors circulating that I was in the pay of the reparations movement (which could hardly pay its own attorneys, much less potential witnesses), I published a comprehensive, fully documented article on slavery in *Railroad History, the* scholarly publication in the field. Presenting only the facts and supportable conclusions, I passed judgment on no railroad which today has a slavery heritage. Not controversial? Not possible. The you-know-what hit the fan. The controversy grew so robust that the following issue of the journal devoted six pages to responses, pro and con. Some "historians" accused me of attacking their beloved railroads by giving ammunition to the reparations movement. Others couldn't accept that black slaves had been "real" railroaders (as if brakemen and firemen of any race weren't actual railroad workers). One critic complained that social history didn't belong in a railroad history periodical, while another charged my article was a tainted "Ain't It Awful" screed. I was accused of exaggerating the harshness of slavery, which, after all, couldn't have been *that* bad. And how about those poor abused Irish and Chinese railroad builders? (This list of brickbats is far from comprehensive.)

On the other hand, I had plenty of supporters who praised the "courage" it took to publish my data (not really). The piece was later nominated for best railroad history article of the year, which was certainly vindication, although it didn't win that award because it was too controversial. Now I'll confess, I've been a tease since childhood, and I took satisfaction in making the feathers fly by stirring up a bunch of rigid, good-old-boy "rivet counters" and "foamers." I was having way too much fun! There was even material for a grad student presentation entitled "Five Easy Ways to Tick Off Historians." Eventually the controversy died down. A federal judge dismissed the lawsuit on the grounds that there were no living ex-slave plaintiffs. The sins of the "fathers" (antebellum railroads) could not be visited upon their present-day "sons." Looking back on it, this dustup was both amusing and gratifying. It's rare for historical prospecting to result in such a gold rush to judgment. If anyone wanted to inspect my "claim," they were welcome to do so. I was prepared, and honored, to defend it.

Railroads in the African American Experience: A Photographic Journey was published several years later, and didn't provoke a similar uproar. Slavery merited a single chapter, although the topic of racism suffused the entire book. Controversial or not, it was the most satisfying achievement of my professional life. Winning the Hilton Prize for best railroad book of 2011 was only icing on the cake. I enjoyed (for the most part) a thirty-six-year career teaching African American and US history, for only three employers (thank goodness for tenure and due process at a public university). But my first love was historical prospecting, i.e., research and writing. Starting with handwritten 3x5 note cards, I ended using a laptop computer with capabilities undreamt of two generations before. That span of forty-seven years, from Santa Catalina Island to black railroaders, might as well have been 470 years, from almost the Dark Ages into the digital age. There's been more change in the speed and scope of research in my lifetime than in any previous half century. But high-speed electronic wizardry has its limits. Many of the documents I perused will never be digitized. The most likely candidates for online access are employee magazines and photo collections. But many historic letters and contracts from the nineteenth century and earlier are too fragile to be run through machines, and hand-placing them on scanners would be prohibitively labor intensive. Where would regional and local museums and libraries get funding for digitizing more than a few popular items unless national priorities shift dramatically from subsidizing corn production to supporting historical preservation?

But I don't regret a minute of the work or time invested. Early on I developed a gold miner's obsession, a quest for the treasure of the Sierra Madre, as I panned day after day for elusive nuggets. How otherwise explain such dogged persistence in archive after archive? I had the faith of a religious zealot that a precious gem lay waiting in the next acid-free file folder. Switching analogies, I was a detective searching for clues not obvious to the untrained eye. Some days were seemingly wasted, lost in a box canyon. But not really. I always learned *something* from what would seem useless, because curiosity always overtook boredom, and curiosity is seldom disappointed. Besides, the next day held promise of finding another spot on the streambed where I would pan again with renewed optimism.

I'll readily admit to a "rush" when holding a newly printed book for the first time. What gold prospector wouldn't bask in the glow of a newly minted double eagle? But the newness quickly wears off. Reviewers with an ax to grind, failure to get noticed by the *New York Review of Books,* or the inability of one's university press adequately to promote the book accelerate the decline. But I'm soon at it again, prospecting for some new seam. Why do I put myself through such efforts when

I know I'll never win a Pulitzer? Or, let's be realistic, a five-figure royalty check? How gratifying is it to prepare a bang-up PowerPoint talk for a library author's event, and then only three people show up? (Yes, that actually happened.) Are your spirits lifted when only your closest friends (or those seeking free hors d' oeuvres) attend your book-release party? More than once I've consoled myself with the wisdom of Carlyle: "Fame is no sure test of merit."

Could I do it all again, I wouldn't be anything but a prospector-historian. Nothing matches the satisfactions of a life of original scholarship, no matter how modest the rewards. Fortune and popular acclaim have eluded me, but I have the inestimable satisfaction of leaving an endurable legacy. There's delight in bringing clarity and meaning where the landscape has been previously obscured. I love pursuing a topic that no one has explored, telling a story for the first time. My first books no longer sell. Last year's royalty check for one of the FBI volumes could buy little more than a Big Mac, supersize fries, and a Coke. But that doesn't matter. A legacy matters, particularly that of my railroad book. There's no higher compliment than the Hilton Prize citation, describing *Railroads in the African American Experience* as "an amazing marriage of text and illustration" recommended with "enthusiasm tempered with awe."

I've been asked to write a children's book on the black railroad experience. If I manage to successfully switch to a juvenile readership, it will be my final book. I'm staring down an incurable degenerative disease. In fact, this essay may be my last publication, period. But like the prospector to whom I've referred many times, I'm not played out. I'll still prefer nonfiction any day, hands down. Historical prospecting still courses through my veins, literally and figuratively. Tomorrow's a new exploration, if only in a good newspaper. Meet me at the streambed. And bring your own pan, gol durn it.

THEODORE KORNWEIBEL, JR.'s latest book is *Railroads in the African American Experience: A Photographic Journey,* which won the Hilton Prize for best railroad book published in 2011. After earning undergraduate and master's degrees in history at the University of California, Santa Barbara, Kornweibel earned his PhD in American studies at Yale. He is retired from a thirty-six-year career teaching African American history, the last twenty-nine at San Diego State University.

Bruce White

A GOOD TURN EVERY DAY

A Boy in Duluth in 1926

Friday, January 1: "I went to a show."

Saturday, January 30: "It was my birthday. I went up to the ski slide. I had a tobban [toboggan] ride."

Wednesday, May 5: "I took my music lesson. I got a hair cutt. I saw the first passen[g]er and freight boat go out of the harbor this summer."

Sunday, October 31: "I went to church. We had a large snow storm."

Monday, November 1: "I shoveled the snow off the sidewalk. The snow was up to my knees."

Saturday, December 25: "I went to church. I got lots of Christmas presents."

Wednesday, December 29: "I went up town. I went to the dentist."

Thursday, December 30: "I went sliding."

Friday, December 31: "I went skating tonight."

The official *Boy Scout Diary* for 1926 had a red cover with black lettering and was a little over two and a half inches wide and five and an eighth inches long. It contained 240 pages, including almost 120 pages of useful information on scoutcraft, weights and measures, and the population of regions in the United States with Boy Scout councils. The actual diary section was 121 pages and included writing space for three days on each page. The first page was headed "My Good Turns. A Scout must do a good turn to somebody every day," and every page had this counsel at the bottom: "DO A GOOD TURN DAILY." This particular diary was well worn, having been kept by a boy living in Duluth, Minnesota, but his name was not recorded in it.[1]

When, around 1983, I saw the little diary in the plastic bag in a Duluth antique store, where it was selling for two dollars, it attracted my attention because it reminded me of a pocket diary I myself had kept in 1962, when I was ten going on eleven. Mine was a Christmas gift given to me at my grandparents' house in Zimmerman, Minnesota, where we often went from wherever we were living to spend the holidays with my mother's parents. In the meager space available for January 1, my diary recorded that we left Milan, Ohio, the birthplace of Thomas Edison, on our way back to Washington, DC, where we were then living. We had spent the night in the town at my insistence, because of my obsession with the life story of *Tom Edison, Boy Inventor*. I had read about him in many books, including one of a series of orange-covered children's biographies published by Bobbs-Merrill.[2]

In the weeks that followed, I chronicled getting a haircut, building a snow fort, earning some good grades in school, and watching Jack Benny on television. On February 20, after watching John Glenn on TV in my fifth-grade classroom, I wrote: "Saw Glenn on TV. Saw when he landed. He circled 3 times." My entries petered out in the spring, with only a few entries in August, including a note mentioning my own birthday.

In the *Boy Scout Diary,* all the entries were in pencil. The first few months were sparse; it was not until April that the accounts began in earnest, continuing almost every day until the end of the year. Like my own diary, there were occasional errors of spelling and grammar.

* * *

Tuesday, February 23: *"We had a History test."*

Thursday, March 4: *"We had a Geography test."*

Friday, May 7: *"I planted onions in our garden. I set up my bird house. We had a history test."*

Monday May 10: *"We cleaned house."*

Tuesday, May 11: *"We cleaned house."*

Saturday, May 15: *"This [is] the first this spring we watered the garden with a hose."*

Saturday, July 17: *"I put up the screen windows."*

From the very beginning, many things in this diary touched a chord in me. The main thing was that it was a boy's story. The kinds of things he wrote down were the kinds of things I wrote down in my own pocket diary and in later diaries I tried to keep during my boyhood. Each entry described a moment marking the day: details of proud occasions, accomplishments, amusements, chores completed.

The author of the diary recorded having gone to several meetings of something called the Four Square Club, but did not refer to the Boy Scouts directly; however, he did mention going on hikes and doing other things that could have been scout activities. He also mentioned receiving an "emblem" on July 30 and a "bar pin" on August 24, both of which could have been Boy Scout awards. As for following the direction to do a good turn every day, the ones reported were chores—contributions to the activities of his home, such as cleaning house, putting up the screens, planting and watering the garden, picking berries, and shoveling snow.

* * *

Wednesday, May 19: "*I took my music lessons. I got my new long pants.*"

Thursday, May 20: "*I played ball. I wore my new pants to school.*"

Friday, July 2: "*I got a new cap.*"

Thursday, September 2: "*I was looking for a suit for myself.*"

Saturday, September 4: "*I got my blue new suit today with two pairs of long pants.*"

Thursday, September 9: "*First day I wear my new suit.*"

Saturday, September 11: "*First day I wear my leather jacket.*"

Tuesday, September 14: "*I got weighed. I weigh 101 lbs. 5 ft. 4 in. tall.*"

Friday, September 24: "*I got a new pair of checked stockings and a pair of Paris garders [garters].*"

Photographs of boys living in cities and towns in Minnesota before and after World War I invariably show them dressed in knee pants, also called knickers, the same kind of pants still worn by baseball players and some golfers. They did allow more freedom of movement when involved in sports or riding bicycles. It may also have been the simplest way to dress a boy who might grow a few inches in a few months. It was not until his growth slowed a bit that it became economical to buy him a pair of long pants. Hence long pants as a rite of passage, as described in accounts such as Minnesota writer F. Scott Fitzgerald's 1928 story "A Night at the Fair," about a boy in pre–World War I St. Paul for whom getting a pair of long pants became suddenly very important when one of his friends got his. Fitzgerald wrote: "Without them he was cut off from his contemporaries." It became a point of pride.[3]

In this diary, the pride in the boy's simple remarks about long pants seems obvious, and this pride in such milestones is an undertone throughout his account.

A snapshot purchased in a Duluth secondhand store in 2013 shows a typically dressed early-twentieth-century midwestern boy wearing knee pants or knickers and stockings. The date on the back, January 13, 1918, suggests that the location may have been Duluth. On that date the city was undergoing a severe winter storm, with snow followed by plunging temperatures.

* * *

Saturday, October 2: *"I went down town to the News Tribune to hear the First World Series [game]."*

Sunday, October 3: *"I went to the Strand to see Douglas Fairbanks in the Black Pirate. I heard the second World Series [game]."*

Tuesday, October 5: *"First day Duluth radio station broadcased [broadcast] at the Spalding Hotel."*

Wednesday, October 6: *"I put up my aerial. I saw a football game."*

Sunday, October 10: *"I went to the 7th World Series [game]. St. Louis won the World Series. The score was 3–2."*

Monday, October 11: *"I went over to a boy's house to test my crystal [radio] set. It worked."*

Tuesday, October 12: *"I put up a long aerial. I got Hotel Duluth, the Spalding Hotel, and Superior."*

Wednesday, October 13: *"I heard the Spalding Hotel band."*

Here's another thing I recognized in the author of the diary: an obsession with sports. The boy who wrote the diary played all sorts of sports, including baseball, football, hockey, and horseshoes. He also was an enthusiastic follower of the sports media of the time. Radio broadcasts of sports games were only beginning and were unavailable in people's homes in Duluth. But in 1926, the city's morning newspaper, the *Duluth News Tribune,* set up a giant scoreboard on Michigan Street, at the rear of the newspaper's office, which used lights to depict players on a giant baseball diamond. With a dedicated telegraph line, the newspaper was able to provide the World Series, play by play, for members of the public.[4]

Newspaper accounts state that the crowds filled the street, blocking traffic. Fans reacted to seeing the game acted out on an "electrically operated baseball field" as though they were witnessing the actual game. New York Yankees fans "shouted themselves hoarse" when Babe Ruth hit three home runs in the fourth game of the series, on October 6—the first time any player had done so. At the same time, St. Louis fans loudly and repeatedly demanded that the St. Louis pitcher be removed.[5]

Coincidentally, in 1926 Duluth was getting its first radio station, WEBC, catching up with the town of Superior across the bay, which already had one. In fact, WEBC had been in Superior earlier, before transferring to Duluth. While radios with vacuum tubes could be purchased in stores, a radio set could be made more cheaply with an antenna wire, a tuning coil of copper wire, a crystal detector, and earphones. The set did not require any source of power.[6]

While apparently no attempt was made to broadcast a play-by-play account of the World Series on the station, it was reported that "the results" would be broadcast during the game. It was the beginning of sports on the radio in Duluth.[7]

*   *   *

Tuesday, August 10: "We had a examination in history."

Wednesday, August 11: "We had a circus on the Grant playground. Polly won first prize in the pet show."

Friday, August 13: "Last day of summer school. I passed into the 7B."

Monday, August 15: "I went to the Zalda [Zelda] to see the Warning Signal."

Historians fault novelists, storytellers, and movie directors for making things up. Historians insist that the truth is much more interesting than fiction, even if the facts they find do not come to them fully formed into stories, but rather appear in scattered bits of evidence, "faint clues and indirections," as Walt Whitman put it, from which they must construct their accounts. It is important to know that raspberries ripen later in Duluth than in many other places, that Polly was probably the family's parrot (though we cannot prove this), and that the Zelda was a movie theater located downtown at 311 West Superior Street.[8]

Historians might well learn from novelists about how to communicate a sense of time, place, and feeling, but novelists could learn from historians too—practicing restraint, resisting facile conclusions, basing too much on too little. From the historian's point of view, the first step is to get the details right, get them down on paper, assuming nothing except that which rises out of the information available. There is nothing "mere" about facts; it is from them that stories can be told.

It is probably not surprising that I am a reader of mystery stories of many kinds. I have read hundreds of them. Historical research resembles the work of detectives in mystery stories, but it's more like the daily work of actual detectives. I once read an interview with a private detective who was asked about what it was like to do stakeouts and tail people down dark streets. He responded that much of his work was not like this. He spent most of his time in the library, looking up people in city directories and other sources. This was before the days of the Internet.

Truly successful historical research requires a tedious yet often rewarding search through all available resources. At the same time, it requires an intuitive sense about where information may be located. The born researcher, if there is such a thing, will early on in a project begin to absorb it, make it part of himself or herself, and become increasingly obsessed with the topic. At this point the researcher becomes hard to live with, but through heightened awareness the greatest research results are achieved. Researchers will sometimes report that in this condition, they can walk over to a bookcase, open a book, and quickly find the answer to something they are seeking. This can be described as mere coincidence, yet it is "meaningful coincidence," Carl Jung's definition of synchronicity. Coincidence is the result of obsession and detailed preparation. As the baseball team owner Branch Rickey put it, "Luck is the residue of design."[9]

I confess that in writing this account, I have followed some of the techniques of mystery writers like Agatha Christie who conceal information from the reader at the beginning of the story to create more suspense, but in this account the chronology accurately conveys the experience I myself had with the diary. At the beginning, I was not obsessed with it. I first read it as a document about Duluth and an anonymous boy living there. It was only later that I began to think I could identify him.

* * *

Thursday, January 28: "Barbara Sturminski['s] Birthday."
Saturday, February 13: "The docter came to ma. I went up to the ski slide."
Sunday, February 14: "Barbara Sturminski died 1926."

My first visit to Duluth was with my family, when I was a child. We ate lunch in a café in the old Hotel Duluth, on Superior Street, which displayed a taxidermied bear to memorialize a famous event—the animal broke through a plate-glass window and ran into the hotel dining room, where after much mayhem it was dispatched with a police officer's single shot.[10]

In the 1970s, when I came to Duluth as an adult, I was struck by the feeling that the city existed in another era. Perhaps it was that I arrived one night during a November snowstorm, and the next morning, despite the usual hardiness of city residents, there were few cars on the snow-packed city streets. But also, Duluth then had not yet felt the full "benefit" of urban renewal. Many parts of the city survived untouched. There were many old buildings, and old businesses still operated in them. Neon signs that seemed to date from the 1940s or earlier were everywhere.

A semblance of time travel can occur through the power of imagination aided by the details of everyday life from the accounts of people who lived it or from photographs depicting the places they lived. When looking at one of these photos, I often wonder what was happening beyond its borders; in my imagination I find myself walking down adjacent streets looking into windows.

For years I had no idea who had written the entries in the diary, although I often had some thoughts about how to find out. There were names and locations that could provide clues. The antique store where I bought the diary was a treasure trove of similar historical mysteries. The owner bought many things at estate sales. Occasionally I would ask her where or from whose estate she had acquired a particular item. I once found an album there filled with sepia-toned photographs of life in a small town from the late nineteenth century. A key piece of information in the images was the signs on businesses in the otherwise unlabeled photos. With information from the woman at the antique store about the identity of the person whose estate the album came from, and some research in midwestern business directories at the Minnesota Historical Society in St. Paul (where I had worked for ten years and where I often go to do research), I was able to identify the place as a little town in central Wisconsin.

In the case of the diary, there were some clues about the author. First, it was obvious that he was a boy. It was apparent that he lived east of downtown Duluth, up the hill, in a neighborhood known as the East Hillside. On the "For Emergencies" page, someone had written that the nearest fire alarm was located at Ninth Street and Seventh Avenue; other entries make clear that this was East Ninth Street and Seventh Avenue East. These entries include a number of references to attending events at Grant School (now Myers-Wilkins Elementary), located then as now at the corner of East Tenth Street and Eighth Avenue East.

Duluth covers eighty-seven square miles of land and water at the western tip of Lake Superior, a good portion of the land still undeveloped. The inhabited part of the city is strewn along a southeast-facing hillside rising up from a magnificent harbor and lakefront. The city is one where it makes sense to refer to an uptown and a downtown, though residents usually just say "by the lake" or "over the hill." The streets lie parallel to the hill and the avenues rise from the shoreline as far as they can go, which is not the same in every case. It is a city that is cooler by the lake in the summer and warmer there in the winter. There are days throughout the year when the whole bay is covered with fog and other days when the air is crystal clear and you can see far across the lake to Wisconsin.

Someone living near East Tenth Street and Eighth Avenue East would be ten blocks uphill from Superior Street, the main southwest-northeast axis of the city, and eight blocks up the Lake Superior shore northeast of Lake Avenue, which is where the city is split into its northeast and southwest halves, though residents simply call these halves "East" and "West." A person standing in front of Grant School looking down the hill early in the morning would, if the weather was right, have a fine view of the sunrise over the trees with Lake Superior and Wisconsin in the distance. Because of the steepness of Eighth Avenue, people walking up from Superior Street would be out of breath when they reached Grant. Even now, driving a car up the same street after a winter storm requires good snow tires. In the 1920s, however, a street-car crossed the hills of Duluth diagonally, heading up Seventh Avenue East just west of the school.[11]

Beyond the school to the north is an opening into the steep bluff called Chester Bowl, the location of a famous ski jump at the head of Chester Creek. In February 1926 the *Duluth News Tribune* told the story of the National Ski Tournament, the culmination of a much longer event, the Duluth Frolic, a celebration of "Duluth's glorious winter" which was "Nature's royal time—when every hill is ermine clad and every tree wears diadems and the air itself is sparkling." Ski jumpers and cross-country skiers came to compete. In the newspaper there were many photographs of the crowds that filled the bowl and of the ski jumpers rising like giant birds in the sky. On February 13, the day before Barbara Sturminski died, the boy must have walked or taken the streetcar up to Chester Park to be part of the big crowd that watched this competition.[12]

* * *

Saturday, May 1: "Barbara Sturminski was buried. I went to the cemetery."

In the 1980s, when I first found the little red diary, census information for residents of Minnesota was easily available on microfilm, both at the Minnesota Historical Society and at many other places through interlibrary loan. Indexing of censuses had begun, but not many had been completed, especially those from the twentieth century. Tracking down someone named Barbara Sturminski and the boy who kept the diary (if I had known his name) in a big city like Duluth would have required having an idea of where they had lived and then searching page by page on the microfilm to locate them. In 1983, the 1910 census was the most recent available, because census information on individuals is not made public until seventy-two years after it has been compiled. So the 1920 census became available in 1992, the 1930 in 2002, and the 1940 in 2012.

As it turns out, I could not have found a Duluth census containing the name of the boy who wrote the diary until the 1930 census was made public, in 2002. But I could have learned a great deal from a Duluth city directory. City directories contain information compiled yearly by private companies on almost every adult resident of many towns and cities. Had I looked up the name "Sturminski" in a directory for Duluth from the early 1920s, I would have been on my way to solving many of the mysteries about the boy and his diary. I never tried this path because the diary was something I was curious about but was not a priority. I had lots of other projects, including research on Ojibwe and Dakota people and their history in Minnesota. This often led me to US censuses, especially the federal censuses of 1900 and 1910, the first to fully record Indian people in an intentional way. But my work left little time for extra projects.

By the early twenty-first century, a great deal had changed in doing census research. Online sources of census information such as Ancestry.com, with indexes to most federal censuses, were now available. In 2004, I signed up for a yearly subscription. It was amazing to be able to use censuses from every part of the country at any time of the night and day, in my own home, whenever I wanted. Occasionally, at home with nothing better to do and bored with the detective novel I was reading, I would look up someone in the censuses to answer some nagging question that had occurred to me over the years. This was a kind of recreational research, a way of honing skills for other projects.

* * *

Saturday, April 24: "I made my bird house and I played ball."
Sunday, April 25: "I went to church and I went to a show."
Thursday, April 29: "I took my piano lesson and I bought myself a book."
Tuesday, May 18: "We got the new book case."

One year on a chilly day in November, I was at home struggling with a stubborn cold when I finally remembered the little pocket diary and wondered if I could figure out who the boy was. The obvious place to start was the 1920 census, the last census that would have included Barbara Sturminski. I went to Ancestry.com and found her listed as living with her husband, Andrew. The census stated that they had come to the United States from German-occupied Poland in 1878—although later I found that the Sturminskis had actually arrived in 1881—and had become citizens in 1888. Living with them was a daughter, Mary, thirty-eight, recorded as single. Their address, 1004 Seventh Avenue East, was right behind Grant School on the same street where the streetcar line ran and fit the information in the diary. But there was no boy listed as living in the house.[13]

The next step I took was to check the 1930 census to find out what had happened to the family after Barbara's death in 1926. I learned that Andrew was still living at 1004 Seventh Avenue East with his daughter Mary. But this time she was identified differently, as Mary Good, and with her was her son, Philip Good, nineteen.[14]

The 1930 census stated that Philip Good was an errand boy for a printing shop. It said that he could read and write but that he had not attended school since the previous September; that he was born in California; that his mother was born in Poland; and that his father was born in the state of New York. But at the Sturminski home in 1930, the boy's father was not listed. There seemed to be a strong possibility that Philip Good was the author of the diary.[15]

Sometimes in doing historical research the facts take an unexpected form. They begin to resonate with a kind of synchronicity in which they make sense not in a cause-and-effect way but in a lateral, almost artistic coherence. Now that I knew the author of the diary might be a boy named Good, the phrase "Do a good turn daily" appearing at the bottom of every page of the diary seemed imbued with special meaning.

* * *

Tuesday, June 1: "We had a[n] arithmetic test. I played ball."
Friday, June 4: "We had a geography test."
Friday, June 11: "We got our Report cards."
Saturday, June 12: "I played ball."

I was able to consult other records not available thirty years ago. Since then, the Minnesota Historical Society has conducted a massive effort to microfilm and index all the death records kept by the Minnesota Department of Health. Now it's possible to check the index online and find a death certificate number, then go into the historical society, get the right roll of microfilm, put it on a reader-printer, and print a copy of the certificate.

Death certificates are wonderfully rich documents, containing a great deal that is useful for personal, family, and community history. Sometimes the full meaning of the information on them is not evident on first reading. Within a few weeks of locating Philip Good, his mother, and many other members of the Sturminski family in the censuses, I found their death certificates. Andrew Sturminski died in 1930, a few weeks after the census taker appeared at the family's house. Philip's mother, Mary, lived another fourteen years at the same address. Her death certificate lists her husband as a man named "Phillip Good." Her son's death certificate from 1981 states his birthday, January 30, 1911, gives his middle name as Joseph, but does not state his father's first name.[16]

The birth date was the definitive proof that young Philip was the author of the diary, because that was the date given by the boy in the diary. Later on I found city directories for Duluth in the 1920s and 1930s that listed Mary Good as the widow of Philip Good. But he, the apparent father of her son, never appeared in any Duluth city directory as a resident of the city.

* * *

Monday, June 21: "I went to summer school. I went to a show."

Tuesday, July 27: "Ann went away to Seattle. I went in a kite contest but I did not win."

Wednesday, June 28: "I got t[w]o postcards from Ann from North Dakota."

Wednesday, August 25: "I got a magazine from Ann from California. I got a bank from Ann from China town."

Monday, September 6: "Ann and Nell went away to Virginia."

There is no mention of Philip's mother in his diary. The woman called "Ma" must have been his grandmother, suggesting that a reference to "Pa" was to his grandfather. Philip's aunts Ann (also listed in some records as Anna) and Nellie, however, were mentioned frequently, and there were several mentions of "Uncle Bill," William Sturminski. There were other relatives who were not mentioned in Philip's diary.

Andrew Sturminski, who was born in 1850, and his wife, Barbara Rzepka, born in 1859, came to the United States on the *Lessing* from Hamburg in March 1881. Along with them was their young daughter Mary, identified as Marianne in a ship's manifest and later sometimes called Marie. The family appears to have reached Minnesota soon after that. Sources refer to a son, named Stanislaus, Stance, or Stanley, born in the United States around 1885. As an adult he was in the navy, serving in both World Wars I and II; he is buried in Arlington National Cemetery. Nellie and Ann were Mary's younger sisters, both born in Minnesota (Nellie in 1891 and Ann in 1892) after their parents' immigration to the United States. Both graduated in 1910 from Duluth Central High School, and both attended Duluth Normal School for two years in training to become elementary school teachers. They both taught on the Iron Range, north of Duluth, in the town of Virginia and possibly later on in Duluth. In the late 1920s, Ann married a Duluth dentist, Francis Barnard, after the death of his first wife. Nellie never married. Another daughter, Margaret, was born in 1890 but died in 1904.[17]

Andrew and Barbara's second son, William Sturminski, who was known also as William Smith, was born in 1887. (This was Philip's uncle Bill.) Throughout his life he had various occupations that took him all over the country, most often tending bar. At the time of his death, in 1958, he was working as a bartender in Moose Lake, Minnesota. He never married. A third son, Frank, was born in 1894 and later lived in California and elsewhere. According to Frank's World War I draft registration, he served in the navy and he shared his nephew Philip's birthday, January 30. At the time of his mother's death it was reported that Frank was living in California.[18]

As the oldest child, Mary was the first to start working. At the age of fifteen, according to the 1895 Minnesota State Census, she was living and working as a servant in the household of Heiman Berthold, a "Capitalist." In 1900, while the "Struminskis" lived on Garfield Avenue near the docks on Rice's Point, Mary, then nineteen, was living with and working as a domestic servant for Walter Singer, a "vessel agent" living on First Avenue West along with his wife. A few years later, according to the city directory, she was a "waiter" at the Hotel St. Louis, still living with her family on Garfield Avenue. Her father worked as a laborer for the Northern Pacific Railway. Her brothers Stanislaus, a messenger, and William, a laborer, lived with them. Her sisters Ann and Nellie were still in school.[19]

* * *

Wednesday, September 22: "I went down to the Soo Line depot to [see?]
Uncle Bill."

Wednesday, December 22: "I got a card from Uncle Bill."

Geographic mobility has been a fact of American life since before the arrival of European Americans, and it has remained significant for hundreds of years. The creation of census indexes over the last twenty years and their availability on sites like Ancestry.com now allow for relatively easy tracking of Americans' migrations. A search of such online databases for the uncommon name "Sturminski" reveals that by 1910 Marie and her brother William had gone to the West Coast and were living in San Francisco. They lived in the Tenderloin, an area rebuilt after the 1906 earthquake. By 1910 it was an area of hotels and rooming houses where many other single young people lived. William was a hotel clerk, possibly living in the same unnamed hotel where he worked, at 364 Eddy Street. Marie worked as a waitress, living with other waitresses, clerks, domestic servants, electricians, and hairdressers in the Winton Hotel on O'Farrell Street, which is parallel to and two blocks away from Eddy.[20]

It was while Marie was living in San Francisco that she gave birth to her son, Philip. I discovered his birth certificate on Ancestry.com from a cryptic entry in an index of births in California. It wasn't until recently that I finally got a copy. Dated January 30, 1911, it lists Philip as "Babe Struminski," but this date provides the connection to the author of the diary. It lists his mother as "Marie Struminski," a waitress with an address in the Fillmore district, an immigrant neighborhood west of her previous residence. The boy's father was listed as Philip Good, a hotel clerk, with no address given. In a box labeled "Legitimate?" the answer was "No."[21]

The story of Marie's relationship with her son's father cannot be fully discovered from the available records. All we have is a bare outline of possibilities. In the 1910 census, there was a young man named Philip Good living in San Francisco in the Arlington Hotel on Ellis Street, the parallel street between O'Farrell and Eddy, the streets on which Marie and William were living. He lived only a few blocks from both of them.[22]

The 1910 census stated that Philip Good was born in New York and was twenty-four (although later sources suggest he was older). His occupation in 1910 was "Casket Trimmer." He soon changed jobs: by 1914, he was the manager of the Hotel Eaton, at 364 Eddy Street, the same address where William Sturminski had been a clerk in 1910. When Philip J. Good met Marie Sturminski is not known, and no marriage license has yet been found.[23]

Good continued to work as a clerk in local hotels. By 1918, he was married to a woman named Susan H., and his draft registration form shows "Jackson" as his middle name and his birth date as November 5, 1882. He was described as being of medium build and medium height, with brown eyes and dark hair. The draft official who examined him that day said Philip had not lost any limbs and had no obvious physical problems that would impede his service but stated, "Claims Feet Bad." In 1920, when Marie was back in Duluth with her parents, Good was still living in San Francisco with Susan. In 1930, still married to her, he was a hotel manager across the bay in Berkeley. He died in September 1931. Marie Sturminski had begun to be listed in censuses as "Mary Good" as early as 1930, and starting that year, even before Philip Jackson Good's death, her entry in Duluth city directories included "widow of Philip J." An obituary of her mother, Barbara, published in the *Duluth News Tribune* in 1926, had already called her "Mrs. Mary Good," though it did not name her husband or son.[24]

* * *

Wednesday, September 8: "First day of school after our vacation."
Wednesday, October 27: "I went to the show at the Grant School."

Many questions remain unanswered. Knowing that the possible sources of information greatly outnumber the ones that have been digitized or even the ones that could be examined given limitless time, the researcher wants to never give up, to leave no stone unturned, but there are so many stones in so many directions.

What was not clear from the research into censuses, death certificates, and city directories described so far is what happened to the boy Philip between 1911 and 1926, the year he kept his diary. He was not listed in the census with his mother in 1920 and has not been located in any other federal census in the country under the name "Philip Good" or "Philip Sturminski."

There was also a continuing mystery about where Philip was going to school. Philip often referred to going to events at Grant, the school in his backyard. He also referred to going to school to take classes, but never said that he was attending Grant. There were other possibilities. He could have been attending a parochial school, perhaps one of the city's Polish schools.

One day after I had written much of this essay, I was in the reading room of the Minnesota Historical Society library and decided to look for school records for Duluth. While many local records have been kept in the places they originated, others have been sent to the state for preservation. In the case of St. Louis County, a number of records of Duluth's Independent School District 709 are now preserved in St. Paul.

Paging through the inventories of the school records, I saw an entry for school censuses, which started in 1912. Within ten minutes, I was looking at the volume of the census for 1920. It was a census of students within the district of each particular elementary school, organized by school and then by student. The entries consisted of the name of each child, birth date, age, parent or guardian, home address, and the school the student was attending, whether parochial or public. Evidence from one such census suggests that they were compiled by an enumerator walking around the neighborhood and knocking on each door to find out if there were school-age children living there.[25]

Within a few minutes of looking through the entries for Grant School, I found Philip Good, with the right birth date, the right age, and the right address, attending Grant School in 1920. What was puzzling was that his parent or guardian was listed as P. J. Good. However, because this information would have been supplied by the family, it was not proof of Philip's father's presence in Duluth. Confusion did occur in such records, based on errors either of transcription or interpretation. Although Philip continued to be listed in the school censuses almost without break for the next seven years, there were a number of incorrect entries. In some, his grandfather, Andrew Sturminski, was listed as Andrew Good, the parent or guardian of Philip Good; in others, Andrew was listed as the grandfather of Philip Sturminski. In only one case, in 1925, was his mother, Mrs. Mary Good, listed as guardian. This is the first known case where she used "Good" as her own last name.[26]

After looking at the school censuses from 1920 on, I requested the box of the earliest censuses, before 1920. There was no Philip Good there, but Philip Sturminski was living at the same address, from 1917, when he was six, the earliest year of school eligibility, until 1919. In the first two years, prior to the construction of Grant, Philip was at Franklin School. After that, Philip was shown as attending Grant School, except in 1927, when he went on to Washington Junior High, located in the center of Duluth on Lake Avenue at Third Street.[27]

Although he does not appear in the 1920 US Census, the school records make clear that Philip Good was living in Duluth from the age of six on. When his mother came back to Duluth from California with him is still a mystery.

* * *

Saturday, December 4: "I went to church. We got a box of presents from California."

From the scrawled handwriting of this entry in Philip's journal it seems possible that the family received a box of "prunes" from California, rather than "presents." In any case, who in California sent the box is not clear. It is possible that it was sent by Philip's uncle Frank, who was said to be living there. It is also possible that it was Philip's father.

Philip's relationship with his father is a puzzle. Whether he ever met his father and whether his father had any role in his life are unanswered questions. It could be that his father helped support him and sent him presents every year for Christmas, and that when Philip's aunt Ann went to California in the summer of 1926, she met with Philip's father.

A novelist telling this same story might, after thinking over the known facts, arrive at an interpretation of Philip's father's character and from that construct a satisfying story, but the known facts do not cover all the possibilities. More than one story about Philip's father is possible: one in which he never acknowledges being the father, another in which he helps support his son until his own death, and still another in which he may not even be the real father of the boy.

In fact, the biggest mysteries involving the boy Philip all relate to his father, whose own background is only vaguely apparent. Who was Philip Jackson Good? Where did he live before he came to California? How old was he? Various sources give various answers. His year of birth was anywhere from 1881 to 1886. His mother was born in New York or Kentucky, but her name or the name of his father is not known. Part of the problem is that Philip Jackson Good was born after 1880. A federal census that could have listed him in his childhood, living in his place of birth, was taken in 1890, but almost all of that data for the entire country has been lost, a portion by fire, the rest through poor bureaucratic decision making—one of the greatest tragedies of American archival record destruction.[28]

It is possible that Philip Good may have been a hotel clerk in Denver before going to San Francisco. In July 1907 a man named Philip Good, who was a bellboy at the Hotel Albany, was arrested for stealing some items from suitcases belonging to two young women, who were passing through town on a short trip. When they returned to Denver the items were missing. The newspaper reported that the policeman had trouble in making the arrest "as Good denied his identity each time he was sent for, and said that he did not know anyone by the name he bears." A few days later Good was acquitted of the charges, after he explained to a judge that the two young women had returned to the city at 3:00 AM and he had given up his bed for them and then they accused him of "stealing a 35-cent fan and a powder box." In addition the management of the Albany Hotel vouched for him. In 1908 and 1909 Philip Good was listed in the Denver city directory as clerk at the Albany Hotel. No further listings for him have been found in Denver.[29]

A novelist might insist that there is an essential truth to be seen in the possibility that the man who denied knowing anyone with the name he himself bore could be the father of the boy in Duluth. The historian would acknowledge that the existence of a Philip Good working as a hotel clerk in Denver prior to the Philip J. Good appearing in San Francisco, where he worked as a hotel clerk, is convincing, but that further research is necessary.

* * *

Tuesday, December 21: "Pa Antie died."

Friday, December 24: "I went to the show to see the Northern Code. I went to a funeral."

Since the early 1900s, every county in Minnesota has been required to submit the death certificates they created on state-designed forms to the Minnesota Department of Health, which then compiled and numbered them alphabetically by county and chronologically by date of

death. This means that by looking on the microfilm of death certificates for St. Louis County, it is possible to discover the name of the
person Philip called "Pa Antie," who died in Duluth on December 21,
1926. It turns out that this was Mary Anna Walkowiak, widow of Jack
Walkowiak. She was born in Poland in 1862, the daughter of a man
named Andrew Sturminski. Assuming this information is correct, it
seems unlikely that Philip Good's grandfather Andrew, who was born
in 1850, could be Mary Anna's father. And since Andrew's own 1930
death certificate listed his father's name as Frank, it is possible that she
was Andrew's cousin or perhaps a much younger sibling of his father,
which would explain that young Philip meant to write "Pa's Auntie."[30]

When people keep diaries they are consciously engaging in history,
selecting from available facts, deciding what is important, picking
the right language to communicate information. Sometimes, knowing that what you are writing will be history, your language becomes
stilted, to convey the gravity of the effort.

When the boy reported the death of Barbara Sturminski, his grandmother, his words were formal, stating the fact the way one might
write in a family Bible or communicate the information to someone
beyond his family who would not have known her the way he did: "Barbara Sturminski died 1926."

In a diary with limited space, a few simple words must encapsulate
a complex experience. It is hard to know the feelings of this boy about
his grandmother, or even if he knew exactly the way he felt himself.
The same must be said about the possibility that Philip never knew his
father. No one can speak of the unexpressed emotion of anyone else's
life in a recognizable way. Who can judge anyone else's grief or whether
it has been expressed too much or too little?

In my own 1962 pocket diary, one short passage conceals a much
longer story. On August 3, I wrote, "Missed train from Chicago. Got
9:30 train." This statement tells nothing of my mother sending me off
by myself early one St. Paul morning on the Burlington Zephyr to Chicago, where I was to switch trains to go on to Washington, DC. I was
going to spend a week at School Patrol Camp, training to be the boy
captain of the patrols in Matthew F. Maury Elementary School in Arlington, Virginia. It does not mention the heron I saw rising from the
water as we headed south from St. Paul. It does not say whether it was
my fault or the Traveler's Aid people's fault that I missed the person

who was going to take me to the other train depot for the connecting train to DC. It does not say that when I finally got on the Baltimore and Ohio train, the conductor asked me, "Are you the boy who caused all the trouble in Chicago?" or the sense of injustice I felt but did not speak. It does not explain my joy at seeing my father, who came to meet me at Union Station in Washington, or how we went to lunch that day at Sholl's Cafeteria, my father's favorite place to eat.[31]

Less than five years later, on a Thursday afternoon in early March, my father died suddenly. By then I was covering basketball games for my high school newspaper, starting to be a writer. I tried to express my grief in the diary I had been given the previous Christmas, but even as I wrote the words, they seemed awkward, and for years I wanted to tear out the page and burn it. The truest thing I wrote was a simple descriptive statement: "As I write this on Friday I still expect him to walk in from sweeping off the car, to stomp his feet on the rug by the door, to place the broom by the bookcase, and to speak to me." I did not know how to mourn for my father. It took me years to know how to grieve properly.

Philip Good's diary stands as a wonderful record of a boy's life in Duluth in 1926. But it does not tell us directly the way he felt. It is only through the selection of facts he makes in writing his account that we can draw any conclusions. The rest we can only imagine.

*   *   *

Tuesday, May 4: "I planted a little spruce tree."

I wondered if the spruce might have been planted in the cemetery near the grave of Philip's grandmother, though it could have been a school project. In the late nineteenth and early twentieth centuries, schoolchildren all across the country planted trees in late April or early May, on the day that came to be known as Arbor Day. After World War I, the planting of trees was sometimes dedicated to honor the memory of the dead from the war. Philip's grandmother was buried in the Polish Catholic Cemetery, almost five miles north of the family home, in a rural section of Duluth, along with other members of the family. Online registers of the cemetery did not list Philip or his mother, but their death certificates stated that they too were buried there.[32]

One day, after I had written most of this essay, a friend and I set out to visit the cemetery. My friend, a resident of the city who had never been to the Polish Cemetery before, was driving. She entered the cemetery on the first entrance to the right from Howard Gnesen Road. I wondered why she had turned there, since it was not the main entrance. She drove a short distance and stopped to reconnoiter. I looked out over the vast cemetery stretching toward the east and wondered how we would ever be able to find Philip or the rest of his family. Then I looked to the left of the car and saw the name Sturminski on a stone next to the car. We got out for a closer look. Philip Good's grave was the closest to the car.

In this Polish cemetery the usual practice was and is for each family to have a large stone marker giving the family name. Each individual buried there had a smaller stone, set into the ground with his or her name and dates of birth and death. Philip's was next to his mother, Mary Good, with Nellie Sturminski to the right of Mary. Also in the plot were Andrew, Barbara, William, and "Pelagia," apparently the Polish name of the sister also known as Margaret, who died in 1904.

Philip J. Good's gravestone

There are spruce trees in the Polish cemetery. I noticed within a foot or so of Philip's grave evidence that a large tree had been cut away to the ground, but I could not tell what kind of tree it was. There was a sign in the cemetery saying that after Memorial Day 1971 tree planting was not permitted on family plots and any trees on such lots had to be trimmed to no more than four feet.

Turf was creeping over some of the markers in the Sturminski family plot. We cleared away some of it, deciding to return later with a knife to do a better job.

* * *

Thursday, August 26: "I had my picture taken by a Kodak."

In one draft of this essay, I wrote: "If I could travel in time, I would first go back to look at this photograph." Perhaps only a historian would say something as silly as this, since it would make more sense to actually meet the boy Philip Good and talk with him. At five-foot-four, Philip was not tall for fifteen, though he still had time to grow. He was a bit old to be just going into 7B, which was the first term of seventh grade. Philip's progress in school may have been affected by things in his life over which he had no control. Other Duluth school records show that Philip may not have started first grade until he was seven, and he had to repeat fourth grade due to illness. But the fact that Philip had two aunts who were teachers, was living in a house with a new bookcase and a piano, and was taking music lessons suggests that his family valued culture and education. In this era, however, many young men left school after eighth grade to get jobs. Philip himself was among them. In the 1940 census, it was reported that Philip, who was then working as a coal passer on an ore boat, had completed eight years of school. During and after the war he was a fireman, perhaps for ore boats, as mentioned in his death certificate.[33]

He never married. After his mother's death in 1944, he continued to live in the same East Hillside neighborhood where he had been living since 1926, with or near his aunts Nellie and Ann. In the 1950s he worked for the Bayview-Zenith Dairies. In his last years, he lived to the east, farther up the hill past Chester Bowl, just south of the University of Minnesota–Duluth campus, in the house on Nineteenth Avenue East where Ann had lived until her death in 1979. He was working as a maintenance man. He died on October 6, 1981. After that either there was an estate sale at the house or the remaining things from his life were sold directly to the owner of the secondhand store.[34]

* * *

Saturday, November 6: "I saw Babe Ruth at the Lyric for nothing."

The free show featuring Babe Ruth at the Lyric was supposed to be only for boys between the ages of seven and fourteen. Philip Good was fifteen, but he went anyway. During the 1920s and later, Babe Ruth was a favorite of boys throughout the country. Raised in a Catholic orphanage and industrial school in Baltimore, where he developed as a baseball player, Ruth had the lifelong reputation of playing baseball with a contagious boyish enthusiasm. According to a well-developed legend, the three home runs he hit during game four of the 1926 World Series were promised to a sick boy in New Jersey, who after hearing of Ruth's success recovered and lived a full life.[35]

I read all the books about Ruth I could find when I was a boy, including the one in the same series as the Thomas Edison biography I had read, *Babe Ruth, Baseball Boy.* In those books, the famous person's career was begun or foreshadowed in his childhood. The middle of his life was seldom mentioned, but at the end, the boy, now a man, would make a triumphant appearance, if not in the place of his youth, at least in front of a community that would give him the acclaim he deserved.[36]

Because Philip went to so many movies in 1926, for a long time I thought his reference to Babe Ruth at the Lyric meant he went to see a free movie. But one day, when it occurred to me that Babe Ruth might have come to Duluth in person, I searched online for the phrase "Babe Ruth visits Duluth," which took me to a page about a man who on the day he died was talking with someone about Babe Ruth visiting Duluth the day before. The man died on November 7, 1926. At the next opportunity I went to the Minnesota Historical Society to look through the issues of the *Duluth News Tribune.* It turned out that the Lyric was not a movie theater but a vaudeville house, and Ruth's appearance was part of a national tour to capitalize on his recent stardom in the World Series. Ads in the newspaper stated that "The Bambino Himself, The King of Swat," who was described as the "Highest Salaried Attraction in Vaudeville," would be appearing in four big shows in the afternoon and evening on Saturday and Sunday, November 6 and 7, along with "5 Selected Acts." In these appearances Ruth, probably dressed in his Yankee uniform, would tell stories of his life as a player and demonstrate some of the secrets of his success with the bat.[37]

Ruth was also set to make a single appearance on Saturday morning, free for boys who cut out and signed the coupon appearing on the front page of the *News Tribune* and presented it at the newspaper office during the two hours before the show. According to a reporter, at the appointed hour "the front doors of the newspaper were stormed . . . by a majority of the boys in Duluth between the ages of 8 and 14. So anxious were the boys to get in and get their tickets to the free show that it was necessary to summon the police to quell the near riot that ensued."[38]

Scrolling through the pages of those early November newspapers, I ran across many photos and features detailing Ruth's coming appearance and his arrival in Duluth. He posed, sporting an impressive fur coat, with Mayor Snively of Duluth and Dave Bancroft of Superior, then manager of the Boston Braves, the team that had traded Ruth away to the Yankees in 1919.[39]

Finally, I found the photo taken in the theater during his appearance before the assembled "Duluth-Superior School Boys" gathered to pay tribute to "their national hero." It was a banquet shot, a panoramic view taken from the front of the theater, with Babe Ruth standing in the middle row surrounded by boys, hundreds of them—actually, two thousand of them. The caption said that the boys could not be quieted

Babe Ruth in Duluth, 1926

as they waited for Ruth to appear and that only Ruth could get them to submit quietly to the "ordeal of posing for a Tribune cameraman." Ruth had to be summoned from his dressing room in his shirt sleeves. His appearance at first was counterproductive, sending "the boys into hysterics, but at Ruth's own request, they finally stopped for the camera." There he is, a figure in white, at the center of the image, Babe Ruth, all boy, the boy of boys, the hero of boys, in a crowd of boys, and somewhere in the crowd, there is a boy about five-foot-four, wearing a fairly new leather jacket and long pants, a boy born in one city by a bay who lived out his life in another, a boy whose first name was given on his birth certificate only as "Babe": Philip Good, the author of the 1926 *Boy Scout Diary*.

NOTES

1.   The author would like to acknowledge the assistance of Patricia Maus and Mags David of the University of Minnesota–Duluth Library Special Collections, Kate Regan, and Marcia Edelen.

2.   Sue Guthridge, *Tom Edison, Boy Inventor* (Indianapolis and New York: The Bobbs-Merrill Company, 1947).

3.   Patricia Hampl and Dave Page, eds., *The St. Paul Stories of F. Scott Fitzgerald* (St. Paul, MN: Borealis Books, 2004), 193.

4.   Descriptions of the scoreboard and photographs of the crowds gathered are found in the *Duluth News Tribune*, October 3, 4, 6, 7, and 9, 1926.

5.   *Duluth News Tribune*, October 7, 1926.

6.   On WEBC radio, *Duluth News Tribune*, October 6, 7, 10, 11, and 12, 1926; also see Roger J. Johnson, "A Technological History of WEBC Radio, 1924–1995," MA thesis, University of Wisconsin–Superior, 1997, available: http://www.northpine.com/broadcast/webc/.

7.   *Duluth News Tribune*, October 7, 1926.

8.   Walt Whitman, "When I Read the Book," *Leaves of Grass* (Philadelphia: David McKay, 1900), 14. In earlier versions of the poem the word *clues* was spelled *clews*.

9.   Carl Jung, *Synchronicity* (Princeton, NJ: Princeton University Press, 1973), 10, 69. The Rickey quotation has sometimes been attributed to the English poet John Milton, though without a specific citation. Branch Rickey used the line throughout his life, with the earliest published reference to him saying it to be found in an article entitled "Life's Boxscore Similar to Baseball Says Rickey," in the *Lexington[Kentucky] Herald*, November 1, 1915, 7.

10. There are many versions of the bear story; for one, see "Sheldon Aubut's Duluth History, Hotel Duluth," http://www.cityhistory.us/duluth/architecture/hotelduluth.htm.

11. The streetcar line is shown on the 1921 McGill-Warner Co. map of Duluth, copy in Duluth Public Library.

12. The history of Chester Bowl is discussed in an article by Nancy Nelson on the *Zenith City Online* website, http://zenithcity.com/chester-park-history -part-ii-chester-bowl-upper-chester/. Full-page advertisement for the Frolic, *Duluth News Tribune*, February 6, 1926. Full-page advertisement for the National Ski Tournament, *Duluth News Tribune*, February 7, 1926; see also photographs and articles for events of February 13, *Duluth News Tribune*, February 14, 1926; see also panoramic view, February 16, 1926.

13. US Census, 1920, Minnesota, St. Louis County, Duluth, District 15, enumeration district 106, sheet 15b, census taken January 12, 1920.

14. US Census, 1930, Minnesota, St. Louis County, Duluth, enumeration district 69–50, sheet 9a.

15. According to the 1930 city directory the printer was the Steele-Lounsberry Co.: see R. L. Polk, *Duluth City Directory* (1930), 128.

16. Death certificates for Barbara Sturminski, Duluth, February 14, 1926, #26368; Andrew Sturminski, Duluth, April 16, 1930, #26222; Mary Good, Duluth, October 5, 1944, #27692; Philip Joseph Good, Duluth, October 6, 1981, #026504; on microfilm at Minnesota Historical Society, St. Paul.

17. Passenger list for *Lessing*, March 9, 1881, included in Hamburg Passenger Lists, 1850–1934, Ancestry.com. Stance Sturminski and his wife Ethel J. are buried in Arlington National Cemetery in Section 41, Grave 1029. In World War I he was a gunner's mate on the USS *Pennsylvania;* see details of Sturminski's service in the records of the Minnesota War Records Commission, University of Minnesota–Duluth Library, Special Collections. Details of his service in World War II have not been located. An article in the *San Diego Evening Tribune*, June 16, 1926, stated that Stance Sturminski had been aboard the *Pennsylvania* for the full ten years following its commissioning in 1916.

At a meeting of the Northeastern Minnesota Educational Association in February 1915, Anna Sturminski was slated to give a presentation on "Primary Reading in the Rural Schools," based on teaching experience in County School No. 56: *Duluth Herald*, January 22, 1915, 4. See the Duluth Central High School yearbook called *The Zenith*, 1908, 1909, and 1910, with photographs of Anna and Nellie in the 1910 issue; Minnesota State Normal School, Duluth *Bulletin, Ninth Annual Catalogue*, May 1911, 34, *Tenth Annual Catalogue*, May 1912, 31. In 1920 both Anna and Nellie taught at the Northside School in Virginia and Nellie also taught evening Americanization classes: *Duluth News Tribune*, September 8 and October 16, 1920.

Death certificate for Guendoline Agnes Barnard, March 21, 1927, #1927-MN-025296. Francis Barnard, his first wife, and Anna S. Barnard are all buried in a single plot in the Forest Hill Cemetery, Duluth. Obituary for Maggie Sturminski, *Duluth News Tribune*, May 20, 1904, 12.

18. Death certificate for William Smith aka William Sturminski, Duluth,

September 11, 1965, #21748. Frank Sturminski draft registration, June 5, 1917, Cass County, Nebraska, from National Archives Microfilm M1509, World War I Draft Registration Cards, 1917–18, image on Ancestry.com; *Duluth News Tribune,* February 16, 1926.

19. Mary Strominski, Minnesota State Census, 1895, St. Louis County, Duluth, First Ward, 8. US Census, 1900, Minnesota, St. Louis County, Duluth, ward 6, 5th precinct, enumeration district 282, sheet 9b; for Marie Sturminski see ward 3, enumeration district 265, sheet 10b. R. L. Polk & Co., *Duluth Directory* (1903), 637.

20. For Marie see US Census, 1910, San Francisco County, San Francisco, 43rd district, enumeration district 290, sheet 10a; for William see 42nd district, enumeration district 285, sheet 6a. The website "Up from the Deep" has an extended account of the Tenderloin District and many of the buildings there, including the Winton Hotel and the building at 364 Eddy Street: http://upfromthedeep.com/uptown-tenderloin/.

21. Birth certificate for Babe Sturminski, January 30, 1911, in the office of the San Francisco County Clerk, San Francisco, CA.

22. See US Census, 1910, San Francisco County, San Francisco, 43rd district, enumeration district 290, sheet 8b. On the Arlington Hotel see http://upfromthedeep.com/uptown-tenderloin/.

23. Philip Good was already listed as residing at 364 Eddy Street in 1912; see Crocker-Langley, *San Francisco Directory* (1912), 725, (1914), 796, 952; image online at Ancestry.com.

24. Draft Registration Card for Philip Jackson Good, San Francisco, September 12, 1918, from National Archives Microfilm, M1509, World War I Draft Registration Cards, 1917–18, image on Ancestry.com. US Census, 1920, California, San Francisco County, San Francisco, Precinct 33, enumeration district 261, sheet 3b; 1930, California, Alameda County, Berkeley, enumeration district 1–280, sheet 23b; death certificate for Philip Jackson Good, September 4, 1931, Alameda County Clerk-Recorder, Berkeley, CA.

R. L. Polk, *Duluth City Directory* (1930), 719. The entry lists her as Mary Sturminski. Later entries from 1935 to 1943 list her as Mary Good, widow of Philip: (1935), XX. *Duluth News Tribune,* February 16, 1926.

25. See Duluth School Census, 1916, Franklin School, which lists for one address "2d trip, no one home": St. Louis County, Independent School District No. 709, Minnesota Historical Society, State Archives.

26. St. Louis County, Independent School District No. 709, Duluth School Census, 1920, 1921, 1923 (Phillip Sturminski), 1924 (Philys Sturminski), 1925, Minnesota Historical Society, State Archives.

27. St. Louis County, Independent School District No. 709, Duluth School Census, 1917, 1918, 1919, 1927, Minnesota Historical Society, State Archives. On the construction and opening of Grant School, see Duluth Board of Education records, University of Minnesota–Duluth Library, Special Collections,

vol. 12; see also data sheet on Grant School, compiled by Special Collections staff.

28. Kellee Blake, "'First in the Path of the Firemen': The Fate of the 1890 Population Census, Part 2," *Prologue* 28.1 (Spring 1996), available: http://www.archives.gov/publications/prologue/1996/spring/1890-census-2.html.

29. Ballenger & Richards, *Denver City Directory* (1906), 518, (1908), 555, (1909), 577. *Denver Post,* July 16, 1907, 12; July 19, 1907, 5. An article in the Denver newspaper at the time of the San Francisco earthquake stated: "Philip Good, a commercial man of Denver, is in San Francisco": *Denver Post,* April 18, 1906, 3. In 1904, a Philip J. Good was living in Kansas City, working as a trimmer for a casket company, which ties in with Philip's stated occupation in the 1910 census in San Francisco: Hoye Directory Company, *Kansas City Directory* (1904), 113.

30. Death certificate for Mary Ann Walkowiak, Duluth, December 21, 1926, #27436.

31. On Sholl's Cafeteria, see John H. Fund, "Sholl's Last Supper," *Wall Street Journal,* December 7, 2001, online at http://online.wsj.com/news/articles/SB1007689909696934480.

32. *Duluth News-Tribune,* May 1, 1903, 6; April 2, 1922, 11; April 27, 1922, 4.

33. According to Duluth School Board records in the special collections of the University of Minnesota–Duluth Library, the first term was 7B and the second, 7A. In particular see Duluth Board of Education, *Report* (1926), 87. Similarly, the Term Standing records in the St. Louis County, Independent School District No. 709, Minnesota Historical Society, State Archives, show that students entered the B term in the fall and the A term in the spring, although some students had to repeat terms due to illness or poor grades. See Term Standing records for Philip Good's time in Grant School from 1919 to 1927, in the St. Louis County, Independent School District No. 709, Minnesota Historical Society, State Archives. US Census, 1940, Minnesota, St. Louis County, Duluth, enumeration district 88–27b, sheet 1a.

34. R. L. Polk, *Duluth City Directory* (1950), 214, (1980), 71, 147; death certificate for Anna Sturminski Barnard, Duluth, November 23, 1979, #29032; death certificate for Philip Joseph Good, Duluth October 6, 1981, #26504.

35. On the mythology about Babe Ruth, see F. R. Lloyd, "The Home Run King," *Journal of Popular Culture* (Spring 1976): 983–93.

36. Guernsey Van Riper, Jr., *Babe Ruth, Baseball Boy* (Indianapolis and New York: The Bobbs-Merrill Co., Inc., 1954).

37. Death certificate for Samuel M. Kielly, Duluth, November 7, 1926, #27283. *Duluth News Tribune,* November 6, 1926.

38. *Duluth News Tribune,* November 6, 1926, 1, and November 7, 1926, A9.

39. *Duluth News Tribune,* November 7, 1926.

BRUCE WHITE is a historian and anthropologist who lives in St. Paul, Minnesota. He is the author of two award-winning books, *We Are at Home: Pictures of the Ojibwe People* and *Mni Sota Makoce: The Land of the Dakota* (with Gwen Westerman). He has researched and written widely in the field of the Native and early European history of the Great Lakes region, subjects on which he works as a consultant for Native communities and government agencies through his firm, Turnstone Historical Research.

Annette Kolodny

CURIOUS ENCOUNTERS IN MY SEARCH FOR VINLAND

*I*n 1961, while still an undergraduate English major at Brooklyn College in New York, I won a scholarship for summer study abroad. Eager to experience life in a country about which I then knew next to nothing, I used the scholarship to enroll in the literature program at the University of Oslo in Norway. My ten weeks in Norway were glorious, not least because my studies introduced me to a literary tradition far older than and very different from the American literary history I had concentrated on at home. Always curious about how literary traditions first begin, I was particularly intrigued by the medieval prose narratives written down in Iceland in the vernacular—that is, the everyday language of western Norway and Iceland. Today we call that language Old West Norse or Old Icelandic. And because they were written in the vernacular, rather than Latin, these prose narratives initiated that great corpus of enormously popular medieval literature known as the Icelandic sagas.

Struggling through texts whose language challenged me with every word, depending for help on dictionaries and English translations of a few of the sagas, I fell in love with the powerful personages, the narrative energy, and the sheer exuberant adventure of the stories those sagas told. What I never anticipated in 1961, however, was that almost forty years later two of those sagas would send me on a great adventure of my own. It began as a research project that, among other places, brought me several times back to Norway. But in Maine in the summer of 2000, it developed into a project that confronted me with people and events so unexpected that I was forced to entirely rethink what I was about.

To explain, I begin with the scholarly context out of which my project emerged. In anticipation of the approaching 1992 quincentenary of Columbus's first landfall in the Americas, the 1980s witnessed a wealth of new research about Europe's earliest contacts with the so-called New World. But following fast on the Columbian quincentenary was yet another significant historical marker that generated even more research and a major traveling exhibit curated by the Smithsonian Institution. This was the year 2000, the millennial anniversary of what is generally believed to have been Leif Eiriksson's first exploration of North America around AD 1000. Leif famously named the land he explored "Vinland" to emphasize its wealth of natural resources, including the abundance of wild grapevines. The story of Leif's exploration as well as the stories of subsequent attempts to settle a permanent Norse colony in Vinland circulated widely in oral tradition in Greenland, Iceland, Denmark, and Norway. Then, about a hundred years after the events they record, these *oral sayings*—or *sagas*—began to be written down by Christian clerics in Iceland. They thus entered the medieval literature tradition that so intrigued me when I studied at the University of Oslo. The two surviving sagas that tell of the voyages to Vinland are "The Greenlanders' Saga" and "Eirik the Red's Saga," known collectively as the Vinland sagas. Although embellished by folklore motifs and medieval literary conventions, the two Vinland sagas are based on real people, real places, and real events.

The stories in these sagas were given a physical reality in 1961, when the Norwegian adventurer Helge Ingstad discovered the remains of a Viking-era site at Épaves Bay, near the fishing village of L'Anse aux Meadows, at the northeast tip of Newfoundland. Excavated in subsequent years by Ingstad and his archeologist wife, Anne Stine Ingstad, the site showed evidence of having been used for Norse ship repair as well as evidence of the presence of women. Consistent with the stories in the sagas, the little settlement could have housed as many as 160 people. In a volume published in 1977, titled *The Discovery of a Norse Settlement in America,* Anne Stine Ingstad detailed unearthing the remains of eight house sites, four boat sheds, a charcoal kiln, evidence of domestic animals, a woman's spindle whorl, a smithy for forging iron, iron nails and nail fragments, and a "ring-headed pin, which is a Viking Age form of jewelry" used for fastening a cloak. Carbon dating of these finds, combined with the specific architectural features of the tiny settlement, led Anne Stine Ingstad to conclude that it "suggest[ed] Iceland as its cultural source," but that it ultimately "derive[d] from Norse Greenlanders and is of an early date, probably of the first half of the eleventh century." In other words, exactly as told in the sagas, those who ventured to Vinland were mostly Norwegians who had immigrated to Iceland, but the main jumping-off point for the voyages to North America were the Norse settlements on Greenland.[1]

Still, there was no conclusive proof that L'Anse aux Meadows was the Vinland of the sagas, and some of the details from the sagas seemed to suggest otherwise. Most notable is the absence of any sign of wild grapes ever having grown at L'Anse aux Meadows. The scientific analysis of ancient soil cores demonstrates no traces of wild grapes growing north of the Penobscot River. During periods of climatic warming—as when the Norse voyaged to North America—wild grapes could be found on the East Coast only as far north as Passamaquoddy Bay. The attempted Vinland colony, therefore, had to have been south of L'Anse aux Meadows, possibly in the Gulf of St. Lawrence, southern New Brunswick, southern Maine, or even farther south. No less important, at the time of the Norse arrivals, there are no indications of Native peoples living anywhere near L'Anse aux Meadows. Yet contacts with Native peoples, whom the Norse called "Skraelings," are a prominent feature of both sagas.

In my graduate courses on the literature of the early American frontiers, I had for many years been teaching the letters and journals of Christopher Columbus. But in 1993, I added English translations of the two Vinland sagas as further required readings. For the most part, my students were excited by these texts, as I had been. Yet while my students were fascinated by stories of a contact that had preceded Columbus by a full five hundred years, they also repeatedly posed the same urgent questions: Where was Vinland located, and what had *really* happened there? And were there any Native American stories about this early contact? In the summer of 1995, I began searching for answers to those questions. The fruit of that search was my 2012 book, *In Search of First Contact: The Vikings of Vinland, the Peoples of the Dawnland, and the Anglo-American Anxiety of Discovery*, published by Duke University Press.

I began my research by trying to identify the Native peoples with whom the Norse might have come in contact. If reports of wild grapevines in the sagas were accurate, then the Native peoples encountered in Vinland were located south of Newfoundland, from the Canadian Maritime Provinces and the Gulf of St. Lawrence to New England and beyond. If the descriptions of Skraelings using "skin boats" (or moose-hide canoes) were also accurate, then the Native peoples encountered in Vinland lived north of Boston. At the time of the Norse arrivals, skin boats were utilized only by Algonquian peoples living north of Boston.[2]

Based on these clues, I tentatively concluded that the Skraelings in the sagas were most probably the ancestors of one or more of the peoples who today comprise the Wabanaki Confederacy. These include the Mi'kmaq, the Maliseet, the Penobscot, the Passamaquoddy, and several closely related groups who identify as Western Abenaki or, simply, as Abenaki. The terms *Wabanaki* and *Abenaki,* sometimes used interchangeably, are respectively the English and French approximations of the Eastern Algonquian word *Wôbanakikiiak,* meaning Peoples of the Dawnland—that is, the people living farthest to the east where the sun first rises. All are Algonquian peoples who speak related dialects of Eastern Algonquian. According to reports from the Smithsonian Institution's Bureau of Ethnology, as late as the 1880s there existed among these groups a significant continuity of many traditional practices, including storytelling. Despite the crushing population losses from disease and warfare, coupled with the cultural impositions that began at the end of the sixteenth century, I wondered: might *any* trace memories of the Norse contact have managed to survive?

As I discovered, there were survivals. Some were faint and barely recognizable, while others were buried in prophecy tales about the coming of the "white man." In long-forgotten printed sources and in oral traditions still very much alive, I uncovered remnant memories of very early contacts with—or sometimes only sightings of—strange men arriving in large vessels unlike anything the Indians had seen before. As a result, I was able to compose two complementary chapters for my book, one titled "Contact and Conflict: What the Vinland Sagas Tell Us" and the other titled "Contact and Conflict Again: What Native Stories Tell Us." I thus came very close to answering my graduate students' questions about whom the Norse encountered in Vinland and what really happened in that initial contact between Europeans and Native Americans. Sadly, as the chapter titles indicate, for both peoples that contact was not entirely a happy one.[3]

Altogether, over the years, this research took me to Norway, Denmark, the Archives of the Indies at the University of Seville in Spain, the Canadian Maritime Provinces, Maritime Quebec, the tip of Newfoundland, and all across northern New England. I visited medieval archaeological sites in Norway and Denmark and talked with scholars at the University of Oslo about the sagas, Vinland, and the excavations on Greenland. I interviewed Helge Ingstad at his home in the woods outside of Oslo. I trudged across thawing mud to make my way to the reconstructed Viking settlement at L'Anse aux Meadows and met in Halifax with Birgitta Linderoth Wallace, the archaeologist who followed the Ingstads and completed the L'Anse aux Meadows excavations for Parks Canada. Yet not until I visited Maine did I begin to understand that I wasn't really searching for the historical Vinland after all, but for the stories that kept it alive.

*   *   *

In June 2000, I made my first research trip to Maine, accompanied by my husband, the novelist Daniel Peters, and my former research assistant, Chadwick Allen, a scholar of comparative indigenous literatures. In advance of our arrival, I had arranged for Moses Lewey (Passamaquoddy) to help with my research as our local guide and assistant. Moses was a Native speaker and knew the coastal areas well. I had been put in touch with Moses by a mutual friend in the Mi'kmaq tribe. The two men had met in jail many years before, both then much younger and incarcerated for public drunkenness. But Moses was now fifty and worked the night shift as the dispatcher for the Passamaquoddy tribal police. That is why he had free hours during the daytime to work with me.[4]

My Mi'kmaq friend had described Moses as "very traditional," but all our contacts to date had been solely by telephone. Moses had sounded very formal in those conversations, and I found them extremely hard work, with lots of silences on his end. So when we met for the first time at the motel I was staying at in Eastport, I was not exactly prepared for someone in a tank top, Bermuda shorts, and black Nike running shoes worn with black socks. He was about my husband's height (five-eleven) but quite lean, with an angular face and mostly dark brown hair (save for some gray on the sides) pulled back in a long ponytail. He said his given name was Richard Lewey, but everyone called him Moses. He never explained why, and to this day I have never asked. After I introduced Moses to my husband and Chad, they all shook hands, and Moses presented me with a red and blue bandanna tied into a small, round bundle.

"Tobacco offering," he stated ceremoniously. Then he followed that up with a gift of a small, multicolored Passamaquoddy woven basket with a glass holder inside for a candle.

In return, we gave Moses a copy of my husband's novel about the Aztecs, titled *The Luck of Huemac,* a couple of cones of southwestern sweet grass, five packets of American Spirit tobacco, and a bouquet of dried lavender from my backyard in Tucson. My Mi'kmaq friend had told us that Moses would need to make offerings to the people he was contacting on our behalf—hence the multiple packets of tobacco.

During our several telephone conversations, I had told Moses about my project and asked him to introduce me to anyone who might be helpful. One of those whom Moses had contacted was a relative by marriage, a revered elder and educator in the tribe named Wayne Newell. Wayne had agreed to meet with us later that day at his home on the Indian Township reservation near Princeton. To fill the time until then, Moses took us on a tour of the Pleasant Point/ Sipayik reservation. It was mostly made up of unassuming single-story red-brick houses, but these were mixed in with a variety of what appeared to be standard middle-class tract homes, some fairly large. It wasn't the most prosperous-looking community, but then nothing in this part of Maine looked very prosperous. And the Pleasant Point/ Sipayik community certainly didn't display any of the signs of abject poverty that I'd seen years before on parts of other Indian reservations in the west. We ended the tour with a drive up to the tall new water tower that stands on a hill overlooking the whole community, and Moses pointed out the two islands in Passamaquoddy Bay that belong to the tribe.

At this point, it was time to start out for our meeting with Wayne Newell. As we drove the forty-five minutes to the second designated Passamaquoddy community near Princeton, I sat next to Moses in the front seat of his car while Dan and Chad followed in the rental car we'd picked up the day before at the Bangor airport. Along the way, Moses pointed out trees with eagles' nests in the topmost branches and in-dicated areas where sweet grass could still be gathered. As I learned later, the mildly aromatic stalks of sweet grass are often woven into the baskets for which Passamaquoddy basket makers are so famous, and they are also twisted into braids and exchanged as gifts. In many of the Indian homes I was to visit over the next days, braids of sweet grass on a table or mantle functioned in place of the commercial chemical air fresheners commonly used in non-Indian households.

With just the two of us in the confined intimacy of his car, Moses seemed to relax and, in answer to my questions, he told me a little more about himself. He was divorced, and with his former wife (also Passamaquoddy) he shared custody of his two sons, one ten and the other thirteen years old. There were no jobs in the area, and between Maine's long-term economic decline and the local prejudice against hiring Indians, his sons had nothing to occupy them during the summer months when school was out. They spent most of their days hanging out at the local playground, shooting hoops. Just as on the reservations in the west, drugs and gangs were beginning to infiltrate Indian communities in the east, and Moses was clearly worried for his boys.

It was mid-June and full spring in the areas we drove through, the grass lush and bright green, speckled with yellow and white wild-flowers and patches of purple lupine. After living in the desert for so many years, I was surprised at how powerfully I responded to the beau-ty of a New England spring.

We continued driving through the town of Woodland, which that day reeked of the pulp stench from the Georgia Pacific paper mill. Then we headed on into Princeton, situated between two large lakes. A bit farther, we drove into a residential area known as Peter Dana Point, which juts out into Big Lake. A stiff wind was blowing, and a few drops of rain fell just as we pulled into the driveway of a small ranch house. Moses went in first and then returned to beckon us in. We met Wayne Newell's mother and his wife, Sandy, in the living room, where they were watching television, and then Wayne led us out onto an enclosed porch at the back of the house. Wayne was a somewhat heavyset man with a round face, black hair parted in the middle, and glasses with lenses so thick they almost obscured his eyes. That day he was wearing a "Walk for Life '98" T-shirt. He offered us chairs on the porch, and he and I sat opposite one another across a small table. Dan sat between us, taking notes; and Chad sat nearby, also taking notes. Moses sat over in the corner, a respectful distance away, listening intently. Through the screened windows of the porch, we looked out on a long backyard leading to a wooden dock where a small boat was moored. The wind was kicking up whitecaps on the surface of the lake, its waters a darker shade of gray than the sky. It was a quiet and—with the soft patter of raindrops on the roof—a very peaceful place to talk.

Wayne listened with amiable bemusement as I explained my project, but he said he didn't know of any stories that were identifiably about the Vikings. He then sounded out the Passamaquoddy word for stranger—a word once applied to "the white man"—writing it down in Dan's notebook as WENUCH and pronouncing it *when-nooch*. He said it literally means "who's this?" or possibly "from where do they come?" Wayne knew, though, that no word like this, or any word even close, appears in the sagas. The two Vinland sagas contain only the Norse word for the Natives: Skraelings.

In fact, it turned out that Wayne knew the Vinland sagas well and had once worked as a consultant on a film about a Viking slave left behind in Vinland by his Norse masters. Wayne's job on the film was to translate parts of the script into the Passamaquoddy language so that the actors who played the Skraelings could speak an Indian tongue. The premise of the film was that the Viking slave happily adopted Indian lifeways and was assimilated into the tribe. There is no basis for any of this in the sagas, Wayne noted, but it reminded him that in some of the stories about Gluscap, the Algonquian culture-hero and symbolic ancestor, Gluscap is described as light-skinned. Nineteenth-century folklore collectors made much of this, citing it as evidence of ancient Viking contact and cultural influence. And even today, Wayne added, there were many white folks convinced that Maine had once been Vinland.

Our conversation went on for several hours. I learned that Wayne had been in a Harvard PhD program designed to restore and preserve Native traditions and languages. He said he had never completed the dissertation, just the coursework, because he wanted to return to his people and use what he had learned. In recent years, he was instrumental in helping to produce the first Passamaquoddy-English dictionary. And he was a major influence on the development of a Native-centered curriculum for both the tribal schools and the Maine public schools. I also learned as we talked that Wayne had a dry and impish sense of humor.

After telling me several stories he remembered hearing as a child and explaining to me the basic grammar of the Passamaquoddy language, Wayne allowed me to press him on questions about the sagas.

He identified the meaning of some of the cultural practices of the Skraelings as reported in the sagas. He explained, for example, that because red was a sacred color for most Wabanaki peoples, their ancestors would particularly have prized even small pieces of red cloth in their trading with the Norse. This helped me understand why, in "Eirik the Red's Saga," the Skraelings continued to trade their fine dressed pelts even after the Norse began to run out of red cloth and so offered shorter and shorter pieces in exchange. Wayne then went on to speculate about the reasons for the gradual decline of oral storytelling among the Passamaquoddies. This he attributed to the introduction of the telephone, then to television, and, finally, to the arrivals of periods of modest economic improvement during which the Passamaquoddies built larger homes with private spaces that separated the generations. Clearly, this was something he had thought about a lot. Through it all, he allowed me to tape-record him, so that most of what he told me—then and in later meetings—eventually became part of *In Search of First Contact.*

By now I realized that it was quite dark and that we had been smelling dinner cooking almost the whole time. As we filed back out through the house, we saw that dinner was all done and set out, waiting on the dining room table, with several family members also waiting quietly nearby. Yet no one had tried to interrupt us or hurry us along, and Wayne hadn't shown the slightest hint of impatience. Clearly, no one had expected us to stay as long as we did, but the traditional Passamaquoddy codes of hospitality had prevailed nonetheless. We apologized and thanked Wayne and then hustled out to our cars in the rain. As we drove into the night, it dawned on me that there was a certain appropriateness in the fact that the first word Wayne taught me that afternoon was *wenuch,* the Pasamaquoddy word for "stranger." I was indeed a stranger in this world, and it would take me many years and many more visits to Maine even to begin to fathom the complex codes of courtesy, politeness, and reciprocity by which this community lived.

* * *

In addition to introducing me to individuals within the Passamaquoddy communities, Moses had also taken the initiative of calling all the local historical societies in the area to inquire about their holdings. Several said they were certain they held ancient Viking artifacts. So a couple of days later, with Moses's car in the shop, we picked him up on our way to the Lubec Historical Society. There a white-haired arche-typal Old Mainer with a bona fide down-east accent greeted us and led us through a cluttered front room that looked like an antique dealer's storeroom. In back of that was a meeting room equipped with some long trestle tables, a few rows of folding chairs, a slide projector, and a portable movie screen. Moses had already given the gentleman an idea of what we were interested in, and the Old Mainer immediately mentioned a Norse Pond "over to Cutler," a town near Machias. He had also heard about a Norse Wall, this from a man named Walter El-liott, who he said died a year ago, or maybe two. Apparently, Elliott had read the Vinland sagas and then searched until he found a place along the coastline in south Lubec that corresponded to one of the landing places described by the Vikings. The Old Mainer unfurled some large maps to show us a sailing route that would have brought the Viking ships around the southern end of Campobello Island and into an inlet above Quoddy Head. It didn't exactly conform to the Norse account, but it was close enough to spark our interest, especially when this gen-tleman said that Elliott found some artifacts in the same vicinity.

Responding to our queries, the Old Mainer offered to telephone an-other member of the society, whom I will call Mack (not his real name). Minutes later, Mack arrived, a man in his fifties, a bit overweight, with gold-rimmed glasses and wispy, reddish-gray hair. He was just retired from the Coast Guard and had gone back to school to get his under-graduate degree. He told us he was fascinated by history and archae-ology. Mack said he had known Walter Elliott and done some explor-ing with him. Then, together, Mack and the Old Mainer brought out a large board covered with aluminum foil on which were mounted a heavily rusted nail and blade, two of the artifacts Elliott found near the south Lubec site. They also produced, encased in a tiny plastic baggie, a round, dark gray stone with a hole in its center, like a miniature stone doughnut. It looked like a spindle whorl, used for spinning thread, and it closely resembled the one found at L'Anse aux Meadows. *That* artifact was one of the key early finds that helped the Ingstads authen-ticate the site as Viking. Dan, Chad, Moses, and I were immediately excited.

But I was also suspicious. This "discovery" process was all too easy and just too good to be true. Where was the state archaeologist's report on these "finds"? Had the society even notified the state or attempted to have the nail, the blade, and the spindle whorl dated and authenticated? The answers to my questions were vague and evasive, and I really couldn't make sense of them. Red flags were going up.

Then Mack began talking about burials and spearheads and some place where a chair had been carved out of the bedrock. He gave us a photocopy of an article about a bronze pin Walter Elliott had found which was supposedly similar to ones in the British Museum. There was also a stone head Elliott had discovered while digging a new well in his yard, and an arrowhead made from either glass or diamond. The more Mack talked, the more skeptical I became. The red flags really snapped to, though, when Mack started talking about another of Elliott's discoveries, the Spirit Pond rune stones. These seemed to have involved Elliott in some legal difficulties. They were found somewhere near Elliott's home in Grand Lake Stream, Mack said, and some of the runes on them were identical to those found on the Kensington Stone.

Oops. Mack made this statement as a validation of Elliott's discovery, but the Kensington Stone is perhaps the most famous Viking fraud of the nineteenth century. Allegedly unearthed by a Minnesota farmer, the Kensington Stone was incised with runes, the ancient Norse writing system, testifying to a Viking presence in Minnesota around 1362 CE. Every rune expert who examined it has pronounced it a modern fake, yet the Kensington Stone has shown great resilience as an object of popular belief.[5]

Absolutely convinced that his home state was the historic Vinland, the Old Mainer was photocopying nautical maps to make his case, while Mack offered us photos of the so-called Norse Wall and gave us the names and phone numbers of other people in the area who also claimed knowledge of Viking presence in Maine.

Then, red flags flying high, I accepted Mack's offer to show us the place where the stone spindle whorl was found, which he said was just a few miles away. We thanked the Old Mainer for his help and walked outside into an oddly bright coastal fog, blown in by an extremely chilly wind. We all got our jackets from the trunk and put them on before getting into our car and following Mack's to the road that led to Quoddy Head State Park. Illuminated by the setting sun, the fog hung like a gauzy curtain on both sides of the road. Once within the park, we left our cars and walked about twenty yards to a place where a large metal culvert ran under the road, emptying into a tidal inlet that still held some water, even though the tide was out. The mossy green grass that grows down to the water, and the brighter green of the meadow through which the inlet winds, appeared extraordinarily beautiful in the golden light glowing through the fog. We climbed down to the band of stones and shells deposited by the tide, which is where Mack said the spindle stone was found. Because of the dampness, my rheumatoid arthritis was causing my knees and hips to ache, so I remained behind as Dan, Moses, and Chad crossed the inlet and climbed to the top of a rocky knoll surrounded by thickets of wild roses in bloom. Even with the fog, they were able to look out over the grass and scrub and see the shore and the open water the Vikings would have sailed in on. But there was hardly much high ground here on which to build a settlement, and at the moment, late in the month of June, it seemed an awfully damp, cold place. However a spindle whorl might have gotten here, this was not the site of the Vinland colony.

We got Mack's telephone number and e-mail address before saying good-bye and headed back toward Eastport. In the car, I asked Moses for his assessment of what we'd seen that day, but all he said was that he found it "all very interesting." My husband Dan offered the opinion that we had entered the *Land of the Cranks,* a term that greatly amused Moses. Not entirely disagreeing, still I scolded Dan on the grounds that both the Old Mainer and Mack seemed genuinely sincere in their beliefs, that they had been very generous in trying to help us, and that we didn't yet know for sure that what they were telling us was untrue. Dan shrugged, saying he was willing to suspend judgment a while longer, though we all knew that everyone's suspicions had definitely been aroused.

* * *

Over many more days, Moses introduced us to people in both Passamaquoddy communities, Indian Township and Pleasant Point/Sipayik. We met the director of the tribal museum, local basket makers, the tribal representative to the state legislature who was researching Passamaquoddy history, and one gray-haired woman who cautioned me against only seeking out men as sources of stories. "Women have our own stories to tell," she informed me. But in fact, when I asked about those who might share old stories regarding first contacts with Europeans, the immediate responses were often uncertain, even reluctant. Even with Moses as my intermediary, I recognized again and again that

I was an outsider here. I had no right to those stories, and Native peoples are necessarily wary after decades of scholars who built careers on misrepresentations and biased interpretations of Native cultures. It would take several years and many more visits to earn people's trust.

By contrast, lots of non-Native Mainers were eager to share their beliefs about first contacts. On another afternoon, we visited the Grand Lake Stream Historical Society Museum. Moses had contacted them, too, and been told that they owned an ancient carved stone spearpoint believed to be Viking. So with Moses's car still in the repair shop, the four of us piled into our rental car and drove out to Grand Lake Stream. The museum itself was a red barnlike structure with a white door and white lettering that read "GLS Historical Society Museum." Dan took a snapshot with our throwaway camera and murmured, "I think we're getting close to the heart of Crankland." Inside, we were greeted by an older, white-haired gentleman who explained that he was retired but volunteered as the museum's part-time caretaker and director. The room we entered was crowded with display cases, old farm implements, an antiquated gasoline pump, and a large canoe. The clutter was neat, but it corroborated the director's contention that the collection had outgrown the space. He began by showing us specimens of arrowheads and larger projectile points, all mounted on boards and labeled with hand-lettered signs. Some were supposedly four thousand years old, others only one thousand, he said, although the dating appeared to be wholly arbitrary. None had tribal identifications.

In response to our questions, he admitted that no one in the society had attempted to contact any of the local Indian communities in order to share their holdings or to inquire about the possible uses, age, or tribal affiliation of any of the arrowheads. "Some might be of great historical interest," I volunteered. Yet with Moses standing right there as a member of our research team, this gentleman asserted that contacting those on the nearby reservations "wouldn't be of much use because Indians don't know anything about their history." Then he continued, "We just store whatever anybody brings in or donates." Clearly, Indian history and Indian artifacts were not his group's keen interest. Instead, as he gradually revealed to us, most of the members of this local historical society were convinced that ancient visitors from Europe or the Mediterranean had once plied the Maine coast and established a settlement for a time. And he offered to show us the society's most prized possession, the stone spearpoint about which Moses had been told.

Unlocking a large wooden wall case, he brought out a rectangular clear Plexiglas box that housed a gray stone about a foot long and six inches in diameter, fluted at one end and pointed on the other. Unfortunately, the Plexiglas box seemed designed to frustrate our desire to photograph and handle the artifact because it wasn't hinged at either end. But Moses took the box, examined it for a few moments, and then, without a word of protest from the museum's director, used the point of a pen to slit the seal around the top. The spearpoint was now out and in our hands.

The incising was shallow and appeared white against the grayish beige of the stone. One side of the stone was relatively flat, and on this side was a crude graven image of some sort of bearded male warrior figure holding a round shield in front of him. It had been found locally years before and donated to the museum, though no record of the place and date of the find seemed to be available, not even the name of the person who first uncovered it. When I explained to the museum's caretaker-director that my husband and I had studied Viking-era artifacts on our trips to Norway and Denmark, he eagerly encouraged us to examine the stone more closely. Dan and I turned the stone over and over, looking at it in full daylight as well as under the incandescent and fluorescent lamps of the museum. We also peered at it through a magnifying glass. "I don't think this is Norse," I told the gentleman. "It doesn't resemble anything I've ever seen in the museums and archives of Scandinavia." "Then it must be Phoenician," he replied, adding, "they were here too, you know." Finally, I asked if Moses could examine the stone, and the gentleman agreed. "No, it's definitely not Indian," Moses declared with conviction. "It looks to me like it was done with a Dremel tool." And so it was. To anyone with a trained eye, it was clear the stone had been incised with a fine-point electric drill.

Obviously, the museum's caretaker-director had hoped that, as a university-affiliated researcher, I might validate and add authority to his and others' belief that the carved stone was an authentic Viking artifact. When I didn't, he immediately switched to his alternate theory that the stone was Phoenician, and he completely ignored Moses's quite accurate observation that the engraving on the stone was modern.

As we drove Moses back to his home on the Pleasant Point reservation that evening, Moses kept asking over and over again, "Why would anybody make these fakes?" and "Why do they want to do that?" Unfortunately, the many and complex motivations behind the forging of ancient artifacts—fame, money, the desire to "fool the experts," a commitment to some particular view of history for which no other evidence is available, or some combination of these—were beyond any of our abilities to explain. One impression was emerging clearly, however. Many non-Native people are fascinated by the mysteries of the remote past, and some of them will hold on to an improbable theory rather than approach their Native American neighbors in order to ascertain whatever insights into a knowable past might be gained by sharing collections of Indian arrowheads.

With Moses's questions still unanswered to anyone's satisfaction, I did a little more digging. I found that I was hardly the first person drawn to Maine by the promise of ancient Viking artifacts. The novelist, essayist, and satiric poet Calvin Trillin had preceded me. And the man named Walter Elliott was once again involved.

In 1971, Trillin reported on a part-time carpenter and jack-of-all-trades from Maine named Walter Elliott who claimed to have found three engraved stones on the banks of the Morse River near where it widens into what is called Spirit Pond in the area of Popham Beach and the township of Phippsburg. Two of the stones were covered with incised symbols, while the third appeared to show a map of Popham Beach. The find generated a great stir of publicity when Elliott identified the strange markings as medieval Norse runes. Based on his discovery, Elliott declared himself "convinced that Maine is Vinland," and many of his fellow enthusiasts began looking forward to the prestige and tourism dollars that would surely now flow into Maine. "As all of the people involved acknowledged" to Trillin when he covered the story for the *New Yorker*, "They *want* to believe the stones are real—to believe that Viking ships once sailed through the islands that lie off Popham Beach and up the Morse River and into the shelter of Spirit Pond."[6]

But the stones *weren't* real. Like a number of other imputed artifacts that Elliott claimed to discover in subsequent years, the Spirit Pond stones, too, proved to have been etched with an electric steel engraving tool (though Elliott denied this to his death). Elliott's attempts to sell the stones for money were thwarted by the fact that they had been found on state land and were thereby legally state property. In the end, Elliott was "encouraged" to turn them over to the state by a $4,500 gift from a private donor. Performing its due diligence, the state had the stones examined by several expert runologists, and all concluded that they were fakes.[7]

Today the Spirit Pond stones are housed in the Maine State Museum in Augusta and, when exhibited, are clearly labeled as fakes. Nonetheless, on this first visit to Maine, so many people told me about the Spirit Pond "discovery" and assured me the stones were authentic that I felt I had to meet with Elliott's widow, Susan. So we arranged to visit in the modest home Susan had shared with her late husband. The front yard and covered porch were filled with what appeared to be weathered ancient pieces of carved stone, including a vaguely classical Greek-looking head from some missing statue. As we entered, my husband, my research assistant Chad, and I were all graciously received. (Moses had a doctor's appointment that day and wasn't able to join us.) A retired schoolteacher, Elliott's widow was happy to share old newspaper clippings and odd "finds" brought home by her late husband over the years. She had no idea why he made the things he did, and she declined to say whether she believed any of his "discoveries" to be authentic. "I just don't know" was her only answer.

Then something prompted Susan to mention that the state archaeologist had sent one of the Spirit Pond artifacts to the Smithsonian as a possible example of a fake. Going into the other room, Susan returned with a newspaper clipping from the first section of the *Portland Press Herald* of June 2, 2000. It contained a front-page story titled "Romance in Old Stones." The story was about Walter Elliott's discoveries, and while it valiantly tried to be evenhanded, it finally came down squarely on the side of the experts. The experts had found the runes to be inauthentic and ascertained that some of these artifacts were created with the help of power tools. According to the article, the *coup de grace* had been delivered by the renowned archaeologist William Fitzhugh, curator of the Smithsonian exhibition on the Vikings, who chose to include one of the Spirit Pond rune stones in his exhibition as an example of a "known" fake.

Dan read all of this aloud to us in as even a tone as possible. But our interview with Susan had clearly reached its conclusion. Her attitude was hard to gauge—perhaps a bit hurt or embarrassed, perhaps resigned to the fact that her late husband was a fraud. She had given us the article herself, after all, and didn't seem angry or eager to dispute its findings. Her modest home testified to the fact that neither the carvings Walter Elliott claimed as his own nor the ancient artifacts he claimed to have found had brought him wealth or fame. At best, they had brought—for his wife at least—an unwanted notoriety.

Yet for other Mainers who sought us out, including those who had helped me make contact with Elliott's widow, the discoveries were *real*. In their eyes, Elliott was a kind of hero, bravely standing up to established authorities who snobbishly refused to acknowledge the contributions of amateurs and "ordinary people." Accompanying and even fueling this stated distrust of "experts" was these Mainers' unshakable belief that Vikings had once visited Maine and settled there for a time. Elliott's "discoveries" were precisely the kind of proof they were eager for.

They had other proofs, too, among them a small pond with an elliptical wall of stones at one end. This, they were sure, was a product of Norse engineering. But when I spoke with expert hydrologists at the University of Maine who had examined Norse Pond, they all assured me that it was a natural feature of the landscape, some ten to twelve thousand years old, and showed no signs of human intervention. Apparently, as my later research revealed, in the second half of the nineteenth century, "rusticators" came up to Cutler from Boston and mistook the elliptical wall of stones for a man-made dam. They decided to exploit the nation's then-current belief that the Vikings' Vinland had been located in New England and named the pond accordingly. It was their way of luring summer tourists to the Cutler area.

To be sure, dedicated amateurs have often made lasting and significant contributions to a number of fields and disciplines. Amateurs have usefully challenged the accepted and sometimes ossified orthodoxies espoused by established experts. Yet amateurs can also let their theories get ahead of the evidence, or, as appears to have happened here, they can accept the wrong things *as evidence*.

In point of fact, there is nothing that definitively excludes the Maine coast from the areas the Norse might have visited during their Vinland venture. There is simply no documentary or hard archaeological evidence that they did. To the regret of historians, the eleventh-century Norse made neither maps nor charts and didn't even have words for these tools in their vocabulary. The geographical locales described in the sagas can be interpreted as describing any number of areas from Nova Scotia, New Brunswick, and the Gulf of St. Lawrence as far south as New York. The finds at L'Anse aux Meadows make clear that that place served as the landing site and base camp for voyages back and forth to Greenland, and the people who lived there made excursions to and established encampments in regions farther south. But just how far south remains uncertain. And we may never know the answer because rising sea levels over the last century have washed away whole swaths of land all along the Atlantic coast, especially in Maine. Any evidence of thousand-year-old turf and wooden buildings erected by the Norse have surely long ago been swept away with the tides.[8]

That said, Moses's still-unanswered questions and these unexpected encounters in Maine gave me a lot to think about. So Dan and I, along with Chad, spent the next day at leisure, walking along the shore on Campobello Island. To and from the island, we again drove through Lubec, passing the turnoffs to Cutler and Quoddy Head, and again passed the Lubec Historical Society, where we were first lured into the world of Viking enthusiasts. But it all seemed disenchanted now, drained of its mystery, no longer capable of sparking our expectations.

We were winding up our research in this part of Maine, and Moses had invited us to dinner, promising "two kinds of moose meat." Moses's house was a blue clapboard duplex, of which he had the lower floor. When we arrived, he invited us into an L-shaped room with an open kitchen on the right, a card table and folding chairs for the dining area, and a living room demarcated by a couch with its back to the dining area. The living room was dominated by a large television in the corner, flanked by standing racks filled with videos, most of them action films that appealed to his two boys. The walls, however, were decorated with pictures and paraphernalia distinctly pan-Indian. There was a wall clock in the shape of a large arrowhead with a depiction of Indians on horseback, wearing feathers and carrying bows and spears. A framed print nearby showed Indians on paint ponies running down a buffalo. Mounted on nails were ceremonial pipes and feathered headdresses, while a beaded dream catcher hung in the window. Over the entrance to the rear hallway leading to the bedrooms was a long narrow banner bearing the word "Passamaquoddy."

In addition to moose meat cooked two ways, Moses made baked potatoes, green beans, corn on the cob, and the Passamaquoddy version of fry bread. A nice merlot would have been the perfect accompaniment, but since Moses doesn't drink—and the reservation is dry—we happily settled for Pepsi and iced tea. The moose was tender and delicious, with no obvious gaminess to distinguish it from beef. After we had finished and many times complimented Moses on his cooking, the four of us sat around the small card table and talked about our recent forays into the wilds of what both Moses and Dan were now calling Crankland. It was our unanimous sense that none of these people were out to con us, at least not in the sense of trying to relieve us of our money. Nor were they trying to fool us into believing something they knew to be untrue. If anything, it seemed they were trying to *share* something with us—the thrill of discovery, perhaps, or the inner glow of being among the cognoscenti, those who share some secret and important knowledge.

Before we left, I gave Moses a check for the agreed-upon fee of one thousand dollars, the promise of which he'd already used as part of the down payment on a much-needed "new" used car. It seemed little enough for all the time he had given us, and for the way he had tracked down whatever leads came to hand. Dan and I had come to appreciate the element of deliberation in his manner, which required a pause before every reply, and no shooting from the lip. The pause gave even the simplest sort of agreement an emphasis that feels flattering: "Yesss."

On our last afternoon together in the motel, Dan and Chad consolidated their notes with my memories. Certain now that even if Vinland had been here once, it has by now gone the watery way of Atlantis, we put down our notebooks and headed out for a lobster dinner.

Later that night, when I phoned Moses to say good-bye, he insisted on coming over to the Motel East to do it in person. To our great surprise, he arrived bearing a last round of gifts. Circular spirit catchers made with leather, beads, and feathers for Chad and Dan, and a fine lidded Passamaquoddy basket for me. Also braided lengths of fresh sweet grass, one for each of us. We were grateful but also embarrassed, stunned by a generosity that so far outstripped our own. All we could do was to thank Moses, grip his hand in a power shake, and say to him in Passamaquoddy, as he says to us, "until next time."

* * *

On the flights back to Tucson, I mulled over the time in Maine. I knew I would be going back, and I knew that Wayne Newell would be—as I put it on my dedication page—one of "my truest teachers." I also knew I would be seeing Moses again, and I made a mental note to bring gifts for all next time. But I knew, too, that this first visit to Maine had confronted me with something I had not previously thought about: for some Americans, the stories we tell about discovery and first contact matter profoundly. The Viking history buffs I met in Maine were deeply invested in an American origin story that began not with Columbus or even with Indians but with the romanticized Vikings of legend. And as I pondered why, another curious thing happened. My research took on an entirely new focus that I had never anticipated.

I came to realize that my real subject was not the geographical location of the fabled Vinland nor the ethnic identity of the Native peoples with whom the Norse both traded and fought. These certainly continued to fascinate me, but they were only my subtext. My real subject, I realized, was the many and complex agendas that had prompted Americans' many and often contradictory stories about first contacts between the "Old" and "New" Worlds. After all, the initial successive waves of immigrants from Europe were well aware that they had invaded, dispossessed, and almost annihilated dense and once-thriving indigenous populations. And whether or not explicitly articulated, this uncomfortable fact has left our so-called nation of immigrants with what I termed in my book "an ongoing anxiety of legitimacy." That is why successive waves of newcomers have repeatedly tried to find ways to claim their right to be here. As a consequence, the tales of discovery and first contact inevitably became intimately intertwined with the politics of who really belongs here.[9]

In sum, a number of curious things happened in my search for Vinland. The Native stories I uncovered had little interest in the specific identity of the first white men they encountered, instead concentrating on the outcome of that encounter for the Indians. Non-Indians, by contrast, were fascinated by the very mystery of *firstness*. As a result, I was offered faked artifacts, and I met people with passionate attachments to a specific, albeit unverifiable, version of Maine history. Neither the absence of hard evidence nor the evidence of fraud could sway them. Yet it was precisely those odd encounters that forced me to reconceive my entire project so that, in the end, my book became less a study of history and more a study of the stories we tell ourselves *about* history. I am convinced that *In Search of First Contact* thereby became a better book. I suspect that many research scholars have had similar experiences. If truth be told, because we somehow have to explain or account for them, it is often the surprises in the research process that teach us the most.

NOTES

1. Anne Stine Ingstad, *The Discovery of a Norse Settlement in America: Excavations at L'Anse aux Meadows, Newfoundland 1961–1968,* trans. Elizabeth Seeberg (New York: Columbia University Press, 1977), 239, 238. Subsequent "AMS radiocarbon dates on twigs and small branches" preserved at the site "date the Norse occupation to somewhere right before or after A.D. 1000": Birgitta Wallace, "L'Anse aux Meadows, Leif Eriksson's Home in Vinland," *Journal of the North Atlantic* 2 (Spring 2009): 121.

2. The Norse explored west and north of Greenland, encountering and trading with Eskimo peoples in the Canadian Arctic. The Norse might also have encountered the Beothuk who once inhabited parts of Newfoundland, and they probably had some contact with the Naskapi and Innu (formerly known as the Montagnais) of Quebec and Labrador.

3. Unquestionably the most important long-forgotten printed source that I uncovered was *The Life and Traditions of the Red Man,* originally written and self-published in Maine in 1893 by Penobscot elder Joseph Nicolar. Nicolar told the story of his people from the first moments of the world's creation through the successive first sightings of, early contacts with, and eventual permanent settlement of newcomers from Europe. In 2007 I published a new edition of this neglected masterpiece, and I discuss it at length in *In Search of First Contact: The Vikings of Vinland, the Peoples of the Dawnland, and the Anglo-American Anxiety of Discovery* (Durham, NC: Duke University Press, 2012), 295–313. A Penobscot story about a first sighting of Europeans which had previously remained in the oral tradition is now published for the first time in *In Search of First Contact,* 276–79.

4. Chadwick Allen's most recent book is *Trans-Indigenous: Methodologies for Global Native Literary Studies* (Minneapolis: University of Minnesota Press, 2012).

5. Despite all the expert testimony, the Kensington Stone was actually exhibited in the Smithsonian Institution as late as 1948, although its authenticity was clearly noted as questionable and controversial.

6. Quoted in Calvin Trillin, "U.S. Journal: Maine. Runes," *New Yorker* (February 5, 1972): 70, 72.

7. In 1977, the eagerness of many local citizens and dignitaries to accept

"discovered" rune stones as genuine became the subject of Trillin's gentle satire in his novel *Runestruck*, set in a fictional Maine town.

8.   See Kolodny, *In Search of First Contact*, 98–99.

9.   Kolodny, *In Search of First Contact*, 14.

ANNETTE KOLODNY completed her PhD at the University of California, Berkeley, in 1969 and has since become an internationally award-winning scholar in American literary and cultural studies. She is currently professor emerita at the University of Arizona, where she previously served as dean of the College of Humanities. Among her most important books are *The Lay of the Land* (1975), *The Land Before Her* (1984), and *Failing the Future: A Dean Looks at Higher Education in the Twenty-First Century* (1998). Her most recent work concentrates on Native American literatures and early transnational contacts with the Americas.

Comanches, Cowboys, and a Political Rock Star

I learned not long ago that I've exceeded the average life expectancy of alligators and great horned owls. I sure haven't had to work as hard for my dinners, and my history of wise choices is not compelling. But I take some satisfaction in my belief that my two best books came after I qualified for Social Security.

One is my second novel, *Comanche Sundown,* which TCU Press published in 2010. The research and writing of the novel consumed twenty-five years, which is no way to make a living. The protagonists are Quanah Parker, the half-white last war chief of the Comanches, and Bose Ikard, a freed slave, Texas cowboy, and drover on trail drives to New Mexico Territory and Colorado. Quanah's mother was Cynthia Ann Parker, stolen at age nine by Nocona, the warrior she later loved and married; she was the cause célèbre of Texans enraged by the Comanches' kidnapping and captivity of women and children. Bose Ikard (pronounced *eye*-curd) was the slave of a homeopathic doctor who freed him toward the end of the War of Northern Aggression, as Southerners characterized the Civil War, but never acknowledged him as the son he clearly was. Quanah and Bose became mirror images, in my mind. They were both half-breeds, as mixed-bloods were called back then, and both knew the humiliation and isolation of being cast out for reasons of their blood. The supporting cast took on two of Quanah's many wives, his mother and father, Pat Garrett, Billy the Kid, Bat Masterson, the bogus Comanche shaman Isa-tai, General William T. Sherman, and Ranald Mackenzie, commander of a cavalry largely composed of freed slaves. Writing that novel was like being aboard a runaway horse or mule. I could neither give up and jump off nor rein the beast in.

The other book I'm most proud of is *Let the People In: The Life and Times of Ann Richards,* which the University of Texas Press published in 2012. Ann was a one-term governor of Texas, from 1990 to 1994. She became a media superstar one night in 1988 with a bravura performance as keynote speaker at the Democratic National Convention whose presidential nominee was the Massachusetts governor Michael Dukakis. Ann is best known for her delivery of a line about George Herbert Walker Bush, then the vice president and soon to be president: "Poor George, he can't help it. He was born with a silver *foot* in his mouth." In 1994, that man's son, George W. Bush, took her down handily in her bid for reelection, a payback that seemed almost Shakespearean.

Ann was a recovered alcoholic, and political foes in both parties vilified her as a closet lesbian. But she was married for almost thirty years to David Richards, a distinguished civil and voting rights attorney, and for the last seventeen years of her life she went steady, as they put it, with Edwin "Bud" Shrake, a charismatic novelist, screenwriter, playwright, and globe-roaming star in the early days of *Sports Illustrated.* Ann's political career was colorful and brief. But she was the first ardent feminist elected to major high office in the United States. Ann put many of the cracks in the glass ceiling that's much discussed today. Hillary Clinton considered Ann her mentor when she was first lady and US senator from New York. I anticipated objection to my writing a biography of Ann because I am a man. But that was part of the challenge and reward. Although I devoted a great deal of care to the female characters in my unprolific fiction, my journalistic career had never afforded me much opportunity to write about women. But the most daunting obstacle to my writing a biography of Ann was that for twenty years she was my friend.

A few months ago a friend in the business world asked me with a grin, "Are you going to explain how you jumped from Quanah Parker to Ann Richards?" Now that a kind editor has asked, I suppose I am.

* * *

In the summer of 1984 my wife Dorothy Browne, my stepdaughter Lila, her best friend Katy, and I were on a plane landing at the Dallas–Fort Worth airport. I had won a grant from the National Endowment for the Arts, the first real money I'd ever had. The endowment recommended that the grant's purpose was for research and travel, so we ignored friends' practical advice on how to invest the small windfall and took off for a six-week jaunt through England, France, and Italy. Except for a few brief excursions in Mexico, it was my first travel abroad, and I came back a much different person. At least I felt I was. Dorothy and I gathered our carry-on bags, the girls their Cabbage Patch dolls, and we walked off the plane into a culture shock: a sea of top hats, balloons, and shouting people dressed in red, white, and blue. They were Republican national conventioneers celebrating their nomination of President Ronald Reagan and Vice President George Bush for a second term. They won with ease that fall.

After weeks in a cramped Peugeot on twisting, narrow, scenic back roads of Europe, on the drive home to Austin in my Chevrolet the interstate highway looked like a giant's carving of the earth. We had hardly unpacked and gotten over the jet leg before I took off alone, intent on getting right to work on a nonfiction book about football. On the way to interview an old friend and coaching acquaintance in southern Oklahoma, I stopped in Wichita Falls, Texas, my hometown until I was twenty-three. It's a small city populated by oil millionaires, roughnecks, rednecks, cowboys, and god-fearing working folk who have treated me warmly all my life, though I was an often-fired beer-joint lout for a time there until I decided to grow up.

That night I accompanied my sister and family to a rodeo in the nearby small town of Henrietta. My maternal grandfather, on leaving his last tenant cotton farm, had been caretaker of that rodeo arena and a squat cinder block building on the grounds that Henrietta folk called the country club. My grandmother shelled bushels of black-eyed peas for the annual rodeo feast. I had written that arena and someone much like my grandfather into my first novel, *Deerinwater*, which Texas Monthly Press would soon publish. Those splintered bleachers and the arena's loose red clay soil triggered an assault of memories and associations, and then the rodeo began. A lone horseman sat out by the fence with a Stars and Stripes and its staff that he held propped against his cantle, the flag rippling in the wind. The horse stood loose reined as the rider held his hat against his heart and people stood and sang the National Anthem. Out behind that cowboy I saw nothing but short-grass pasture and a fading blue twilight sky.

The next morning I drove across the Red River to Lawton and had a good time talking to my high school friend. The Oklahoma town is much like Wichita Falls, except for the Indian population and soldiers stationed at adjoining Fort Sill. (Note of preference here: I have it on good authority that an excellent way to get the tires and wheels removed from your car is to go around a reservation saying the words "Native American." The ones I've known call themselves Indians with pride.) After the interview I drove out west through the small pretty range of Wichita Mountains. Several Indian tribes attach spiritual significance to those well-timbered peaks and valleys. Comanche parents told children they'd better be good, for their tribal bugaboo, the Great Cannibal Owl, occupied a cave in those mountains and gobbled bad children at night. I drove on out through a federal preserve stocked with buffalo and found Quanah Parker's Star House at a place called Cache. One of his Texas rancher friends shipped the lumber to build it from Wichita Falls across the Red River, a quicksand stream that then had no bridges. The favor bestowed on the reservation chief a fine two-story home with private bedrooms for his seven wives and white five-point stars laid among the blue shingles on the roof. I didn't cross the fence to the empty house for it was on private property and no one was around. But it was a pleasure just to stand outside the gate and let all the stories sift through my mind.

After the Comanches' defeat, Quanah had been championed by Texas cattlemen who were nostalgic for the old days—also because he leased them grazing rights to the rich prairie on the short-lived Comanche-Apache reservation. In 1905 Quanah and Geronimo rode their horses in Theodore Roosevelt's inaugural parade. Weeks later, Quanah and his cowboy friends took Roosevelt on a ballyhooed wolf hunt on the 480,000-acre Big Pasture of open range. There weren't many if any wolves left for their greyhounds to run down, but coyotes abounded, and one day the president snapped the head off a rattlesnake with a quirt. At the end of the president's adventure, he and the cowboys and Quanah galloped down the main street of Frederick, Oklahoma, with their elbows flapping.

Back in Texas, I stopped for the night in Seymour. The motel's owners were Indians of Asian ethnicity, and as I was registering in the lobby, the door opened and a legless man walked in on his fists. He inquired, "Y'all know if there's a radiator shop around here?"

However far I roam, these are my roots, my home country. The rolling savanna wasn't settled and farmed until the Comanches and their allied Kiowas and Southern Cheyennes were finished in 1875. I grew up knowing no Indians. Their forebears had not been welcome in Texas, and they got the hell out. The Comanche-Apache reservation, which before that had been a Choctaw reservation, was scrapped into 140-acre grants in the last Oklahoma land grab. Lawton sprang right up in tents. I learned nothing of Indians in my formal education, and there were no statues or museums that I knew about. (Fort Sill does have one.) But west of Wichita Falls along the Red River is a little town named Quanah. To the east is another little town named Nocona, for Quanah's equally ferocious war chief father, also called Peta Nocona in the whites' attempt to catch the Comanches' unwritten dialect of Shoshone. A novel was brewing in my mind based on the life of Quanah Parker. And I had concluded my first research trip.

* * *

Despite having a war chief father, Quanah was jeered by other boys for his half-white blood. It made of him *tuibitzi*, a braggart youth. In the Nokoni or Wanderers band of his birth he also came to be shunned as a harbinger of bad luck. The war between the Comanches and Texas settlers was an endless exchange of vengeance raids. Nocona, as I choose to call him, led one such raid in early December 1860. They laid waste to farms and ranches, reportedly killed twenty-three settlers, and struck terror in the small settlements of Jacksboro, Belknap, and Weatherford. They raped, scalped, and shot arrows in a woman who was several months pregnant. The next day her child was born dead, and she lived four days, screaming, before she died. The Texas rangers were then a loose mounted paramilitary of Indian fighters. The enraged Texans mounted a punitive expedition that included an unpopular twenty-two-year-old ranger called Sul Ross, a scout named Charles Goodnight who wore an ocelot skin vest, and a detachment of US Army dragoons singing Irish chanteys.

The horse tracks of Nocona's big raid led the Texans to a Pease River Comanche camp comprised of old people, women, and children. The men and able boys were off hunting buffalo. Sul Ross claimed that he allowed his Mexican servant to stop the death song of a wounded Nocona with a shotgun blast, and that he recognized that a captive woman with a small child had blue eyes. (Goodnight, who was remembered by the surviving Comanches as "the Leopard Coat Man," claimed he was the one who first saw that.) She was Cynthia Ann Parker, who had lived twenty-four years as a Comanche called Naduah. In every way but her blood she was Comanche. In 1886, as an

ex-Confederate general and state senator, Sul Ross would run for governor backed by an adoring biography endorsing his record as a great
Indian fighter. He served two popular terms and was the revered first
president of Texas A&M University. Aggies pitch coins at his statue on
the campus for luck in taking their exams. A small college in Big Bend
is named for Sul Ross.

Comanches scoffed that the man killed by Ross's rangers that day
was a civil chief supervising a skinning camp, and Quanah always
claimed his father died one day after picking plums that grew wild on
the Canadian River in the Texas Panhandle. But if Nocona was hunting buffalo with Quanah and his younger brother Peanut that day, he
still suffered horrendous losses. His wife and young daughter Prairie
Flower were taken into a second captivity among the white Parker clan.
Cynthia Ann lost Prairie Flower to an illness and horrified her kin by
slashing her breasts in grief, a Comanche custom. She lived in misery
until about 1871, never knowing what became of her sons and husband,
if it's true that Nocona wasn't killed that day on the Pease. Also slain
that day was Nocona's younger wife, like Cynthia Ann a captive, only
she was from Mexico. Not long after the raid Quanah's brother Peanut
died, most likely of smallpox.

After all that bad luck, Quanah felt unwelcome enough among
the Nokoni that he rode onto the remote treeless plains and serpen-
tine canyons of the Panhandle and joined the Quohadi or Antelope
band. In October 1871 he proved himself as a warrior by handing Ranald Mackenzie's cavalry a devastating defeat in Blanco Canyon. After
the nighttime raid a sudden norther and blizzard saved the fleeing
nomads from being overtaken by the soldiers and perhaps wiped out.
The battle left Mackenzie with a serious arrow wound in his leg, and
among dozens of horses Quanah stole Mackenzie's favorite, a gray
pacer. Right after that he incited near inter-Quohadi warfare by running off with a woman whose father had promised her to a man who
had many horses, the Comanche standard of wealth. Quanah and
his followers based themselves along the Middle Concho River, near
present-day San Angelo, and they were the wildest Comanche bunch
of all. Welcomed back into the Antelope band because of that prow-
ess, in June 1874 Quanah and the shaman Isa-tai forged an unprecedented warriors' alliance of Comanches, Kiowas, Southern Cheyennes,
Kiowa-Apaches, and Arapahos. Quanah meant to drive the Texans out

into the Gulf of Mexico in boats, as the Honey Eater band and a war chief named Buffalo Hump had done twenty-four years earlier.

But Quanah's greatest day of valor came in a losing cause. At a lonely place on the high plains called Adobe Walls, the great alliance was blown apart by the .50-caliber long guns of vastly outnumbered buffalo hunters who called themselves hide men. The Comanches called Mackenzie "Bad Hand," for one had been left a claw by a rebel bullet in the Civil War. In September 1874 Mackenzie tortured a comanchero trader into revealing the location of the last holdouts in a sheer ravine called Tule Canyon. The soldiers gaped, then went skidding and tumbling down the canyon walls at first light, catching the Indians by surprise. Few on either side were killed in the gunfight, but afterward the soldiers destroyed the Indians' food supply and buffalo robes, burned two hundred lodges, and captured a huge horse herd. The next morning Mackenzie's soldiers started shooting the horses. They were killing two a minute, and the job took them all day. Quanah's band held out one more hungry winter, then a Methodist minister who spoke Comanche persuaded them their war was over. Mackenzie rode out to meet Quanah with the formality of Ulysses S. Grant accepting the sword of Robert E. Lee.

Quanah's world and the life he anticipated were crushed and extinguished when he was just thirty years old. Though he was treated with respect, his warriors and peers were thrown raw meat over a Fort Sill wall by jeering soldiers. General William T. Sherman ordered him taken in chains by rail to a dank, deadly prison in Florida, but Mackenzie appealed on his behalf, and Grant countermanded Sherman's order. Quanah lived on for thirty-seven years as a reservation chief, a friend of ranchers he had battled when they were frontier rangers, residing in style at the Star House with his seven wives. Father of eighteen surviving children and grandfather of dozens, he had a deaf-mute driver called Dummy and with Oklahoma cowboy pals starred in a 1908 movie. He died in 1911, just a year after winning permission, with help from Charles Goodnight, "the Leopard Coat Man," to move his mother's remains to Comanche soil in Oklahoma.

I should also say this of his attraction to me as a character: Quanah Parker was the Timothy Leary of his time.

My novel might have joined a considerable parade of books focused only on the warrior and his mother. But I was riveted by the brutality of the Comanche horsemen and the fear and hatred they aroused in Spaniards, Mexicans, and Texans in a war that lasted two and a quarter centuries. The Spaniards just gave up and on maps identified sprawling parts of present-day Texas, Oklahoma, Kansas, New Mexico, and Colorado as Comanchería. Bose Ikard was a trusted drover on trail drives of cattle to distant markets that were led by Goodnight and Oliver Loving, best known these days as Gus (Robert Duvall) and Call (Tommy Lee Jones) in the enduring miniseries *Lonesome Dove,* which was adapted from Larry McMurtry's Pulitzer Prize–winning novel. McMurtry fictionalized Bose in the novel, then killed him off with an Indian lance. Bose in fact lived to age eighty-two, in his later years as a tenant farmer and handyman. A grade school in Weatherford, Texas, is named for him. Bose crossed over into my fictional scheme when I discovered, in a 1937 book by G. A. Holland titled *A History of Parker County and the Double Log Cabin,* a ten-paragraph account of a running fight near Weatherford in April 1869 between Comanche horse thieves and young cowboys. Bose was one of those cowboys, along with his white half brother. That battle was the Texans' first recorded sighting of the Comanche who came to be known as Quanah Parker. He was taller than the others, but what stood out most was the utter arrogance of his wearing a blue US Army jacket. The battle went badly for the cowboys and Indians, with fatalities on both sides. I wrote my version of that battle in a hotel room in Quito, Ecuador, where I was on a magazine assignment about oil exploration in the Amazon. And so I plunged off in a mental and creative wilderness of my own.

*   *   *

At a birthday party in San Antonio in October 1980 I was introduced to Dorothy Browne by my friend Pete Gent, the former Dallas Cowboy receiver and author of the fine novel *North Dallas Forty.* I was a thirty-five-year-old bachelor living in contentment with dog and cat in a cabin overlooking a pretty valley called Rogues Hollow that was fifty miles from Austin and far removed from its politics. Dorothy was a single mom working for the Texas chapter of the ACLU that shared a two-story building with the *Texas Observer* of Molly Ivins's tenure and the office of David Richards and his law partner Sam Houston Clinton. On a group expedition to Laredo and Nuevo Laredo, Mexico, David was among the first to wave me into an Austin gang that in time would be like extended family.

Dorothy had been married twice, first to Bill Brammer, his birth name Billy Lee. In 1960 he had published *The Gay Place*, a superb novel about Texas politics structured as a triplet of novellas bound together by a governor called Arthur "Goddam" Fenstemaker. The character was a composite, as are most in fiction, but he bore a remarkable resemblance to Lyndon Johnson, for whom Billy Lee had worked as a senate speechwriter. The novel was received as a roman à clef about LBJ and shared billing with Joseph Heller's *Catch-22* as one of the top debuts of that year. On a par with Robert Penn Warren's *All the King's Men* and Joe Klein's *Primary Colors*, it's considered one of the finest novels about American politics. Billy Lee was hailed in some quarters as the next Scott Fitzgerald, but he never finished another book; the temptations, diversions, and substances of the nineteen sixties and seventies derailed a great talent. Billy Lee had been one of my mentors in the early days of *Texas Monthly*, and his last published piece of writing was a review of my first book about the explosion of live music in Austin, *The Improbable Rise of Redneck Rock*, which Heidelberg published in 1974. I was devastated when he died at forty-seven from an accidental overdose of amphetamines. Many years later, one of the most gratifying moments in my career came when the gifted San Antonio writer Jan Jarboe Russell wrote that *Let the People In* and its domineering politician Ann Richards were the lineal and literary descendants of *The Gay Place* and LBJ as Arthur Fenstemaker.

I hadn't known Dorothy when Billy Lee was alive. After seven topsy-turvy years with Billy Lee, and another marriage of the same duration to a handsome, promising, then burned-out liberal legislator named Arthur Vance, she was not too inclined to take another long-term emotional chance on a writer whose prospects were hardly certain. But a love affair ensued, and one Sunday night in late 1980 I found myself parked on a sofa observing her and a boozy crowd of foursomes playing "gonzo bridge." It was the first time I'd seen Ann Richards. She and David were then separated, and she had just been through a brutal ambush and intervention by David, her two oldest children, and close friends over her out-of-control addiction to vodka. The night of the intervention she had flown straight to a month in a Minnesota rehab facility that was no luxury spa. She wrote a friend involved in the intervention that she feared coming home. She didn't know if she could be funny if she wasn't drinking. But Ann dominated that bridge party. I couldn't take my eyes off her. She had adopted her hairstyle of a silver, firmly sprayed bouffant—part of a calculated persona she created for herself when she got into politics as a county commissioner—but at forty-seven she was sexy as all get-out. And she knew it. At one point she leaned back, analyzing her cards, and said, "I've just got to tell you all about *Club*. We have such a good time at Club. We just talk and talk. And when we get to the end, we vote on what'll be our next topic of discussion. I think I'm going to propose *vaginal itch*." Months passed before I realized with that joke she was talking about her newfound devotion to Alcoholics Anonymous. She attended those meetings the rest of her life.

Dorothy and I married in 1982 and invited Ann to the wedding. She sent us a nice gift with a note to Dorothy, who was a social friend, that coming to a wedding "would be like touching a warm burn." She and David divorced the next year. But with all that turmoil and change in her life, she took advantage of an incumbent state treasurer's indictment on felony counts of official misconduct and became the first woman elected to Texas statewide office in fifty years. David contributed $94,000 to her $300,000 campaign. Dorothy had resigned her position with the ACLU, and following our 1984 trip to Europe, in her job hunting she wrote a shy, tentative letter to the new state treasurer. Ann fairly squawked when she talked on the phone. "Darthy, come on down here!" she commanded. (She pronounced that name with precision, for she had gone by her first name of Dorothy until she started high school.) Dorothy told Ann that she didn't even know what the treasury did. "Oh, nonsense," Ann replied, "you can do anything you set your mind to. We're gonna teach you all about *money*."

Dorothy's initial job was drafting correspondence in a way that approximated Ann's voice. They often worked late. I would be gone on a magazine assignment or off researching my historic novel, and my stepdaughter Lila—whose father Arthur Vance became my good friend—spent many evenings doing her homework at the treasury; she and Dorothy smiled at each other on hearing the sounds of Ann padding down the hall in her stocking feet.

Ann liked writers and accumulated many friendships with them. Among them were the *Texas Observer* editor and satirist Molly Ivins and two sportswriters turned magazine journalists, novelists, nonfiction authors, dramatists, and screenwriters—Gary "Jap" Cartwright and

Edwin "Bud" Shrake. Cartwright's swarthy and distinctive features actually derived from a Comanche grandmother, not anyone of Japanese heritage; the politically incorrect nickname was tagged on him by a cranky newspaper editor in Fort Worth. He was the offbeat craftsman and stylist leading the charge at *Texas Monthly,* the magazine where I got my start. Bud was six-foot-six and handsome as a leading man in the movies. He was one of the top contributors of *Sports Illustrated* and a novelist of real gifts. Their circuitous lives and careers brought them to Austin about 1970, the year I arrived. At an old-style booze and chop house called the Raw Deal and the music emporium that made Willie Nelson Austin's instant favorite dope smoker—Armadillo World Headquarters—they were wacky, funny, and hard drinking; Ann and David Richards were co-founders of their short-lived salon called Mad Dog, Inc.

Ann was an avid and opinionated reader. My first novel, *Deerinwater,* which came out in 1985, bestowed a pretty Indian name on a homely plains town much like Wichita Falls. Ann told me she enjoyed the book, narrated in first person by a former high school football star. But she frowned and said she had trouble with the ending, in which the protagonist and his wife and little girl escape town following a scandal over oil field theft and a nighttime gunfight in which the protagonist shoots a corrupt cop dead. The young killer's father, the district attorney, and his friend and boss, the county sheriff, set their feud aside and use their power to get rid of the cop's body and cover up the mess. I made it clear that the onetime running back fired in self-defense, but Ann let me know that her moral sensibilities were offended. In her big voice she said of the killer and his wife: "They just *drove away?*"

* * *

The high plains stretching toward Canada are broken from the plowed fields and overgrazed pastures of my youth by an arrangement of erosion gullies becoming canyons called the Caprock. The most spectacular of the canyons are Palo Duro and Tule, where Mackenzie's cavalry surprised the Indians and killed all their horses. In 1986 *Texas Monthly*'s editor Greg Curtis asked me to write a feature about Palo Duro Canyon. From her ACLU days Dorothy knew a cowboy lawyer in Amarillo named Selden Hale who took pro bono cases for them and rode mules in Palo Duro, the steepest reaches of which you cannot navigate by vehicle and would not wisely descend afoot like Ranald Mackenzie's soldiers. After an alarming descent and one runaway on a big black mule named Stagger Lee—Selden hollered at me, "Try WHOA!"—the two days in that stunning netherworld with my new friend and Dorothy and the subsequent writing of that essay set my Quanah Parker wheels churning in earnest. In the town of Canyon, in a little state college now named West Texas A&M, I found a treasure trove of Comanche and Quanah lore called the Panhandle-Plains Historical Museum. I flew back to Austin my briefcase bulging with reams of notes and my brain swimming with germs of inspiration.

In 1985 Larry McMurtry had published his blockbuster *Lonesome Dove* after first declaring that the rural and historical tradition in Texas letters was bankrupt. Larry had grown up in a little town and on a family ranch just twenty miles from Wichita Falls. His first four books, especially his second novel, *Leaving Cheyenne,* were among the spurs that first urged me to write. His epic about the cattle drives and Indian fights heavily mined the material I hoped was my quarry. To say his wonderful book made me nervous is an understatement. But Quanah Parker made only one very brief appearance in it, and by then my research had persuaded me I could connect the downfall of Quanah's Comanches with Billy the Kid's horse-stealing operation and wooing of lasses that led to his demise in New Mexico Territory.

Then one night Dorothy and I were at a seafood restaurant in Austin with Ann Richards and Bud Shrake. I had enormous admiration for Bud, in part because he helped define the literary western with a 1968 novel called *Blessed McGill.* Bud was always full of news about publishing and movies. He remarked, "McMurtry's coming out with a new one about Billy the Kid."

I reached for my wineglass as Dorothy blurted, "Oh, Jan, you've done all this work on a Billy the Kid novel."

Bud had known nothing about what I was working on. Ann told Dorothy the next morning that she felt just terrible for me that moment, and I had to see it on her expressive face that night. *Anything for Billy* proved to be one of McMurtry's most forgettable books, but I panicked. I made the mistake of believing that in the leap of faith of writing any novel you can know and predict the market. I should have just kept digging and writing, but I put the novel away and started another one far removed from Texas and the nineteenth century. It's a love story and thriller involving the Basque separatists ETA in the north of Spain. I thought I knew the American and his Basque lover, but the plot seemed more and more problematic, and I hit a wall midway through the draft. I thought, "That was brilliant. Now I have *two* half-finished novels." (I've now gone back to the Basque novel, also after twenty-five years, and I'm making progress. You can go home again, or anywhere else, if you wander around long enough.)

And so in 1990 I crept back into simultaneous research and writing of the story that I thought I had abandoned. I had heard stories that Quanah had been a leader in the peyote cults and had fought attempts to criminalize use of the drug. I called the Oklahoma Historical Society for more on this. The librarian who took my call was snippy and haughty. She scolded me: "I know the literature of this, and I can assure that never, ever happened." Months later I grinned in delight. In my part-time speech-writing work I was in Washington, and I made time to go to the library of the Department of the Interior. I found a book by William T. Hagan, *United States–Comanche Relations*, published in 1976. In it was a remarkable passage about how Quanah learned the peyote ritual from Mescalero Apaches in the course of one of his periodic adventures in Mexico, and in the reservation years he shared it with the Poncas, the Otos, tribe after tribe. Songs he composed for the all-night rites are still sung. The delegates to the constitutional convention for Oklahoma statehood in 1907 were trying to make peyote possession and consumption a crime. And in a photo in Hagan's book there stood Quanah in white man's suit with other members of "the Peyote Delegation." They lobbied well, and the proposal was voted down.

I discovered something else that deepened my skepticism about the ways conjectural history becomes the authentic account. In 1886, as Sul Ross was running for governor, James T. DeShields wrote the first book about Cynthia Ann Parker. It was "dedicated by permission" to General Ross, and DeShields rhapsodized about the Battle of the Pease:

> The great Comanche confederacy was forever broken . . . The blow was a most decisive one; as sudden and irresistible as a thunderbolt, and as remorseless and crushing as the hand of Fate . . . Divining Ross's purpose, the watchful Peta Nocona rode at full speed, but was soon overtaken, when the two chiefs engaged in a personal encounter, which must result in the death of one or the other; Peta Nocona fell, and his last sigh was taken up in mournful wailings on the wings of defeat.

Today the genre would be called campaign biography. Forgotten was Ross's report at the time that he simply let his Mexican servant kill the Indian. And the frontier war lasted with much savagery for fifteen more years. But in 1889, with Ross in the governor's office, J. W. Wilbarger reprinted portions of DeShields's book verbatim in *Indian Depredations in Texas*, which purported to be a definitive work of scholarship. In my research I came across an account by Horace Jones, the army's interpreter when Cynthia Ann Parker was captured on the Pease. With no apparent reason to lie, he claimed that Nocona approached him at Fort Cobb, Indian Territory, in 1862, and frightened him badly. He went on that Nocona said he only wanted to smoke a pipe with him— he was just trying to find his wife and daughter. Jones said he told the alleged dead man that he had no idea where they were. For his part, Quanah did not speak out strongly against Ross's claim until 1896. He had been trying to get his mother's remains moved to the Comanche reservation in Oklahoma, and he was enough of a politician himself that he did not want to cross swords with Texas's governor. But with Ross out of office he held forth: "Texas history book tells General Ross kill my father; he no kill him. I want to get that straight up. No kill my father. *He not there.* I see my father die."

An essential skill of any research is a grasp of what you can use and what you can't. My primary interest was in Quanah's untamed years, not those on the doomed reservation. But because it seemed relevant to young Bose Ikard, a house slave in Weatherford in 1860, at the University of Texas's Dolph Briscoe Center for American History I found and used a jewel concerning Cynthia Ann Parker. John Baylor was a wild-eyed madman in Weatherford who hated all Indians and published the only newspaper on that frontier, a rabid sheet called *The White Man*. In his column "Late Indian News," he celebrated soldiers' scalping of Comanches and he would break the story of Cynthia Ann Parker's re-capture on the Pease. But long before that, Baylor was obsessed with Cynthia Ann. On the front page of *The White Man* he wrote a serial fiction about Old Hicks the Texas ranger and his relentless search for the imagined Cynthia Ann. The invented account of her rescue by Old Hicks is in an issue preserved by University of Texas archivists:

> When we overtook them, she held quite a large round pebble in her small hand, which was upraised above her head, as if in the act of hurl-ing it in our faces. I could see an expression of unutterable defiance

in the flashing of her black eyes, and in the compression of her thin, delicate lips. I saw at once, from the fairness of her complexion, not only that she was not an Indian, but felt this must be the face that so possessed my imagination. She was a clear brunette, and evidently a foreigner. I signed as eloquently as I could, for I knew how to express friendliness and good will by gestures. She paid no attention to that but sharply asked me, "Qui êtes-vous?"

I speak French very lamely, and answered, as best I could, "Texans, Americans, et amis." She smiled brightly, threw away her pebble, and came bounding down the rocks to join us. That night her small, graceful head lay upon my shoulder, while the long and silken hair streamed in a raven cloud to my feet. She was very lightly clothed, since the only garment of civilization her captors had given her was something like a chemise of fine linen, which left her breast exposed and her arms naked; she, however, had thrown over her shoulders, as a cape, the brightly rosetted skin of an ocelot, but this had now fallen off. From an instinct of delicacy that does not desert even rude backwoods men, I swept her long hair as the most appropriate veil over her bosom. It was sacred to me!

A Texas ranger who spoke French!

Some of my research just involved driving and reflecting on what I'd seen. One time on southern Oklahoma's Fort Sill I found the sheer black cliff above a clear-running creek that the Comanches called Medicine Bluff. They would go up there to have their visions, and ailing old ones would sometimes sing their death songs and plunge off headfirst. That day soldiers were practicing rappelling on the cliff, as if adding insult to injury. Another time I took off with a friend named Bill Hauptman, and for several days that spring we roamed through west Texas, western Oklahoma, and the Texas Panhandle. We walked through the slim remains of the zany onetime health resort of Mineral Wells, which became the 1909 setting of my novel's epilogue. We climbed over the Medicine Mounds near the town of Quanah—an eerie jutting of four sandstone hills that had great spiritual significance for the Comanches, at least until the 1860 vengeance raid by rangers and Irish dragoons on a nearby curve of the Pease River. Bill was a Tony-winning playwright and had written the best novel set in a fictionalized Wichita Falls, a story about tornado chasers called *Storm Season*. He had been watching the weather channels every night when we got to our motel rooms. Bill and I rolled on through Panhandle ranchland and with my lawyer friend Selden Hale's direction found the site of

Adobe Walls, where besieged buffalo hunters that included young Bat
Masterson stood off and shattered the great alliance led by Quanah
and exposed the shaman Isa-tai as a fraud. Now it was just a stand of
tall lovely cottonwoods surrounded by rolling prairie. But I had all but
memorized the narrative of *Adobe Walls,* a 1986 book about the desperate battle by the historian T. Lindsay Baker and archaeologist B. Byron
Price. We could see the ridge where the hide man Billy Dixon shot an
Indian off his horse three-quarters of a mile away. Then, off to the
east, in a towering white cloud we saw a super cell form. It was almost
like Bill had called it up. It was a beautiful thing to observe, at a safe
distance. About an hour later as we were driving east of Amarillo, we
heard a man yelling from a little radio station in Oklahoma: "Get to
your cellars, there's two of 'em on the ground!"

* * *

Ann Richards was astounded when she got the call to deliver the keynote at the Democrats' 1988 national convention. On different occasions she had been tongue-lashed personally by Lyndon Johnson and
Jimmy Carter in their days of overweening ego and power. Though
Michael Dukakis proved no match for George Bush, her speech made
her a media darling and vaulted her into position to run for governor of Texas. That was also when her longtime friendship with Bud
Shrake blossomed into romance. They were in their mid-fifties, with
four failed marriages and six grown children between them.

I was Ann's volunteer adviser on environmental issues during her
1990 race for governor. Ann kicked off her campaign with a fact-finding
tour of the Texas Gulf Coast on a leased yacht. It was a free television
bonanza, with dolphins frolicking in the wake as she took a turn at the
pilot's wheel the first sunny day. Dorothy had taken vacation time to be
her boss's aide for the weeklong duration, and my purpose was to help
Ann if policy questions backed her into a corner; Dorothy and I shared
a cabin, and it was quite some boat. It was a floating series of business-
like policy briefings by experts who would come aboard for a stretch
then depart, but the third night we witnessed the Richards campaign
in meltdown. Political reporters on board had learned that neither the
owner of the yacht nor his son had their oceangoing pilot's licenses
in order. The political team of Attorney General Jim Mattox, who was
furious that Ann was in the race, was pushing the blunder and story.
What if the Coast Guard boarded and seized the yacht under the watch

of those gleeful reporters? One young Richards aide declared that we were going to jump ship. Ann was going to sputter up the Houston Ship Channel the next morning on a shrimp boat with no air conditioning. While Dorothy and I slept, cooler heads prevailed. The owner and his son would leave the ship, and the first mate, who was licensed, would pilot the yacht the rest of the way. Still, the sun was far from up when Ann summoned me to her cabin to ask what I thought. I told her I had thought the shrimp boat was a terrible idea, but then added, "I just feel bad about the old man."

Her eyes narrowed and she said, "What?"

"Well, he's been enjoying himself, the television and all, and it *is* his boat."

I might know about beach erosion and ocean dumping of ships' plastic refuse, but her expression let me know that in politics I was a rank amateur. "Jan," she rebuked me, "I didn't take him to *raise*."

Later in the campaign, I had recruited a team of volunteers of widely varied expertise. One afternoon as we were meeting in the crummy campaign headquarters, the candidate appeared, and it was the only time I saw her fabled temper. I can't recall why she tore into us. I just remember thinking, "These people aren't getting paid a nickel for trying to help you." But it had been a long day, and her feet hurt.

The Democratic primary was brutal. The press turned into a howling mob one night at a Dallas debate when she refused to answer if she had ever taken illegal drugs. She had developed a fondness for marijuana to go along with her vodka in the seventies. It almost knocked her out of the race, but she hung on to defeat the pugnacious Mattox and a former governor, Mark White. The *Los Angeles Times* headline read: "Richards Wins Mudslide."

She should have had no chance against the folksy Republican oilman and rancher Clayton Williams, but he made a joke about rape to reporters invited to his Davis Mountains ranch and taunted her in sexist ways. They never debated, but at a joint appearance at the Dallas Crime Commission, in front of TV cameras he called her a liar, said he was "going to finish this deal," and refused to shake her hand. Afterward in the van, she startled aides who had been with her in Dallas that terrible night of the screaming press gauntlet by declaring, "Boys, this sucker is over. He must have lost his mind." Williams's gaffes soon had middle-class suburban women dying to get to a voting booth and send him back to his home on the range. And in the stretch Ann became the candidate people thought they had seen when she was making her breakout speech. In a state whose demographics had already flipped Republican, she won by 91,000 votes. She was the beneficiary of one of the most spectacular self-destructions in Texas political history. After it was over Williams allowed with his good-natured grin, "I'd shoot myself in the foot, then load'er up and blast away again."

Dorothy was one of the senior aides who went with Ann to the governor's office. Ann and her campaign manager turned chief of staff, Mary Beth Rogers, initially made Dorothy second in command in the criminal justice division. Ann had promised she was going to shake things up, and, on issues ranging from insurance regulation to toxic pollution, for the first two years of her term she did. In the governor's office a tight group of former detectives and narcotics agents were dealing out millions of dollars that had been granted to the state in the federal War on Drugs, and Ann wanted someone to keep an eye on what they were doing. And she and Mary Beth took delight at the thought of those guys looking at the résumé of their new superior and seeing she had once worked for the ACLU. After a few months Ann reassigned Dorothy to start from scratch a program of drug and alcohol abuse treatment programs in the prisons. Texas shot from fiftieth to first among the states in such programs in a matter of months. It was the high point of Dorothy's working life.

In six months Ann completely reversed the public's distaste for her during the campaign. She went after agencies that were controlled by the interests allegedly regulated, and in her primary legacy she overturned the old white guy monopoly on government that had reigned since Reconstruction. She appointed women, blacks, Latinos, Asian Americans, gay men, and lesbians to positions of responsibility and power. The media in New York and Washington adored her, and celebrity suited her just fine. On Christmas Eves, Dorothy, Lila, and I dressed up and went to her small party of aides and friends in the grand Governor's Mansion. It was great fun while it lasted.

Ann's term was an almost perfect parabola—two years up and two years down. She was stymied in the second half of her term by her own mistakes, bad luck with major appointments, and a hostile lieutenant governor who had once been a mentor and drinking buddy. Her relationship with the lieutenant governor, Bob Bullock, turned poisonous—he reviled her administration as a bunch of hairy-legged lesbians. And in real ways she was undone by her own celebrity. That was her liquor now, and she couldn't stay away from it. But she was a micromanaging governor to the end. She was tired and out-campaigned by George W. Bush and his political guru Karl Rove. She gave the former president's son a pass on his questionable service in the National Guard during the Vietnam War, and one night at the end of what had been a masterful swing through the state, in Texarkana she got carried away and called him "some jerk." She and campaign manager Mary Beth Rogers knew what a terrible mistake that was. Like Clayton Williams, Ann had succumbed to hubris—the *very idea* that he would challenge her.

The pundits back east were startled when Bush beat her by over 300,000 votes, attributing the upset to a nationwide GOP sweep. Bill Clinton called that night and said it was his fault. The health care plan managed by Hillary Clinton had gone down in flames, and the House had been taken over by Newt Gingrich's "Contract with America" Republicans. New York governor Mario Cuomo, long considered a top presidential prospect, had gotten the boot too. But a Dallas friend of Bush, Bob Beaudine, who was heading the search for a new Major League Baseball commissioner, told me he had been asked to come to Bush's office one day; Beaudine also wrote about the meeting in his self-help book *The Power of Who.* "We talked baseball for a while, then some politics. He got serious and said, 'Bobby Boy, you might as well get me the commissioner's job because these people have me running for governor, and I don't think I can beat Ann Richards.'" I don't know who all of those people were. I assume some of them were members of his father's political machine in Washington and Texas. But I still believe Ann blew that election.

Given the future direction of the country, what-ifs abound. What if Bush had gotten that job running big league baseball? What if Ann had won and Bush had lost? What if she had not run for a second term and sought the vice presidency or even the presidency, as some aides advised? Those questions, which were often asked in Texas, could only be answered in a novel.

* * *

In 1998 Ann was four years out of office, and Dorothy had another job she loved, directing Gulf Coast programs for the land office and its commissioner, our friend Garry Mauro. Then in April of that year I was shot and nearly killed by an armed robber in Mexico City. Of that, let me just say here that it was a long road back, and it involved my friendship with the boxer Jesus Chavez, a two-time world champion, now retired and living in Dallas with a green card. But in my opinion he had been unjustly deported to Mexico, a country where he was born but had never really lived, during three years of his athletic prime. All the money in boxing is related to television exposure in the United States. I had written a *Texas Monthly* story about his plight, and with younger colleagues at the magazine had gone down to watch his first bout in Mexico. After three delightful days in the Mexican capital, we got in the wrong cab. The hijacking and robbery turned deadly, and one thing led to another.

Excellent physicians in Mexico City saved my life but diagnosed me as a paraplegic. Irked by the press attention but not inclined to pursue any investigation, the police balked at allowing me to leave the country when doctors discovered I was capable of voluntary movement of one foot, and a rush ensued to get me back to Texas and started in physical therapy. Later I would come across a checklist of things Ann and former governor's staff were doing on my behalf, and among the contacts made, with many notations in Ann's big hand, were President Clinton's chief of staff Mack McLarty, secretary of state Madeleine Albright, and Lloyd Bentsen, secretary of the treasury. In not too many hours my wife, stepdaughter, and I were allowed to board the rescue jet to Houston.

And that was not all Ann did. Our lives seemed shattered, our finances in certain ruin, and while I was still in a Houston rehab hospital, friends in Austin cooked up a benefit that raised a great deal of money and, to Dorothy's surprise—she expected a grim or at least melancholy affair—it was a great bash of a party emceed by Ann. I didn't get to see it because a computer feed to the hospital didn't work, and nobody thought to bring a video camera, but by all accounts it was an evening of hilarious, ribald, and at times sage remarks by writers Gary Cartwright, Larry L. King, John Graves, and Kinky Friedman and the former University of Texas football coach Darrell Royal. At one point Ann quieted everyone down and said, according to the *Austin American-Statesman*, "Those of you who know me well know how reluctant I am to offer an opinion. But I've got to say it's high time that someone printed an anthology of Jan's work. I know that, in this audience, there are people who can make that happen. And I want you all to get busy and get it done . . . We are proud of his work and friendship—and grateful to be able to help when he needs us."

At that point it had been twelve years since any book had appeared with my name on it. The next morning I was sitting in my hospital bed in Houston eating the breakfast fare and preparing to go downstairs for my morning rehab exercises when the phone rang. It was an editor from the Texas A&M University Press saying she would be proud to publish a collection of my magazine pieces, which became *Close Calls*. Ann's setting that in motion was about the nicest thing anyone ever did for me. I later wrote about the Mexico misadventure and my recovery in a 2002 Broadway Books memoir, *The Bullet Meant for Me*.

I'm a very lucky man. I now walk with a cane.

*   *   *

More years passed. Four more nonfiction opportunities materialized and the books saw print. I talked to my agent David McCormick about giving the novel one more shove. A former editor at *Texas Monthly,* and my best one, he had been with me throughout the long journey. He told me it was worth finishing, and I started over. I jettisoned plans for a long section about the years after Adobe Walls and the Indians' rout by the cavalry in Tule Canyon. In the central plot Quanah and Bose, those young firebrands and mixed-bloods who started out trying to kill each other, would grow into knowledge they were friends. That was my approach to historical fiction. Plausibility was my compass: not what historians claimed had occurred, but what *could* have happened.

I decided to keep Billy the Kid as the street urchin and boy psychopath he was. Tall and violent Pat Garrett filled a role as well. I saw a photo of Bose Ikard, the only one I found, in which he appeared to resemble Chuck Berry. I wasn't going to have him burst into "Sweet Little Sixteen," but the connection told me a great deal about shaping his character and hearing his voice. In Colorado, Charles Goodnight had told Bose, his most trusted drover, to carry his money sacks to banks in Denver on the theory that no bandit would think a black man had any money. Then he told Bose to go back to Texas, where there were people of his own kind. I made him first a scout for Mackenzie's cavalry, then a deserter for good reason who somehow had to get away with it, and then a captive of Quanah. In the climax I would throw them all into the chaotic mix of the battle at Adobe Walls. Some readers would tell me that Bose stole the starring role.

But I still didn't see how my novel would end, until one New Year's holiday when my wife and I were returning homeward from a celebration in Big Bend and paused at a roadside park with a long overlook of the Pecos River and forbidding yet magnificent country beyond. There I experienced that epiphany that sometimes but too seldom occurs for writers of fiction. Characters start doing things you didn't know they were going to do. It's what keeps writers coming back to the novel.

A Mescalero Apache woman stepped out of the confusion and showed me the way. Her name was To-ha-yea, and she exists in history as little more than a name. She was Quanah's first wife. He gave her father six mules for her on his way back from one of his adventures in Mexico. The Apache culture was vastly different from the Comanches', and she was soon made miserable by the life of the nomadic buffalo hunters. Quanah sent her home to her people and their sacred mountains. I had found a stunning photo of Apache girls in the attire of their puberty rite, an extended affair known as White Painted Woman. I picked out one in a pose suggesting that her spunk and spirit matched her beauty and decided that was To-ha-yea—the same way I drew character from that photo of Bose that resembled Chuck Berry. The Apache girl stood there in my mind and beckoned, "Come this way." And at long last *Comanche Sundown* found its way home.

*   *   *

I have structured this essay in part to demonstrate I had accumulated a great deal of information about Ann Richards and insight into her personality and character before I had a clue I might one day write about her. Along with Garry Mauro's resounding loss to George W. Bush in the 1998 governor's race, a first lap in Bush's 2000 race for the presidency, a Republican was elected land commissioner, and in the partisan broom sweep Dorothy was once more dislodged from a job she loved. Since then she has been the chief of staff for an Austin legislator, Elliott Naishtat, a Queens, New York, native who had signed up as a VISTA volunteer and was sent to Eagle Pass, Texas, on the Mexican border when he was expecting San Francisco. He went to law school and rode Ann's coattails in 1990 to election in what may be the most liberal district in the state, and the redistricting manipulators have largely left him alone. One day in March 2006 Dorothy answered the phone at the capitol and the familiar voice pitched right in: "Darthy, I've got a young woman who doesn't know what she wants to do with her life." Ann said she served with the young woman's father on "the car wash board" and wondered if Dorothy might help find something that exposed her to the inner workings of government. Dorothy took down the details, and the young woman eventually served an internship in Elliott's legislative office.

Then Dorothy asked her friend and mentor, "How are you doing, Ann?"

There was a pause, and then she said, "Not so good." It was one of the few times Dorothy ever heard her voice sound small. Ann said that the day before she had been diagnosed with esophageal cancer. Her father had died that way in 1994. Ann sounded frightened. Who wouldn't be?

For all of Ann's faults, and they were many, I am still amazed that the first thing she did on the second morning of absorbing that terrifying turn in her life was to make a call on behalf of a young woman she didn't know.

The radiation and chemotherapy at the MD Anderson Cancer Center in Houston left her too weak for the surgery that was planned next, and she died at seventy-three on September 13, 2006. I was startled but flattered when Evan Smith, the editor of *Texas Monthly*, called and asked me to write a memorial essay about her. I had written for the magazine since its infancy in 1973 but had never been one of its political reporters or analysts. He explained he thought I could bring a personal dimension to it that others could not, and he wisely gave me only four days to deliver. I couldn't get all tangled up in research. It would have to come off the top of my head.

Published that November, "Ann: An Appreciation" was well received by her children and people who had worked for and admired her. Ann had a legion of younger women whom she had inspired. One was Clayton McClure Brooks, a doctoral candidate at Princeton who had been commissioned to assemble an anthology of original essays titled *A Legacy of Leadership: Governors in American History*. She saw the *Texas Monthly* piece, contacted me through the magazine, and asked me to contribute an essay focused more on Ann's policy achievements or shortcomings than her personality and politics. (It also profiled other women governors of both parties who had followed Ann's lead;

I fancied myself as the first person in Texas who knew about Alaska's newly elected Sarah Palin.) In the course of researching "The Case for Ann Richards," I discovered that a wealth of materials, the essential documents for a biography, were in the Ann W. Richards Papers compiled by archivists at the Dolph Briscoe Center for American History at the University of Texas in Austin. The index alone runs to seven hundred single-spaced pages. The library was just fifteen minutes from my house. So I conferred once more with my agent David McCormick. He had been in Austin in the nineties and remembered her flair and term in office well. So the chore of crafting a proposal, never a pleasure for me, began anew. The directors, editors, and a supportive board at the University of Texas Press came forward with the enthusiasm and resources, and I cleared everything else from my desk. The book took me three years to research and write.

At the start I saw that important sections in the index bore the proviso that authorization by the former governor would be required. I asked the lead archivist, Evan Hocker, what that now meant. He hesitated and said he would get back to me. A day or two later, he reported that most capital punishment and some personnel files would remain confidential and closed. Happily, all the rest was open to me. Ann had stipulated that a year and a half after her death, she wanted scholars and interested citizens to have access to whatever they might find and learn. That desire for transparency into the raw material of one's legacy is very rare among politicians today.

Because my association and friendship with Ann was no secret, I knew I would get creamed by reviewers if I delivered a hallelujah about her virtues and an apologia for her flaws. One editor in New York had wanted to know if I was really going to dig in after juicy details about her sexuality. Well, to the degree they were pertinent, but I didn't believe it was any of my business what transpired in her bedroom; I wouldn't want people snooping around mine. But I was going to be as hard on her as thoroughness demanded and fairness allowed.

I knew that on this book I couldn't be slipshod and cavalier with facts. But I had just spent years working on a long novel. I was in that rhythm of storytelling, and it struck me that the span of her life's narrative arc and the richness of her milieu lent themselves to a novelistic voice. I conducted more than a hundred interviews. David Richards, their four children, and most of Ann's senior aides were eager to help me. Some of the best material came from those face-to-face encounters. One gem was Shelton Smith's account of the wrangle over the Higgs boson, or "God particle," and the Superconducting Super Collider. The enormous scientific project under the rolling plains and farmland south of Dallas proposed that stupendous magnetic energy could simulate the Big Bang and prove a widely held theory of physicists about the creation of the universe. Governor Bill Clements had committed $150 million to the project, but with the collapse of the Soviet Union, the surprise election of Bill Clinton as president, and a projected cost that reached $8.25 billion, ardor for its completion in Washington had cooled. Ann dispatched Smith, a plaintiff's attorney and loyal supporter and contributor, to Washington to lobby for completion of the project, and then when that became impossible, to get the state's investment back. Shelton described the meeting between President Clinton and Ann, who were old friends. He was the only other one in the room.

> She said to President Clinton: "I want you to understand something, pal. You owe me a lot of money, and if you don't pay it back, I'm gonna sue you." Then she turned and pointed at me and said, "And this is the guy who's gonna do it."
> Clinton's a big guy. He had turned beet red. He sat there glaring, both hands on his thighs, and said, "How much are you gonna sue me for?"
> I said, "I don't know for certain, Mr. President, but it's probably gonna be four or five billion."
> "Do you think you can win it?"
> "Yes, sir, I do."
> He turned and stared at Ann a while longer, then he got this huge grin on his face, and he said, "Well, Governor, I guess we'd better get you your money."

The boxes of files came in trucks from an off-campus storage facility, six or seven at a time. I had an able research assistant, Shawn Morris, who had been Dorothy's assistant in the governor's office before taking her doctorate in international studies. She was familiar with the people and subjects, required minimal guidance from me, and brought an unexpected bonus—the perspectives and reflections of people who had been in their twenties during those years. It wasn't just work; it was their social life. I found a vile anonymous letter by a purported high school friend in Waco who claimed Ann was an atheist and ongoing drunk who "left her husband for the bed of another woman" while pulling wool over the public's eyes. Two slightly different versions went out to all the small-town Baptist ministers and newspaper editors in the state on January 1, 1990. I found a long graceful letter from her speechwriter Suzanne Coleman—one of the best of her generation—addressing Ann's sudden if brief loss of heart at the prospect of taking on that beast of a race.

In *Shrub: The Short but Happy Political Life of George W. Bush,* by Molly Ivins and Lou Dubose, I had read that Ann believed her stand on guns had cost her the race in 1994. Looking for evidence of that, in the papers I found a riveting diary of the Branch Davidian siege near Waco from February to April 1993 written by her then chief of staff, John Fainter. Alcohol, Tobacco, and Firearms agents had commandeered use of Air National Guard helicopters and surveillance equipment on the pretext, never proven, that the followers of David Koresh were cooking methamphetamines in the compound. Ann was titular commander of the National Guard, and one of the helicopters was shot up at the cost of $300,000 in the botched raid and gunfight that left at least ten people dead, including four federal agents and Koresh's two-year-old daughter. That day Ann had planned to wax nostalgic about her high school and college years at a "Waco Day," but her speech was thrown out. Reporters quoted her, "The sad part about a situation like this is that you're trying to make sense out of a senseless event. I'm worried about those children in the compound. I want them to get those kids out. If the adults make a choice that they want to be there, then they have to live with the consequences. But kids don't have a choice." When a reporter asked, she answered that she would take "a serious look" at legislation to ban assault weapons in Texas.

The outcome stamped on the nation's consciousness a uniquely Texas image of explosions and inferno. And politically, the blood was in the water for the National Rifle Association. The legislature was signaling that it would pass a bill allowing private citizens to carry concealed handguns. Ann had compromised many of her principles, but she dug in her heels on this one. She parried one legislative thrust with humor: answering legislators' contention that women wanted to carry handguns for protection, she wisecracked that she didn't know a woman who could find a gun in her purse in an emergency. She promised to veto the concealed-carry bill, and she did, but it came back in a special session. An aide of the lieutenant governor told me that when Ann led a crowd of reporters with TV cameras into his chambers to determine his position, that was when "the relationship of Ann and Bullock was ripped for good." She didn't just disagree with her adversaries; she ridiculed them. At a press conference with police chiefs, sheriffs, and constables, she said, "I especially want to thank you for choosing to stand by me on this day when we say no to the amateur gunslingers who think they will be braver and smarter with gun in hand."

One of Ann's top aides told me the governor just got tired of hearing about it. She lost her patience one night on the campaign trail in characteristic fashion. Ann said she wouldn't mind so much if the trained shooters were required to hook their pistols to chains around their necks. That way, others could yell, "Look out, that one's got a gun!"

George W. Bush didn't have to run on the issue. All he had to do was say he would sign such a bill. The NRA would do the rest.

* * *

The archives revealed lighter moments as well. Several people had told me about "the Bum Phillips roast," but the hearsay was vague, and the archive contained no press clips about that evening. But then I found it in a video file. Bum Phillips was a crew-cut, drawling, hugely popular coach who came up a journeyman but then made the Houston Oilers, now the Tennessee Titans, one of the top four franchises in the NFL in the 1970s. After Ann's keynote speech but before she had to decide whether she was a candidate for governor, she waltzed into the blue-collar town of Port Arthur, where Bum had begun his career as a high school coach, and into an über-macho forum that included University of Texas All-American, Heisman Trophy winner, and Oilers All-Pro running back Earl Campbell and Jimmy Johnson, a Port Arthur native who had just been hired to replace Tom Landry as the Dallas Cowboys' head coach. After a bewildering firing by the Oilers and a stint coaching the New Orleans Saints, Bum had since retired to his horse farm. Ann's performance went in part:

> You know, men and women react to football in completely different ways. Women react to a big play, but you watch a man, and you can see the drama—watch his eyes bulge and he licks his lips and leans forward in his La-Z-Boy recliner, and clamps his hands on his Miller Lite, and he tenses up like a cheetah ready to spring . . . Now I have heard the complexity of football compared to chess, but you know, you don't see a lot

of deep thinkers on the football field. Like Bum says, "If he can count to four, he can play for me."

After long days and weeks of practice, running through all those used tires, they finally get to play somebody. They get to the stadium early, because it takes forever to get dressed. They shave their legs, and they wrap tape around them, and they put on these corsets—the kind women wore when I grew up years ago—and they smear mascara *under* their eyes, and they put on the shoulder pads and helmets and color-coordinated arm bands, and they put on shoes that will keep them from slipping on the AstroTurf, and they wrap more tape over the shoes to make sure their ankles are protected.

Well, they get all this rigging on, and they start making themselves into a state, and it's called psyching yourself, and it's all about convincing yourself that you're going to be involved with people who commit felonious assault for a living, and you *like* it. And when they're good and ready, they run out on the field, and the boys slap each other on the fanny two or three times, which produces an adrenaline rush . . . To me, it seems kind of strange that they have a penalty called unsportsmanlike conduct. The uniform alone would make a normal person surly. What would you *expect*?

Now, all I can say, Bum, is that it's a hell of a way to make a living. And I know you're glad to be out of it, and into something where you can deal with the front end of horses.

But I understand why you loved it. Because you know what they say, politics is a lot like football—you have to be smart enough to play the game and dumb enough to think it's important.

She had them whooping and pounding the table in glee, and it was an example of why on the day she would be voted out of the governor's office with just 47 percent of the vote, she still had a popularity rating of 53 percent. Mary Beth Rogers, manager of both her gubernatorial campaigns and her first chief of staff in the governor's office, had known Ann since they lived in Dallas in the 1960s, and for hours she relived and coached me through those years. David Richards took exceptional pains to help me get the story right. He offered his help in snatches of social conversation and important brusque phone calls when he and his children saw advance reading copies. The only time we attempted a formal interview we got nowhere because we met in an Austin bar, and people kept drifting over to chat.

Though Bud Shrake contributed choice details in our social occasions, we never got to have the long talk we planned about his relationship with Ann. He was diagnosed with lung cancer shortly after I started work on the biography. He went out with a blaze of creativity, finishing two novels and a play before the illness claimed him, and I liked and admired him too much to impose on his time. But in my research the greatest pleasure and surprise of all was discovering Ann's correspondence with Bud. The correspondence, which had never been published or remarked upon, began in earnest when Ann got the call to deliver her keynote speech in 1988. Both of their lives were moving too fast for traditional letters with stamps and envelopes, and telephone conversations were difficult. But they discovered that by use of fax, they could communicate in real time. It was e-mail without the computers and Internet. Ann's notes were always handwritten. She didn't like to type.

The faxes flew back and forth between the funny and literate pair, and with deepening emotion they provide a remarkable inside tour of her gubernatorial race in 1990. The onetime out-of-control liberal alcoholic from Austin pulled even with the rancher and oilman Clayton Williams in the last week, then got another huge break when he volunteered that because of his business losses one year when a Texas oil boom went bust, he had paid no income taxes because he owed none. True statement, but his aides were alarmed enough that they opened the bar early for reporters on a whistle-stop rail tour, then changed reporters' hotel reservations to Nuevo Laredo, Mexico, where it would be very hard to make phone calls to their editors. Ann wrote:

Dear Bud,

It is almost midnight. Long day. Texarkana, Longview, Nacogdoches, Angleton, and Houston. Pay dirt today—Williams says he didn't pay any income taxes in '86. We'll see if it plays big.

It would be a treat for me to have you in the mayhem of election night. I'll be home in the afternoon on election day and we'll plan.

Some of the kids and I are going to Padre Island after the election. Depending on the outcome, I've been thinking about asking you to come for some part of the time and I've feared that we might not like each other with constant exposure. Does that make sense?

I know that the root of it is in the lingering anxiety I have about rejection . . . The fatigue is invading my brain and this probably makes little sense but there won't be time to write from here on. I'll be home again Sunday night late.

It's great to come to home to your fax notes

Fondly, Ann

She won the race going away, but as it often happened, Bud was not where she wanted him to be right after the election. He had promised to attend a Fort Worth reunion at his alma mater, TCU.

Dear Bud,
The crown got heavy today. No list of things that *must* be done. No hourly frenzy. I tried some Christmas and inaugural shopping for the family but I could not get much done for shaking hands. I feel trapped in the house and outside too. All of this will take some getting used to—and I am a little frightened.
. . . Another manifestation of my weird state of mind is that I don't feel like I have anything to say—even to old friends. Transition talk spurs gossip or breaks confidences and I think I am tired of being entertaining.
I'd *love* to go to the movie Sunday. What time shall I expect you? I only wish it was not such a long time until then. Maybe I'll clean out some closets.

Love, Ann

Bud said they talked about getting married but just never got around to it. When she died in 2006, Bill Clinton came down to Austin; there is a moving photo of him holding Ellen Richards as she wept and told him how much his friendship had meant to her mother. At the memorial service in a University of Texas coliseum Hillary Clinton was tender and funny, saying Ann was always telling her someday she was going to have to figure out what to do with her hair. That morning at the cemetery, there had been a private service. Lily Tomlin told a choice and funny story about her friendship with Ann in New York. But the most eloquent words came from Bud.

I was there that morning, but I wasn't taking notes, and it wasn't the kind of farewell you could paraphrase. But I played a hunch, and, sure enough, Bud placed the typewritten sheet in his archive at the Wittliff Collection at Texas State University.

For the last seventeen years Ann has been the anchor of my life.
We don't know what life really is, or where life comes from, or what to do with it while we have got it.
But we know that life is far grander than just chemistry. We are beings of spirit.
And even across the divide of death, Ann's spirit remains an echo in our hearts this morning.

Father Taliaferro says hell is being in heaven and not liking it.

I think that's Ann's message to you.

Put a smile on your face, and a good thought in your heart, and try to do the right thing—and you will find Ann standing beside you with a fresh bag of popcorn.

Thank you, Ann. I love you.

Ah-men. And Ah-women. And Ah-Ann.

At the state cemetery in Austin, the words on the back of Ann's gravestone were taken from her speech when thirty thousand people came from all over the state to join her march down Congress Avenue and crowded on the state capitol grounds to see her inaugurated as governor. "Today we have a vision of a Texas where opportunity knows no race, no gender, no color—a glimpse of what can happen in government if we simply open the doors and let people in."

Hence the title of my book. Bud is buried next to her. The red granite marker bears just his name, Edwin "Bud" Shrake, and the dates of his birth in 1931 and his death in 2009. Under that is the carefree motto that sustained him all his productive life and captured the spirit that made him the second great love in Ann's life.

"So Far So Bueno."

JAN REID won the Texas Institute of Letters' lifetime achievement award in 2014. *Let the People In* was honored as the book of the year in 2012 by the Texas State Historical Association, and the *Houston Chronicle* rated it one of the ten best nonfiction books published in the United States that year. His novel *Comanche Sundown* won the Texas Institute of Letters' 2011 award for best fiction, an honor whose previous winners include Cormac McCarthy, Larry McMurtry, and Katherine Anne Porter. Reid is nearing completion of his thirteenth book and third novel, *Sins of the Younger Sons.* He lives in Austin with his wife, Dorothy Browne, and their collie, Gus.

THE MAD BOMBER GUY

I

During the week of January 21, 1990, I received a letter from George Peter Metesky, serial pipe bomber, injured utility worker, devout Catholic, paranoiac, Marine veteran, inventor, and compulsive letter writer, who had been arrested at his home in the Brooklyn section of Waterbury, Connecticut, on January 21, 1957.

Metesky had sustained a lung injury on September 5, 1931, while working at the Hell Gate generating station at 134th Street and Locust Avenue in the Bronx. The station's parent company, Consolidated Gas, the forerunner of Consolidated Edison, had, in a common practice at the time, paid him benefits from an employee-supported fund until the statute of limitations for filing a workmen's compensation claim had expired, leaving him unemployable, sick, embittered, and angry. He put his energy and considerable technical skill into waging a terrorism campaign against his former employer, perfecting small explosive devices in his garage.

The text of the letter was handwritten in neat blue script on a yellow legal sheet, and the printed return address label carried the logo of the National Rifle Association:

Bruce Miller   January 20 – 1990   Chicago, Ill.
   Dear Sir:
   I have neither desire nor intent to assent to any of the suggestions outlined in your letter post-marked January 9th 1990.
   For the past 7–8 years I have turned down requests even from friends offering monetary benefits. 1989 was a "banner year."
   I am 86 years old—still drive a car and work cross-word puzzles. When walking alone I use a cane for "balance."
   Such are the facts in this case.
   George P. Metesky

Detectives inspect the garage were Metesky made his bombs and check the Daimler he bought in 1934. Journal-American *photo courtesy of photography collection, Harry Ransom Center, University of Texas at Austin.*

I read the letter quickly, my excitement fading as I realized the aged former bomber had no interest whatsoever in speaking with me. I had written him a rather fawning letter asking for "an hour or two" of his time. Metesky had to know I had been trying to reach him for about nine months, because the previous April, lacking his home address, I had written to one of his nieces inquiring about Uncle George, aided in that action by Father Shea, pastor of St. Patrick's Church in Waterbury, where Metesky had been a parishioner after his release from detention in 1973.

"George was very faithful to his church attendance, faithful to mass and to the sacraments," Father Shea told me during my visit to his church in April 1989. "He came to church every Sunday. I never brought up the subject of his arrest or anything like that, because I didn't feel it was my place to do that." Father Shea never broached the topic of Metesky's past, yet he volunteered to call Metesky's niece in my behalf, to ask if she had received my letter. She told him that her uncle had moved, and that she would pass along the letter. I suspect that she did.

When I received no answer from George, I wrote to his niece two more times in May and once again in August. When I returned to Waterbury for a second research trip in October 1989, at city hall I searched the bound books that contained an alphabetical listing of vehicle owners. Within minutes, I had found it! George Metesky lived at 1229 Winsted Road, Unit #30, in Torrington, a town less than twenty miles north of Waterbury. On the back of a pink "While You Were Out" message slip, from a pad I happened to have in hand, I eagerly wrote the address and license plate information of the Cadillac registered to George P. Metesky: 83 CAD NV5888.

He had always liked high-end cars, driving his Daimler to White Plains to send hate mail or down to New York to plant his bombs.

So, thanks to the state of Connecticut, I was finally able to send my unwelcome letter to the correct address. The envelope of Metesky's reply was addressed to me in block printing, all caps, a muted version of the notorious handwriting that distinguished his many anonymous threatening notes and letters, like the one postmarked March 1, 1956, and mailed to the city desk of the *New York Herald Tribune:* "WHERE EVER A WIRE RUNS—GAS OR STEAM FLOWS—FROM OR TO THE CON. EDISON CO.—IS NOW A BOMB TARGET."

The unsuccessful and long-running search by police for the anonymous pipe bomber had centered on the handwriting in his notes. Joe McNally ran the document examination section of the NYPD laboratory during most of the 1950s, and by the time of his retirement in 1972 had worked for the police department for thirty-two years, rising to the rank of captain. I met him at the New York City Department of Human Services in June 1989, where he worked on welfare fraud and white-collar crime for the city's department of investigation. His memories of the Metesky case were undimmed, his sense of humor about it infectious.

McNally first saw Metesky's hand printing in 1946, the year he started at the laboratory, learning about document examination from Frank Murphy—then the only handwriting expert in the police department. The Anonymous Letter File contained all manner of threatening missives, including Metesky's notes railing against his former employers as "the monsters of 4 Irving Place," written on postal cards and envelopes and mailed to the Consolidated Edison Company, newspapers, theaters, and well-known retail stores:

Postmarked, December 7, 1941, 8:30 PM MANAGER THE RADIO CITY MUSIC HALL RADIO CITY Mr. Hanuford N.Y. CITY "WHERE A WIRE RUNS OR A LIGHT BURNS" IF YOU SHOULD HEAR THE BLAST OF A "PINEAPPLE" WITHIN YOUR THEATRE—"THANK" THE "MONSTERS" AT THE CON. EDISON CO. INC. #4 IRVING PLACE. IT WAS DELIVERED WITH THEIR COMPLIMENTS—THEY THINK THAT ONLY THEY—HAVE A MONOPLY [sic] ON "RUTHLESSNESS."—FOR INFORMATION SEE THE MAYOR OR BOMB SQUAD OR N.Y. TIMES. F.P. [Fair Play]

For Metesky, the missives were missiles, each one a cumulative indictment: "People pay more attention to the noise of a bomb than to the written word," he said during a court hearing about six weeks after his arrest. "I used the bombs merely to draw attention."

For six years or more, McNally had been briefing detectives on the

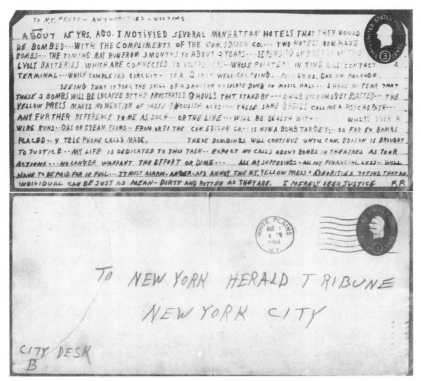

Metesky's letter to the New York Herald-Tribune *postmarked March 1, 1956. Police department files.*

peculiar "G" and other distinctive features of the handwriting of the illusive "psycho" who had placed small pipe bombs in Grand Central station, movie theater seats, the New York Public Library, and telephone booths at various Manhattan locations. This information about identifiable features was used in combing through the handwriting of suspects in motor vehicle registrations, employment applications, and other sources of writing.

"It's like recognizing an individual," McNally told me.

> You see the individual time and time again, and after a while . . . you recognize the individual . . . you have to add up all these little pictures . . . The "G" was a "C" with two horizontal lines. The center line on the "M" comes all the way down to the baseline of writing. The "Y" is a "V" at the top and you've got a vertical on it. The "S" seems to flat out at the bottom. And then the pictorial effect of it . . . it's sort of an arrhythmic type—it's just sort of jumbled, there's no rhythm to it, no regularity to it. If you look at the slant pattern, at one time it's vertical, then forehand, and it jumps back and forth.

Beginning with the first bomb of record in 1940 (Metesky placed others on Con Ed property before this date that were never reported)—an unarmed demonstration model left on the windowsill of a Con Ed substation—and continuing through 1956, his three different bomb designs were picked apart and analyzed, and wide-ranging attempts were made to trace their components—watches, flashlight bulbs, .25-caliber bullets, batteries, springs, pipe couplings—without success.

From 1951, when his activity resumed after a hiatus, until Metesky's arrest, police detectives within the police laboratory and various squads and (beginning in 1955) the specially created Bomb Investigation Unit tried to figure out some rhythm, some regularity, a pattern to the timing and placement of the bombs, examining everything from the days of the year and time of day to the interval between occurrences and the phases of the moon. After consulting psychiatrists, desperate detectives turned to psychics.

Bill Schmitt, the detective whose forceful personality dominated the bomb squad in those years, had learned about explosives as a navy man in the Pacific during the Second World War. Like his father, Schmitt became a policeman, entering the detective bureau in 1946 and the bomb squad in 1950. He retired in 1981.

"In the very beginning the firing device [on Metesky's bombs] was

Bomb squad detective Bill Schmitt. Photo courtesy of Bill Schmitt.

so intricate that I was sure that it was part of military ordnance," Schmitt told me during an interview in the old train station at Dover, New Jersey, in 1989. "I checked all the United States ordnance and it wasn't that . . . one of them worked on the same principle as a depth charge in the Navy works . . . Who would know that this guy would take a solid metal rod and hollow it out, why wouldn't you buy a pipe that was hollow? . . . [Metesky] used to get his jollies doing all this . . . He had his lathe, he was a professional mechanic—he made things."

Among the things he made was an electric snowplow and a "Solenoid Pump," the latter granted a patent on September 23, 1941. He demonstrated the snowplow for his tenants Anthony and Angela Mendillo. The Mendillos rented the third-floor apartment in Metesky's three-family home from 1949 to 1951. He told them his design had been published in a mechanics magazine. Metesky was an avid reader of *Popular Science* and an admirer of Charles Proteus Steinmetz, the brilliant engineer, public intellectual, and socialist who immigrated to the United States from Germany, overcoming poverty and disability to have a successful career at General Electric.

In an interview after his release from detention, Metesky said that he had always been technically inclined and that for him making bombs was as easy as "slicing a piece of bread."

"The patient knows that what he did at times endangered the general population, and he expresses remorse and regret in this respect," wrote Dr. Daniel Schwartz of Kings County Hospital on January 24, 1973, after an interview with Metesky. "Nevertheless, he shows a kind of child-like enthusiasm when he describes in detail the mechanics of his bombs. He himself says the contrivances were something out of Rube Goldberg. At such times his child-like enthusiasm completely overcomes his remorse. He is more involved with the mechanics of the bomb than the danger it presented to others."

II

When I first read about George P. Metesky in the *New York Times* on Friday, February 19, 1988, I was at home in the Beacon Apartments, a severe-looking steel and concrete 1960s high-rise at 2930 North Sheridan Road in Chicago. The building was a haven for elderly Jewish women, some on walkers, who could have been my relatives and who had lived there for decades. Now a younger crowd of single women and men had begun wheeling their bicycles or walking briskly through the lobby.

It had been a mere five months since my new girlfriend, Julia Anderson, an artist and stand-up comic known as "Betty the Enlightened Waitress," had left Minneapolis and moved into my newly rented two-bedroom apartment on the sixteenth floor. I had moved out of a one-bedroom place on fifteen in anticipation of her arrival. I had seen Julia perform at Dudley Riggs's Experimental Theater Company in a revue called *What's So Funny About Being Female?* and I had visited her at a diner called Peter's Grill where she worked as a waitress.

The extra bedroom gave me a place to stack the glossy, 8x10 catalogs I received twice a year from the book publishers for whom my younger brother Eric and I worked as sales representatives, calling on bookstores throughout the Midwest. More than once I'd stepped on an errant shiny booklet and slid backwards or forwards as if the carpet were a skating rink, so having a designated spot for work paraphernalia made life more comfortable.

Gradually, after a year or so, alongside the catalogs (and the brand-new, must-have fax machine), stacks of newspapers and magazines, note pads, photographs, and police records about the Mad Bomber case began to pile up. After walking into that room and finding a small black address book filled with the names of New York detectives, reporters, and a bomber and his relatives, Julia was sure I led a double life.

The *Times* had begun publishing its national edition in 1980, and I moved into the city in 1982, so even six years later it still felt like a novelty to walk outside my building and buy the day's issue from the vending box at the corner of Oakdale and Sheridan. Since daily newspapers played an essential role in the entire Mad Bomber saga, reading about it in the *New York Times* provided an apt beginning for my own misadventures, discoveries, and ruminations about this strange and long-drawn-out case.

The article—"Workplace: Unseen Signs and Unexpected Explosions" by Glenn Collins—dealt with a shooting in Sunnyvale, California, where a computer programmer entered the building of his former employer and murdered seven people. Collins went on to discuss other cases that involved "an old grudge": "George P. Metesky conducted a 16-year vendetta against Consolidated Edison in New York City in the 1940's and 1950's. He had been hurt in an accident while working for Con Edison in 1931. He later planted explosives on the utility's property and public places. Thirty-seven explosions were attributed to him before his arrest in 1957."

After reading Collins's article, I wanted to know more about the mysterious accident and the bomber's obsessive grudge against Consolidated Edison. He had been hurt in 1931, yet more than twenty years later he was fighting his secret war, placing bombs around Manhattan. It struck me as one of the oddest stories I had ever heard. I searched for a book about him and his vendetta, but there was none. Eventually, I decided to research the case by reading 1950s New York newspapers.

At the Evanston public library, using the *Times* index, I read a couple of stories: "Suspect Is Held as Mad Bomber; He Admits Role," from January 22, 1957, and the lengthy front-page piece from January 23, "Bomber Is Booked; Sent to Bellevue for Mental Tests" by Meyer Berger.

Berger was a Pulitzer Prize–winning journalist and the author of several books. His detailed, colorful piece about the case further piqued my curiosity about the eccentric bomber, his family, and Waterbury, Connecticut. Metesky, he wrote, "lived in Waterbury's Lithuanian District . . . with two older, spinster sisters," and "the factory-workers' district where the Metesky's [sic] live is, curiously, called Brooklyn after Brooklyn in New York City. The Naugatuck River cuts it off from the rest of the town, and all of it is drab and drear." Berger quotes Benjamin Schmier, a Legal Aid Society lawyer initially assigned to Metesky, who told the felony court magistrate in Manhattan, "The defendant speaks fluently and speaks very well. He is a man who could easily pass for your next-door neighbor."

"The prisoner," added Berger, "resembled a smiling church deacon . . . Lights in the rather dimly lighted court chamber reflected from Metesky's gold-rimmed spectacles. His somber blue suit with pencil stripe, his neat shirt and tie, his shoes, all bespoke the neat, careful citizen."

I had no idea my initial curiosity would quickly turn into an avocation, a distraction, a preoccupation, and, ultimately, a Gordian knot. But I was in my energetic thirties and grew up in a family that considered time-consuming avocations normal. Wasn't it always more gratifying to concentrate on something other than what one was supposed to be doing?

From the start I felt I needed *every* article from the major New York papers (and also from the *Waterbury Republican* and *American*), and not just articles published post-arrest, but any piece that dealt with the bombings. These are the newspapers I sought out: *New York Daily Mirror, New York Daily News, New York Herald-Tribune, New York Journal-American, New York Post, New York Times, New York World Telegram and Sun.*

The *Times* on microfilm was widely available, but the others were more difficult to find. I went to New York twice a year for publishers' sales meetings, and I had friends in Westchester County with whom I could stay on additional trips, so I was able to use the collections of the New York Public Library.

The Wilson Library at the University of Minnesota had the *New York Daily News,* the *Herald-Tribune,* and the *World Telegram and Sun.* Since I traveled to Minnesota to call on bookstores and visit in-laws, I was a regular at the Wilson. I overheard one staff member refer to me as "the mad bomber guy."

The Center for Research Libraries on Chicago's south side had a complete collection of the *New York Journal-American*, the newspaper universally credited with helping to catch Metesky because of its "Open Letter to the Mad Bomber" that established a dialogue with him and prompted him to reveal the date of his injury and other telling facts about his life. After Metesky was arrested, all the newspapers had to acknowledge the preeminent place of their competitor, "an American newspaper for the American People," to quote the motto that ran on the front page under its logo: an eagle holding arrows in one talon, an olive branch in the other—an adaptation of the Great Seal of the United States.

The *J-A* strove to be the newspaper of the people, offering readers a chance to win money in bright red type at the top of the front page (as in, "It's Fun to Play 'Stop and go' for $130,000 (turn to page 8)." And by giving "The *New York Journal-American* Public Protector Award" to

On January 22, 1957, Metesky enters New York City police headquarters escorted by detectives Jimmy Martin (to his right) and Mike Lynch (to his left). Journal-American photo courtesy of photography collection, Harry Ransom Center, University of Texas at Austin.

policemen for acts of heroism. The *New York Daily News* had its own version, "the *Daily News* Hero Award."

A certain American veteran in Waterbury, Connecticut, apparently preferred the *Journal*; maybe its tone appealed to him. As for the *Times*, he had written off that newspaper in one of his most bizarre anonymous letters, postmarked May 4, 1941, and sent to Con Ed. After suggesting the utility company send him a message via the *Times* "personal column," he added, "As a rule I do not read the N.Y. Times at all."

As Metesky emerged smiling from the police car that took him to New York from Waterbury, he proudly held up a copy of the *Journal-American* with its headline, "LETTERS TO JOURNAL TRAP THE MAD BOMBER."

As I sat in front of a microfilm reader at the Center for Research Libraries, copying the many pages of that very article, next to me stood an entire library cart filled with pleasing, square, gift-like cardboard boxes, each one holding a single reel containing one month of the *Journal-American*. After a couple of days I was scolded for hogging so many reels at once and politely asked to return about half a cart's worth.

I found the columns of print, the violence and pathos in multiple typefaces, absorbing and revelatory in a way that led me to my unspoken rule of research conduct: when in doubt, print it out. In addition to photocopying articles directly related to the Mad Bomber, I found myself filling file folders marked "Unrelated" and "Tangential" with articles like "Spellman Lashes Movie 'Baby Doll,'" which reported, "Roman Catholics today were barred under 'pain of sin' from seeing the movie 'Baby Doll,'" or "Riesel Takes Stand, Tells of Acid Attack," in which "Acid-blinded Victor Riesel groped his way to the witness stand today and told a federal court jury how 'a deluge of acid burst in my face' and deprived him of his sight forever."

As my research efforts pressed forward, I copied articles like these and many others that caught the tenor of the times, because these stories had relevance to my subject in ways I planned to articulate later. I carried in my mind the unstated conviction that the Metesky story, as presented in the press, was a kind of code, a complex language of its own, a strange poem requiring explication that I might only understand in historical context.

I also saw the Metesky case as an ironic reflection of post–World War II political and social culture. It was a case of the 1930s—like microfilm hidden in a hollowed-out pumpkin—haunting the 1950s. Metesky was no red, nor did the NYPD, the FBI, or anyone in authority ever regard him as subversive or as a political actor of any kind. But, just as the surveillance culture of the McCarthy witch-hunts examined suspects' associations during the New Deal period, the Mad Bomber was a creation of the working conditions of an earlier era.

Waterbury's industrial history of factories, brass mills, workplace injuries, and labor strife is absorbing as a subject in its own right, but the irony of George Metesky, the toolmaker or mad machinist, using watches, bullets, and brass plugs—items at the heart of Waterbury's manufacturing enterprise for more than a century—to make his bombs is startling.

In the course of my research, the face-to-face interviews I conducted in New York, New Jersey, and Connecticut's Naugatuck Valley, as well as on the telephone, gave me the greatest pleasure of my working life, even though the work was unpaid labor.

I liked to joke that I became the Studs Terkel of the Mad Bomber story. Somehow, in the voices and stories that no one else had bothered to record I found an irresistible pull. Sitting in a bar and grill in downtown Manhattan interviewing Roy Metcalf, a former *Daily Mirror* police reporter who gave me a concise, engaging description of being a journalist in the 1950s, I heard a man at the bar telling stories about his experience using dynamite to help build the Cross Bronx Expressway. I reflected how infrequently the working lives of people are recorded, the drama and mundane details often lost forever. I dreamt of starting an oral history project focused not on kings and counselors, but on the rest of us.

Over a period of roughly ten or twelve years (but never ending unequivocally) that included three moves from one apartment to another, I gathered information. I wrote letters and made phone calls to journalists, psychiatrists, detectives, utility workers, and even an expert on the operation of steam boilers. I sent Freedom of Information Act (FOIA) requests to the NYPD, district attorneys, the FBI, the Department of the Navy, and the post office.

In June 1989 I spoke with a man named Murray Butchen in the office of the New York county clerk, at the state supreme court, 100 Centre Street. He told me the court records were sealed. He gave me the number of the file and said I would need to go before a judge to get them unsealed. So, I took the dreary elevator up to part 50, room

1130, where Justice Carol Berkman was presiding. I saw some toughs in handcuffs and Justice Berkman, a severe-looking woman with a penetrating voice, staring out at lawyers and defendants over her half glasses. Immediately, I was cowed.

I stood waiting at the back of the room, and when she finally called my name I stepped forward. Before I could say anything, she loudly asked a two-word question: "Unseal documents?" She sort of spoke the question to everyone in the large courtroom. And then, without giving me a chance to explain or even say a word, she said loudly and decisively, "No!"—as if I had asked her to free a convicted murderer or to take her clothes off. The strange thing is, six years later, in 1995, a lawyer friend of mine also visited the clerk's office and was given a huge file of documents to photocopy, no questions asked, including the record of Metesky's police interrogation in Waterbury and handwritten motions filed by Metesky. Had a statute of limitations run out in the meantime, or was I just an unlucky interlocutor?

I visited the morgue at the *New York Post,* housed in the same building on South Street that once served as the offices of the *New York Journal-American.* Before he very kindly gave me photocopies from the morgue, the man in charge came up to me with a very serious look, saying, "the Mad Bomber file just imploded!"

I accumulated articles about boiler construction and operation and about the Hell Gate plant. I visited twenty libraries, including Waterbury's Silas Bronson Library, the Mattatuck Museum, and the library of the *Waterbury Republican-American* and, in New York, the Con Ed Technical Library at 4 Irving Place, the Municipal Library, the New York Public Library Annex, and the New York Public Library on Fifth Avenue.

I acquired books about New York City and Waterbury, Connecticut. I bought an undetermined number at a bookstore called New York Bound at 50 Rockefeller Center, including *New York, the Wonder City, 1932,* a reprinted classic the store sold under its own imprint and that had photographs and histories of the buildings of Manhattan around the time Metesky had lived there.

At the Old Erie Street Book Store in downtown Cleveland I found a copy of *The Consolidated Gas Company of New York: A History* by Frederick Collins. Published in 1934, this book explained the complicated corporate history of the company that became Consolidated Edison.

Duttenhofer's Bookstore in Cincinnati had an unsurpassed section of books about all regions of the United States, and many on the history of New York City. Ohio was part of my bookselling territory.

I amassed material about the history of the workmen's compensation law in New York State. When I was unable to purchase a copy of a book, as in *Casebook of a Crime Psychiatrist* by James A. Brussel or *Is It Safe to Work? A Study of Industrial Accidents* by Edison L. Bowers (1930), I photocopied the entire book by hand.

But there was a trinity of things inside the holy grail of my research, documents or material I never found, the lack of which preoccupied me and obstructed my writing: the sanity report issued by a panel of three psychiatrists, the file of Metesky's workmen's compensation case, and a better understanding of the mechanics of the accident. I also wanted to know more about working conditions at Hell Gate and the day-to-day procedures of Metesky's job. I wanted to know *everything* there was to know before I sat down to write. Little did I know how impossible the mission I set for myself.

III

George Peter Milauskas, born in Waterbury, Connecticut, on November 2, 1903, had always been a quiet boy who kept to himself. He had three older siblings, Anna, Mae, and John. His parents, George and Anna, both immigrants from Lithuania, shied away from the close relationships of the Lithuanian social clubs, according to Edward "Hap" Lasky, a man who had known them well and whom I interviewed at his Waterbury home on Lawlor Street in December 1989.

The family name, "Milauskas," was also construed by Waterburians as "Molusky" and "Metesky." All three names were listed on the mailbox at 17 Fourth Street, the three-family house where the Milauskases had lived for many years after moving from a house on Third Street that was built in 1915 by George Milauskas, who worked as a night watchman at JE Smith lumber company. "Metesky" stuck as a last name with the brothers, George and John. The sisters appear to have kept the original family name, Milauskas, but then I was told by the Waterbury Buckle Company, where George's oldest sister Anna had worked as a foot press operator, that company records identified

The three-family house at 17 Fourth Street in the Brooklyn section of Waterbury where Metesky lived on the first floor with his sisters Anna and Mae. Journal-American *photo courtesy of photography collection, Harry Ransom Center, University of Texas at Austin.*

her as "Anna Mikutas." Why in a town of immigrants from France, Ireland, Italy, Lithuania, Poland, Russia, and other places the name "Milauskas" caused such difficulty I have no idea.

After attending St. Joseph's Parochial School, Metesky enrolled at Duggan Elementary, where he shunned participation in team sports and made no "pitch for the class beauty," according to a detailed and amusing six-part series, "Now the Real Story," put together by a team of five reporters, among them Martin Steadman and Marilyn Bender (both of whom I interviewed) that ran in the *New York Journal-American* in late March 1957. A Duggan classmate, Louis Jannetty, told the *J-A,* "George would literally not step on an ant, he was that averse to hurting anything. He was a meticulous boy. Always dressed well. He wouldn't talk to you unless you made the first advances . . . he was quiet to the point of eccentricity." George had no friends. He went on to attend Crosby High School for two years.

I learned through visits to the Mattatuck Museum in Waterbury that a significant number of Lithuanians along with other immigrants in Brooklyn had been closely involved in the Waterbury labor movement. The Ansonia, Connecticut, plant of the Waterbury Farrel Foundry and Machine Company was struck by its employees in 1919, very likely while George Metesky was working for that company at its Waterbury plant. At the age of fifteen he had taken a job as a machinist's apprentice. The *Journal-American* quoted a man named Phil Sacco, who described the novice employee as "a strange one. He came to work all dressed up in a suit and collar and necktie. He tried to learn the machine business dressed like that, and he hated to get his hands dirty."

In *Metal, Minds and Machines,* Cecelia Bucki recounts, "On June 18th and 19th over 8000 metalworkers, men and women, skilled and unskilled, struck Waterbury's brass mills and factories." In that same month, city guardsmen were assisted by World War I veterans in patrolling the streets, forbidding assembly or parades of any kind.

In March and April of 1920, "8 to 10,000 Waterbury workers struck to resist wage cuts." Troops were deployed, and in July an unexploded bomb was discovered hidden in the bushes outside a house formerly owned by police superintendent George M. Beach, the alleged target. Two New York City detectives, as well as a federal agent, were called in to dismantle the bomb.

George P. Metesky enlisted in the US Marine Corps on April 13, 1920, escaping the turmoil of his hometown. He served in the Dominican Republic during his first tour, earning a good conduct medal before his discharge on March 24, 1922. His sister Anna told the *J-A* she had seen photographs he had taken while in Santo Domingo of people with their heads cut off. George's sister also said that two maternal aunts had suffered from mental illness, and one of them had been committed to the Norwich State Hospital in Connecticut. (The hospital was still in existence when I began my research. When I wrote to them I was told medical records were private, but also that they could find no record of her.)

Metesky reenlisted on August 15, 1925, serving on Guam for a year as chief ordnance mechanic. He was then sent to China for twenty-two months, where he became a specialist electrician, helping to run a power plant in Peking. The corps allowed him to end his tour of service a few months early, in May instead of August 1929, to take a job in the parts department of a car-repair garage in San Francisco, but the place went bust, forcing George to ask his parents to send him money so he could travel home.

Twenty-six-year-old George Metesky began his job as a "generator wiper" at the Hell Gate station, 134th Street and Locust Avenue in the Bronx, on December 11, 1929. The United Electric Light and Power Company, a subsidiary of Consolidated Gas, ran Hell Gate. He rented a furnished room in a five-story Renaissance Revival building at 103–9 West Eighty-eighth Street, between Columbus and Amsterdam avenues, built in 1893 (as of this writing the building still stands). Jamie James, a writer who interviewed Metesky for *Rolling Stone* in 1979, wrote, "Metesky loved his job . . . even now, almost exactly fifty years later, he talks about it with pride, 'you have to know where every single switch in that powerhouse is, you have to know what to do if a mistake is made. They never send one man by himself; it's too dangerous, a mistake could be fatal.'"

The young Metesky was swiftly promoted from his entry-level job to a gallery man, throwing switches and clocking out feeders to safeguard the flow of electrical currents. The "United We Stand" section of *Metropolitan Electric Topics,* a monthly publication of Consolidated Gas, reported that an employee named George McDonald "was promoted from generator wiper to gallery man," so this path was apparently common.

Ann Zemaitis, a retired reporter for the *Waterbury American* whom I befriended, had written about the case. Ann gave me the background notes she had compiled for her articles. She noted that Metesky claimed he had reached the "top employee rating equal to that of men who had been there twenty-six years." But his career ended abruptly when he was hit by a blast of gas—a possible boiler backfire—while opening a generator door in the boiler room, and the combustion gases ruptured his weaker lung, causing pneumonia and later tuberculosis.

Immediately following the blast he spat blood on the floor, Metesky said, and two coworkers witnessed this. He notified the foreman of his injury, but the man ordered Metesky to perform taxing physical labor, "carrying heavy wood." After twenty minutes he collapsed, lying on the boiler room floor for two hours without help of any kind. "There were 12,000 'danger' signs in the plant," he said in a letter to the *Journal-American,* "yet not even first aid was available . . . Mr. F. W. Smith [president of Con Gas] was riding around on the soft cushions of a 16 cylinder Cadillac. Me, laying on concrete."

After two hours he got up off the floor and returned to his furnished room, where he lay in bed for a week. On the advice of a doctor, George's brother John drove to New York and took George home to Waterbury. A doctor visited him there as well and sent him to Waterbury Hospital to be treated for pneumonia. In the hospital he began to suffer lung hemorrhages and was advised to go to Tucson, Arizona, to convalesce. He went to Tucson in 1932 where, after another bout of hemorrhages, he was diagnosed with tuberculosis.

While in Arizona, Metesky wrote to his former employer asking for financial assistance beyond payments he had received from an employee benefit fund, as his money was running out. In response from the company he received a claim form to apply for workmen's compensation benefits, which he did on January 4, 1934, but the statute of limitations had already expired. The first two hearings on the matter were held in his absence, one on May 24 and another on September 27; after the latter his claim was disallowed. Metesky returned to Waterbury in 1935. The following year he was granted hearings again on March 5, April 2, and September 23. The claim was definitively rejected September 28, 1936.

The stage was set for gentle, smiling George who would not hurt an ant to commence his terrorism campaign.

IV

The Consolidated Edison Company's denial of requests by the New York City Police to examine employee files from the 1930s is an astonishing aspect of the Mad Bomber story. Manager of the Property Protection Department John J. Holland, point of contact for police officials, is cited often in reports from detectives and memos from commanders as the person in charge of Con Ed security. For years Holland said the company no longer had employee records earlier than 1940. Holland held regular meetings in his office at 4 Irving Place with the commanding officers of the bomb squad (Peter Dale, and then his successor, John O. Dale) and police laboratory (Howard Finney), of which the bomb squad was a part.

Joe McNally of the police laboratory document section was not welcome at those meetings because he was vocal about his certainty, based on Metesky's notes and letters, that the bomber was a present or former Con Edison employee. Holland always dismissed this idea, preferring to speculate on what other company might have inspired the bomber's anger.

During one of the most interesting and entertaining series of interviews I conducted, McNally talked at length about Holland, mocking the absurdity of his assertions about the possible identity of the bomber: "Look at that they put it [a pipe bomb] in a telephone booth up at Grand Central, must be one of those railroad guys up in Grand Central Terminal! Then the other one, it has to be a post office employee because it [the anonymous letter]'s coming out postmarked at the post office at Grand Central Annex. The Pennsylvania Station, whup! gotta be Pennsylvania Station! Then they had one [bomb] in the subway, gotta be a subway employee."

Holland was successful at convincing the bomb squad commanders to adopt his point of view. "Johnny Holland was a very affable gentleman," McNally said. "He was a hail-fellow-well-met. He had an office up there would really startle ya, it was so big, luxurious you know . . . a great Con Man in my opinion, laughin' 'ha ha ha ha.'"

What made Mr. John J. Holland an effective "Con Man" was his willingness to appear cooperative by providing irrelevant and useless information. Hugh Sang's experience with Holland illustrated this point. Sang started working as a detective in the document section of the police lab in 1951, a banner year for Metesky, during which he placed seven bombs. Just as McNally had learned about document examination from Frank Murphy, Sang learned from McNally.

A memo of December 17, 1954, from Howard Finney, commander of the police laboratory, says that Sang and fellow detective William Larkin were given permission to use an office in room 200 at Con Edison's corporate headquarters to examine personnel folders provided by John Holland. Sang spent a couple of hours a day there for many weeks examining handwriting samples, trying to find one that would match the bomber's distinctive printing. "I kept after Holland," Sang said in an interview, "and he said 'I'm having trouble with the legal department.' And they weren't that interested in giving him any extra, 'cause the stuff I was getting was crap! Troublemakers. Anybody that made an anonymous call, but no meaty files. They didn't want you goin' through that stuff. But it kept us running."

"Mr. Holland is cooperating and the work is being done quietly without causing any suspicions of the Consolidated Edison employees," Finney's memo explained. "Some 300 personnel folders are currently involved . . . if these 300 folders are examined without results, Mr. Holland will make available other personnel folders which would pertain to other possible suspects." Holland was as good as his word, always ready with documents that would yield nary a clue.

Joe McNally said, "I think they knew who it was all along." I asked bomb squad detective Bill Schmitt what he thought of that. Schmitt, McNally, and Sang had spent more hours, weeks, and years on the case than anyone else. Schmitt estimated that, for at least a couple of years, he spent nearly three-quarters of his time as a bomb squad detective searching for the Mad Bomber.

"I'm sure of that," Schmitt said about McNally's assertion regarding Con Edison. "I feel that way too . . . If they didn't know in 1940 . . . they certainly knew by 1951. And I'm sure, again I say, I'm sure John Holland never knew [the bomber's identity]. If nothing else I pride myself in saying you couldn't lie to me for four years and me not find something out."

I told McNally what Schmitt said: "the man had to lie to me every day that he didn't know and I can't believe that."

"I believe it," McNally said, "because at one particular time there . . . [the detectives] were asking like [about] the files, 'where do you keep the files?' And Holland says 'they're all here in 4 Irving Place' . . . I said to my brother, who worked for Con Ed, do they keep all the files at 4 Irving Place? 'No, they don't keep any files up at 4 Irving Place,' he says. 'At Hester Street, they have a whole building there, takes up a square block, that's where the files are.' So, that's when I told 'em, I said, this guy is conning you, they don't keep their files at 4 Irving Place. So . . . [one of the detectives] went up to speak to him, and they said to Johnny Holland, 'what about the place down at Hester Street, your building down there, don't you keep the files down there?' He turns to someone else, he says, 'Do we have some place else where they keep files?' A whole square block, and he didn't know it was there?"

Ironically, when Metesky was finally identified, the newspapers gave credit for the file's discovery to the very company that had hidden it from police for so many years. It was technically true that a senior Con Ed employee named Alice Kelly found the file at 4 Irving Place amongst a batch of "troublesome" cases, but McNally, Schmitt, Martin, Sang, Norris, and nearly all the detectives I spoke with said detective Mike Lynch was very close to locating Metesky's file in Albany (in the New York State Workmen Compensation Board files) based on the handwriting and facts revealed in his letters to the *New York Journal-American*, when Kelly, who worked in the Insurance Department, suddenly "discovered" it.

It is very interesting to note that Alice Kelly refused to accept the $26,000 reward offered by the city council and the Patrolmen's Benevolent Association, telling deputy police commissioner for legal affairs Aloysius Melia (whom I interviewed) in private that her Irish mother considered the reward to be "blood money" and said she should not accept it. Perhaps a Con Ed lawyer advised her not to take it?

Joe McNally and Howard Finney went to Con Ed's Hester Street file facility as soon as they got the information about Metesky's workmen's compensation file from Mike Lynch, one of the four New York detectives who went to Fourth Street in Waterbury to take Metesky into custody.

> I went to Hester Street the day they picked Metesky up. I was there with Finney. Ordinarily, the file would be down in Hester Street, because that's where they kept those files. From the workmen's compensation reports that they had up in Albany, Mike Lynch had gotten the information up in Albany [at the main office of the New York State Workmen's Compensation Board]—the date and everything and what it was filed under [the board had this information about Con Ed's files]—And we went to that place [at the Hester Street warehouse] looking for the file, and the file was gone. We looked, it's not there, and there's no out-card. I'm accustomed to the filing system, as a kid I worked in the mailroom of the Department of Sanitation, and if they took a file they put an out-card in. They didn't have an out-card on it, and that's a no-no.
>
> It was missing. And it was quite a gap there where they were missing. *In other words it looked like they had I'd say, easily it seemed to me, about six or seven inches of files on this particular guy* . . . I can look back at any case I had that gave me a lot of trouble and I would remember it. Johnny Holland, he's the guy that it gave a lot of trouble, they had notes all over the place from him [Metesky], they had the big file on this guy, and you'd ask him, ya got any suspects? And [deep mock-serious voice], no, he had no suspects.

Dorothy Ellison says in "Smiling George," a chapter from the unpublished history of the Consolidated Edison Company she wrote as an employee, "the police ran down every promising lead. Detectives scanned literally *millions* [italics added] of Con Edison records—of every current and former employee with the initials 'F.P.;' application forms of people who had applied for a job and been turned down; employees fired or disciplined for infractions of company rules; letters from angry customers; and all of the crank-type letters received over a number of years."

I have no doubt the police went through hundreds of thousands of records, but only a portion of those were from Con Ed, because they also went through motor vehicle records, employee records from the New York Central Railroad, handwriting samples of thousands of suspects. For Ellison to say in her company-sponsored history that police covered "millions of Con Ed records" is to obscure the fact that police never got the company's cooperation. If police saw "millions" of pages, then surely they saw everything! It is interesting that her list includes not a word about workmen's compensation cases or injured employees, since the Consolidated Edison Company had many of both, a fact the company must have been eager to obscure.

V

An anomaly of the post-arrest story is the tale of Metesky's two legal representatives. While his criminal defense attorney, James D. C. Murray, was saying that the workplace injury Metesky claimed to have suffered was a delusion, a product and proof of his insanity, Bart J. O'Rourke was attempting to reopen Metesky's twenty-three-year-old claim for workmen's compensation that had been repeatedly denied because it was filed too late. The one-year limit was sometimes extended to two years, but Metesky filed his claim two years and four months after his injury.

In his appeal to the Workmen's Compensation Board O'Rourke used the argument that Metesky missed the deadline because he had been insane, even at the time of the accident in 1931. If he was insane while he worked at United Electric, then maybe the accident was a delusion just as his criminal attorney suggested? Of course, this was simply a desperate legal maneuver to try to reopen Metesky's case and win benefits since nothing else had worked.

O'Rourke told the press that what happened to Metesky was not an isolated incident. He described a "pattern" of behavior on the part of employers to keep injured employees from receiving workmen's compensation benefits. Such employers refrained from reporting an accident to the state, instead paying the employee from a company fund for two years, by which time the "limitations for filing for Workmen's Compensation Board benefits had passed. The workers were then unable to collect compensation for their disabilities from any source."

"The employer [Con Ed] put Metesky into the Employees' Benefit Fund," O'Rourke continued, "a fund he and his fellow workers helped support. Evidently, the employer did not report such an allegation of accidental injury to the Workmen's Compensation Board, so the Board could determine whether the accident came within the meaning of the law."

For all the ink spilled over the years on the subject of the Mad Bomber, it is at heart a sad and simple story. A man is injured on the job, and his employer fails to inform him of his right to apply for workmen's compensation benefits.

Frances Perkins, in her interview at the Oral History Project of Columbia University, talks about her time as a reform-minded member of the New York State Industrial Commission to which Governor Al Smith appointed her in 1919. She describes working with newly appointed Moreland Act commissioner Jerry O'Connor to reopen workmen's compensation cases that had been improperly handled. Some cases had been closed without a hearing:

> Either the insurance companies, or the employers, or all of them together, had been conniving at quick settlement. A great many workmen, not represented by unions and not represented by anybody, just would be told, "This is all you get. We're going to pay you $200 and that closes your case." The workmen would agree and have to sign the paper. Yet sometimes they had a continuing permanent partial disability, which they didn't know they were entitled to collect for. Sometimes they would have a physical situation which had been lit up and aggravated by this accident that would haunt them forever. They didn't know they were entitled to claim for that.

Metesky's case was heard by the Workmen's Compensation Board, but two of the hearings took place in his absence while he was convalescing in Arizona. The details may be different, but in effect, these cases are the same—an insured employer finds ways to avoid paying an injured employee.

In Dorothy Ellison's chapter "Smiling George," we have the company's version of the story:

> The old Con Edison records show that Metesky's company career was fairly brief. He was employed by a Con Edison predecessor in 1929 and assigned to Hell Gate generating station. He became ill in 1931 and was diagnosed as having tuberculosis. Although he maintained his illness was caused by "gas in the air" at the station. He remained at home from 1931 until sometime in 1932, when his physician advised him to go to a tuberculosis sanitarium in Arizona for treatment. He did go there and remained for three years, during which he wrote several letters to the company, blaming his illness on "the performance of my duties" and demanding "full payments."
>
> The company urged him to get in touch with the Bureau of Workmen's Compensation if he thought he had a case, but he refused to do this until 1934 . . . under the company's sickness pay plan . . . Metesky received 80 percent of his pay for 26 weeks—a total of more than $700. He also received payments totaling more than $2000 under a company-sponsored Travelers Insurance Company group policy covering totally and permanently disabled employees.

I should add that Consolidated Edison refused to allow me to see the Ellison manuscript, although Joe Pratt, author of *A Managerial History of Consolidated Edison*, consulted it for his book. I telephoned Ellison's next of kin, a brother, and he said, "if the company doesn't want you to see it, then I won't show it to you." After a brief, contentious exchange of letters with a Con Ed vice president, the company mailed me this single chapter.

Ellison says Metesky was paid insurance "covering totally and permanently disabled employees," and yet his injury was never reported to the Workmen's Compensation Board. The "26 weeks" of pay fits the pattern O'Rourke identified and also, in effect, the practice discussed by Frances Perkins whereby the employer says, "this is all you get."

The *Journal-American* article includes a response to Bart O'Rourke from "John Keegan, Chief Counsel for Consolidated Edison": "We have the correspondence with Metesky and the United Electric Light & Power Co. for the years 1931–1933 . . . United Electric did notify Metesky to report his accident to the Workmen's Compensation Board before the statutory period expired. According to the records we hold, there is no indication Metesky notified the company that he suffered an accident until a year and a half after it happened. And, so far as the company knew then, Metesky had only a nose bleed."

The company had no idea he had suffered an injury, but it paid him "under the company's sickness pay plan." It is also interesting to note that both Ellison and Keegan refer to detailed records covering the period of Metesky's employment, records they denied possession of despite years of questioning by police.

An item in "United We Stand," the employee news section of *Metropolitan Electric Topics,* said, "George Metesky, Hell Gate Station, who has been off duty since the early part of September, is resting at his home in Waterbury, Conn." This note appeared in the issue of February 1, 1932, a tacit acknowledgement of his injury.

Frances Perkins witnessed the violent act of another man who had not received his workmen's compensation benefits.

> He was a man who was some kind of construction worker working on an excavation upstate. He had been hit on the head with a bucket. He was unconscious, bled from the nose, mouth and ears—typical concussion symptoms. They'd paid him workmen's compensation immediately. He was covered. They paid for the time he was ill. Then he got better. When he was better and healed up they stopped paying him. They said he was all right. He tried to go to work, but nobody would keep him. He began to have all these mental troubles. He got worse and worse mentally.
>
> Then somebody made a claim. [Perkins described] that his condition of great irritability, irritation, flights of fancy, instability and so forth was the result of having been hit on the head by a steel bucket weighing so many hundred pounds. [She continued,] "But" said the insurance company, "certainly not." They brought in a lot of expert testimony to the effect that he was a "constitutional mental inferior."
>
> [Perkins went on,] The man representing the insurance company was Mr. Geddings. [She stated] He opposed our decision [awarding the man benefits] and said he would take an appeal or ask for rehearing. This [injured] man therefore had had an award made and hadn't got any money. So he came to my office and thought that since I had made the award, I should give him the money. He was as deranged as that. He pulled out his knife. [The secretaries] saw it and were alarmed to death, but they let him go into my office because they knew I wasn't there. [Perkins continued,] He went out into the hall. By pure accident Mr. Geddings was there in the hall coming to my office to discuss this

case with me. I stepped out of the washroom, and what did I see but this man with a knife in his hand and Geddings bleeding from the throat. It didn't kill him, but it almost killed the rest of us. It was the most terrible sight I ever saw.

I've included Perkins's story because it creates a context for the Metesky case, a way of thinking about it as one of many cases where the awarding or withholding of benefits has life-and-death consequences.

More recently, in November 1996, a man named James L. Dailey, distraught over a denial of worker's compensation benefits after he was injured on a construction site and unable to work for several years, took hostages at gunpoint in the offices of the Bureau of Worker's Compensation in Columbus, Ohio. A spokesman for the Ohio Industrial Commission, which shared office space with the bureau, told Maria Gallagher of Ohio Public Radio's Statehouse News Bureau that he had witnessed "bomb threats" and other suggestions of violence from claimants. Bureau employees said it was not unusual for them to encounter people "depressed and angry over the status of their Worker's Comp claims."

The *New York Times* ran a three-part series beginning on March 31, 2009, about the failings of New York State's Workers' Compensation system and the various ways injured employees are denied benefits or discouraged from filing claims. So Metesky's case as an insurance claimant still has relevance viewed as part of the contentious history of the workmen's compensation system.

In New York State, the original workmen's compensation law establishing the system was passed in 1910, and it was declared unconstitutional by the court of appeals in 1911. After legislative action and the electorate's approval of an amendment to the state's constitution to permit the law, the system was reestablished in 1914. Between 1914 and September 1931, the month of Metesky's accident, the law had been amended by the legislature ninety-seven times.

The remaining mystery of the Mad Bomber case is why Con Ed hid Metesky's employee file containing his massive correspondence (he says he wrote two to three hundred letters to the company) and the voluminous record of his workmen's compensation case so many years after the accident and the dismissal of his insurance claim. Further, why did Consolidated Edison bother to send three witnesses to a Workmen's Compensation Board hearing even though they knew

Metesky's claim was invalid under section twenty-eight, the statute of limitations?

Chief of detectives James B. "Lefty" Leggett interrogated Metesky about his actions and his compensation claim in Waterbury at 4:40 AM on January 22, 1957:

> Q. [Leggett] At the particular time, the third hearing, the persons at that hearing were Cavanaugh, Lawson and Purdy, three of the men who had been employed with you at the powerhouse.
>
> A. [Metesky] Yes.
>
> Q. Each of them testified?
>
> A. Yes. Purdy admitted that I was working that day but said that I did not feel good. Cavanaugh said I had a nosebleed. Lawson testified I did not work that day.
>
> Q. At the conclusion of the hearing what happened?
>
> A. The referee was going to make an award in my favor but the company claimed section 28 [statute of limitations].
>
> Q. When did you get a fourth hearing?
>
> A. I got another hearing on the appeal [September 23, 1936] and at that time Hamlin and Company [the insurance company] claimed a defense under section 28. The hearing officer said he could not reverse and denied compensation.

I believe the reason the company blocked Metesky's claim had to do with fear of massive liability for silicosis, tuberculosis, and occupational diseases as discussed by Frances Perkins in her Oral History Project interview as she recounted the struggle, during Franklin Roosevelt's governorship, over what diseases would be covered under the workmen's compensation law. This period coincides roughly with that of Metesky's employment and injury at the United Electric Light and Power Company. Perkins reported,

> We made some additions to the workmen's compensation coverage, primarily in the field of occupational diseases which had not been covered previously, but we had to make very tentative approaches because the employers of New York were up in arms through their association against having a general coverage of occupational diseases. They wanted it specific. Particularly, they were frightened of getting caught with silicosis, which it is true is difficult to diagnose in its earlier stages. It is

difficult to distinguish between silicosis and pthisis—the medical name for the state of the lung being filled up, which is tuberculosis, before they know that the tubercular germ is there.

It is difficult to distinguish whether it is tuberculosis or silicosis filling up the lung and some of the earlier symptoms will be not unlike—fatigue, coughing and that kind of thing because the breathing apparatus is interfered with when the lung is filled up with silica dust.

Nine times out of ten silicosis also leads into tuberculosis as a terminal episode [Perkins explained]. So, the employers were very anxious to evade silicosis as an occupational disease, because of the fact that [it] is so easily confused with tuberculosis and because the two do run into each other. They didn't want to be stuck with all these long, long tuberculosis cases of total, permanent disability, nor the death rate from tuberculosis cases.

So they fought shy of a general coverage of occupational diseases. This was the principal legislative battle that we had throughout the Roosevelt administration, because we recommended continuously the general coverage of all occupational diseases.

Following is a quote from the "New York State Workmen's Compensation Law and Industrial Board Rules, With Amendments, Additions, And Annotations, to September 1, 1931," issued under the direction of Frances Perkins:

Disease or Infection—In a multitude of cases the Department of Labor, without reversal by the courts, has held that "such disease or infection as may naturally result" from an accidental injury includes disease antedating the accident if aggravated, accelerated, developed or hastened by it. For example a heavy strain or other accident may develop an unknown heart defect and cause sudden death, or injury by the upsetting of an automobile may light up latent tuberculosis and cause life-long disability. Disability may be partially or wholly due to disease concurrent with but not consequential from an accident.

So, under the rules as set out here, companies like Consolidated Edison, running so many plants under varying conditions, must have striven to reduce their liability wherever possible, afraid that the vulnerable lungs of their many employees, often working in dangerous or dirty conditions, might sink them in a sea of valid compensation claims.

The explanation of the remaining mystery—why the Metesky file was kept hidden for so many years (in the "troublesome" case cabinet), with manager of property protection John Holland repeatedly telling detectives he had no old employee records—has to do with a kind of corporate paranoia dating to the establishment of the very same work-men's compensation coverage outlined above. Whether Holland—an older man by all accounts—took the initiative himself based on compa-ny procedures of the 1930s or was directed by his superiors will never be known.

VI

One of the curiosities of obsessive research is its similarity to the psychology of collecting—books, objets d'art, paintings, stamps, bits of string, anything. The pursuit is never satisfied because one object sought and found either leads to new questions or simply becomes an occasion for another search. When I set to work on this essay, I made discoveries among the documents I had accumulated and gained a fresh outlook on old material.

For years I had been focusing my attention on the countless things I was unable to obtain—a report on Metesky's bombs from the Pica-tinny Arsenal, the sanity report, his workmen's compensation file, vid-eo footage missing from CBS archives—and therefore had overlooked the valuable substance of what I had on hand. From this experience I have learned not to wait for fulfillment of real or imagined research goals before using everything acquired to begin the beguine of writing.

In blue ink I had transcribed by hand the first tape-recorded inter-views I conducted, with detectives Bill Schmitt and Eddie Lehane. The next round was done on a typewriter, and, starting in 1991, each new interview was entered into a small, beige, boxlike computer with a gray screen. These transcripts were tangible proof I had brought to light an original piece of history—unprompted, unassigned—that no one else had found. The recording of these conversations presented sto-ries, biographies, and a chronicle of my own fumbling joy at being the conduit for such narratives. I would read them over and over, finding music in the language of each subject and his or her verbal expressions.

On October 20, 1989, during one of the research trips I made to New York, I met with Marty Steadman at the public relations firm where he worked. He was the sort of person who could immediately put you at ease. He spoke with me as if I were an old friend, explaining how things worked at the *J-A* when he was a reporter there and telling me several funny stories. I soon learned that among newspaper reporters and editors, the Mad Bomber case, although a serious source of deadline angst, was more comic than anything else. In his New York accent, vaguely reminiscent of Bugs Bunny, Steadman invited me into his 1950s newspaper reporter's world.

"The most ironic thing about the whole Mad Bomber story," the quick-witted Steadman said, "was that . . . [Metesky] was writing to all, virtually all the newspapers, and copy boys on the desk were throwing them away. They thought he was a nut, you know, and for the longest period of time he just couldn't connect with anybody until the story became a huge running story in New York." The hard-bitten copy boys throwing away newsworthy but apparently irrelevant letters might serve as a metaphor for a researcher who disregards what turns out to be valuable material as he searches for that one true unreachable thing.

In the 1950s, American psychiatrists, buttressed by a general consensus around Freudian orthodoxy, rose to a position of great influence as authorities on what was normal behavior and what was not. One of my bookcases filled up with works like *The History of Psychiatry* by Franz G. Alexander, *The Manufacture of Madness* by Thomas Szasz, and *The Vital Balance* by Karl Menninger. My interest in the dominance of Freudian medical notions grew out of my Mad Bomber project.

Steadman was laughing when he quoted criminal courts *Associated Press* reporter Jimmy Ritchie, who described the three court-appointed psychiatrists, John H. Cassity, Theodore S. Weiss, and Albert A. LaVerne, as "Patty, Maxene and LaVerne," a reference to the Andrews Sisters, the famous female trio that sang hits like "Bei Mir Bistu Shein," "Shoo Shoo Baby," and "Boogie Woogie Bugle Boy." These psychiatrists were asked to determine whether the bomber was fit to stand trial, whether he understood the charges against him.

Steadman's thorough reporting of the Mad Bomber story inspired the publicity-seeking Dr. LaVerne to suggest that Steadman team up with him to write a book about the case. LaVerne started calling Steadman "all hours of the night and in the morning and everything . . . when he finished with his patients he'd call me up and then spend an hour and a half on the phone with me . . . finally I said forget about it, that's not my discipline, I don't do that, I'm a reporter, I'm not a writer." Steadman also had doubts about the ethics of the psychiatrist's plans.

Dr. LaVerne was clearly an ambitious man and saw the Metesky case as a watershed moment in his career. His recitation of his own qualifications at the Kings County court hearing on Metesky's sanity went on for eight sentences. The following exchange shows not only that LaVerne was determined to win his case and convince Judge Samuel S. Leibowitz that the indicted man should be committed rather than tried as a criminal, but that he found it necessary to resort to hyperbole to exaggerate the importance of the case and, by implication, himself.

Q. [Judge Leibowitz] As the man lies there today, if he were set free, he would be a dangerous man wouldn't he?

A. [Dr. LaVerne] Undoubtedly

Q. A homicidal maniac?

A. I would say, your honor, of the thousands of schizophrenics I have had the opportunity of examining and seen, in my opinion he's one of the most dangerous to society, and one of the most psychotic I have ever seen.

Fifteen years later another psychiatrist, Daniel W. Schwartz of Kings County Hospital, reported that Metesky told him "that when he was examined at Bellevue, following his arrest on the current charges he was coached and instructed by one of the psychiatrists [most likely LaVerne], that is, taught how to give crazy answers."

Schwartz found that "Despite . . . paranoid feelings and delusions the patient shows no evidence of a thinking disorder." Metesky neither was schizophrenic nor was he any longer a danger to society. "He never showed the withdrawal and the lassitude," Schwartz explained to me, "and lack of interest in the world that schizophrenics are supposed to show with time. He just never did."

I located LaVerne through the American Medical Association after his license to practice medicine in New York State had been revoked for unethical behavior having to do with a program for curing drug addiction with a "Carbon Dioxide Treatment." He was living in Omaha, Nebraska. When I told him during one of our phone conversations I was researching a book about the Mad Bomber case, he said he had "500 pages in a vault" about Metesky and "it takes a lot of money to write a book." One evening he surprised me with a phone call, asking me to travel to Omaha so that we might meet with the governor of Nebraska. "You're a writer," he said. "You can help me persuade the governor of the benefits of club soda. It can save the state a lot of money. Are you aware of what a serious problem drug and alcohol addiction is?"

As I look back on this very strange moment in the adventures of my research, I see it as one more example of a road I followed into a dead end. I had sought Dr. LaVerne in the hope he might share with me the final sanity report and perhaps his notes, but I was left with a rather sad tale of an elderly man trying desperately to recapture the professional success and standing of his younger days. And yet, he was such an unusual character I cannot say I regret having talked with him. It is daunting to think of how many people may have been affected by Dr. LaVerne's questionable medical practices.

James A. Brussel, another psychiatrist involved in the George Peter Metesky saga, was assistant commissioner of the New York State Department of Mental Hygiene and author of *Casebook of a Crime Psychiatrist*. The first chapter, "The Mad Bomber," discusses the case that made Brussel a celebrity. But, sifting through my files and storage boxes, I discovered that Brussel was apt to make things up.

Brussel is known for having provided the police department with a profile of the anonymous bomber that turned out to be, in part, accurate. Following is the version that appeared on page thirty-one of the *New York Times* on December 25, 1956: "Single man, between 40 and 50, introvert, unsocial but not anti-social. Skilled mechanic. Cunning. Neat with tools. Egotistical of mechanical skill. Contemptuous of other people. Resentful of criticism of his work but probably conceals resentment. Moral. Honest. Interested in women. High school graduate. Expert in civil or military ordnance. Possible motive: discharge or reprimand. Feels superior to critics. Resentment keeps growing. Present or former Consolidated Edison worker. Probably case of progressive paranoia." On December 30, the *New York Journal-American* published an edited version with several ellipses.

If the version published in Brussel's book is accurate, then both newspapers made the same error in printing "interested in women" rather than "not interested in women." Brussel says in his book that "all the New York newspapers carried stories about my theories . . . the most concise appeared in the *New York Times* on Christmas day,

1956 . . . this didn't contain all my predictions, but it crystallized the major ones." He says nothing about any error, changing the profile as published in his book to cover up a flaw in his predictions. In an earlier version dictated to police (Brussel declined to put this in writing), he posited various possibilities, a flexible profile that allowed him plenty of wiggle room.

But the most astonishing and bald-faced lie Dr. Brussel told in connection with this case was when he claimed credit in his book for the police department's change in policy that ended the news blackout surrounding it: "'By putting these theories of mine [the bomber profile] in the papers,' I argued, 'You might prod the bomber out of hiding . . . there's a chance someone might recognize him—a mail carrier, a local merchant, a fellow employee.'" Brussel claims police commissioner Stephen Kennedy took his advice, and thus in a matter of weeks the bomber was caught. I can see how a man like Brussel, an author who apparently sought public attention, might want his bomber profile to be given to the press.

And yet, Walter Arm, the deputy commissioner of police in charge of community relations, has gone on record saying that *he* was the person who suggested a change in policy. A reporter in New York for many years, Arm had earned a reputation as a man of integrity and thus had been hired by Commissioner Kennedy in 1955. Arm had published *Payoff*, his book about the police corruption scandal involving a gambling boss named Harry Gross who bribed hundreds of cops, in 1951. In 1969 he published another book, *The Policeman: An Inside Look at His Role in a Modern Society.*

Somehow, I located one of Arm's daughters, and, when I met with her in lower Manhattan, she very generously gave me a copy of her father's unpublished autobiography, *A Reporter's Life for Me—And You.* "Commissioner Kennedy," he wrote, "agreed to my suggestion that after years of no publicity we reverse our policy and give out everything we knew about the bomber. 'There must be someone somewhere who will recognize him and we may get a letter from them' I argued."

Not only did Arm report that the policy change was his idea, and in language oddly similar to Brussel's, but he asserted that a "psychologist" argued *against* such a change. "The Commissioner," he said, "overruled the protest of his detective commanders and the advice of a psychologist and gave me permission to get out everything we knew.

His foresightedness led to the capture of the bomber in less than sixteen weeks." Arm continued, "The psychologist had given us a good description of the elusive bomber . . . saying that he had to be a skilled mechanic, a widower or bachelor who lived with his mother or sister, and that he came from upstate and was in his fifties. He also warned that the policy of publicity would feed his ego and predicted that he would make larger and more dangerous bombs."

Arm's accurate description of a version of Brussel's profile convinces me that "the psychologist" is actually Dr. Brussel. If there was any question about whom to believe—Walter Arm or James A. Brussel—it was resolved when I found a memo confirming Arm's version of events, that Brussel had argued against publicity, in the files of police records released to me after my FOIA requests in 1990.

The memo from Howard Finney, commanding officer of the police laboratory, is dated February 27, 1956, and was sent to the chief of detectives, James "Lefty" Leggett:

> Dr. Brussel, Psychiatrist and Assistant Commissioner of New York State Department of Mental Hygiene who has been consulted on a prior occasion regarding this case, was again consulted on October 18, 1955 at his office, 270 Broadway, New York, N.Y., as to the relative merits of:
>
> a. Releasing to the press all available data regarding this case; or
>
> b. Appealing to the perpetrator through the media of "personal display ads" in New York City newspapers. *Dr. Brussel stated that in his opinion, if this department were to adopt any of these measures, it would encourage the perpetrator to make and place a bomb, larger than any we have yet experienced* [italics added]. Dr. Brussel offered his complete cooperation to this department in any further phases of this investigation.

Dr. Brussel was consulted again in April 1956, according to a memo dated April 18 from Sergeant James Falihee, who sometimes acted as head of the bomb squad: "The undersigned contacted Inspector Walsh. It was decided that personal contact with Dr. Brussel would produce better results." And then, according to *Casebook,* shortly after an explosion at the Brooklyn Paramount Theater on December 2, Dr. Brussel was consulted again. It appears his advice was consistent.

In addition to Walter Arm's writings and the memo from police files, the *Journal-American* reported that "Chief of Detectives James B. Leggett praised Deputy Commissioner Walter Arm, in charge of community relations, for his 'integral part' in the Bomber's capture. After a bomb explosion in the Brooklyn Paramount Theater had injured seven persons Dec. 2, Leggett said Arm insisted that police reverse their policy of secrecy on the Bomber and give him all possible publicity."

The *Herald-Tribune* ran more complete coverage of this matter, quoting Chief Leggett at length and confirming that Commissioner Ken-

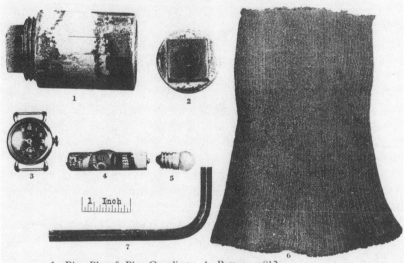

POLICE DEPARTMENT
CITY OF NEW YORK
NEW YORK 13, N. Y.

January 1, 1957

COMPONENT PARTS
(Pipe Bomb)

The objects illustrated below are the COMPONENT PARTS OF A PIPE BOMB.

If such parts come to your attention, either in reference to a PERSON or PLACE that should be connected to the BOMBINGS, immediately notify the New York City Police Department at CAnal 6-2000 or SPring 7-3100.

1. Pipe Plug & Pipe Coupling
2. Pipe Plug & Allen Screw
3. Wrist Watch
4. Battery =912
5. Flashlight Bulb
6. Top Portion of Man's Sock
7. Allen Wrench

STEPHEN P. KENNEDY,
Police Commissioner.

One of a series of flyers released by the New York City Police Department as part of its new policy to publicize the Mad Bomber investigation. From police files proved by Detective John Justy.

nedy had, unlike the story Brussel tells in his book, favored Arm's idea to end the news blackout on the Mad Bomber case.

Brussel hindered rather than aided the capture of the Mad Bomber, since his misguided notion that the pleasure of publicity would encourage the erection of larger, more dangerous bombs actually frustrated Metesky, causing him to build bigger bombs, with the idea of leaving one in the recently constructed New York Coliseum. "They did not publish anything in the papers for years," Metesky told Jamie James of *Rolling Stone* in 1979. "They got some stupid advice from some psychiatrist, 'if you don't bother with him he'll stop.' And that just made me work all the harder."

As for Brussel's *Casebook* depiction of George Metesky and his Brooklyn neighborhood of Waterbury, many of his points have no basis in fact. Neither George Valiulis, a former tenant in Metesky's house, nor reporter Ann Zemaitis had heard anything about children calling Metesky "Mr. Think," as Brussel claimed. There is no evidence anywhere for the extravagant fairy tale spun in his narrative:

> The relationship of the three was a neighborhood mystery. Some said the man [Metesky] was a polygamist, married to both women [his sisters Anna and Mae]. Some said he was the illegitimate son of one of them. Others, first-generation Middle Europeans steeped in Gypsy lore . . . thought they might be witches. These theories were discussed over back fences and on creaky porches Sunday afternoons. Everybody on the street had his own theory. The single point on which all the neighbors agreed was that something dark, something sinister went on in that house, behind its curtained windows and its ever-locked front door.

"On questioning," wrote Dr. Schwartz of King's County Hospital in his report of March 20, 1972, "the patient [George Metesky] states that he has read Dr. Brussel's account and he describes it as '99% false. It was written to disparage me.' As one example of his inaccuracy, he states that he was never the meek man Dr. Brussel described him as being."

I think Brussel's purpose was self-aggrandizement and a desire for the rewards of successful authorship. Maybe he was aiming for a new career in television or the movies. I can imagine a script for a TV series, "Dr. Brussel, Crime Fighter of New York!" moldering in a drawer somewhere.

I don't know what percentage of his chapter is true or false, but among the many things I believe he made up out of whole cloth is the story that Metesky called him one night at 1:00 AM. Metesky was not known to stay out quite that late, and he and his sisters had no telephone. Furthermore, Brussel gives no date for the alleged phone call:

> The phone was ringing when I returned home from a late night in the city.
> "Hello?" I said.
> "Is this Dr. Brussel, the psychiatrist?" The voice sounded calm, assured, controlled.
> "Yes, this is Dr. Brussel."
> "This is F. P. speaking. Keep out of this or you'll be sorry."
> I started to say something, hoping to keep him talking long enough for the police and phone company to trace the call. But F. P. was too clever to fall for a trick like that. Without even waiting to hear my reaction to his threat, he hung up.

And Brussel, too, was clever enough to wait twelve years before telling this fatuous tale along with his whopper about saving the day with his brilliant advice to the New York City Police Department.

VII

The picture of George Metesky that emerges from the material I revisited for this essay includes a stark reality to match the spare décor of the rooms he lived in with his sisters. I said earlier that the entire Metesky affair struck me as a case of the 1930s haunting the 1950s. Metesky and his sisters never left the thirties. Not only was he doomed day in, day out to relive, in memory and in consequence, his 1931 injury, the event that ruined his life, but the Metesky apartment on the first floor of the three-story house on Fourth Street was like a museum: "the clean six-room apartment has lace curtains and is filled with old-fashioned furniture given to them by their father," said one of the Waterbury newspapers. "It contains four expensive radio sets and an upright piano but no television or telephone. One of the radio sets is next to Metesky's severely plain iron bedstead."

Genevieve Valiulis, who lived on the second floor for seven years with her husband Vytautas and their son George, told me her son had the bedroom just above Metesky's: "it was like a hallway with one window" facing the house next door and "*it was like a jail cell*." She later mailed me a hand-drawn diagram of the layout of the Metesky house.

Metesky used to come up to their apartment to fix the electricity or make repairs. He talked mostly with Vytautas, telling him that he wanted to sell the house, split the money with his sisters, and move away from them to a climate more hospitable to his lungs. Genevieve reiterated later in our conversation that Metesky had no compensation and "could not get away from sisters. He wanted to live like a normal person." Metesky and his sisters never had any visitors. His brother John never came to the house.

Genevieve saw Metesky almost every day, going to and from the garage. They were not friends exactly, but said hello to each other. Once a month he would come home late at night. Metesky always said he was going to visit his brother in Hartford, but it turns out he went to New York to plant his bombs. "He was very inside mad, not crazy or anything," Genevieve said. "He was not mentally ill at all—very clever person—honest person, he was interesting to talk to."

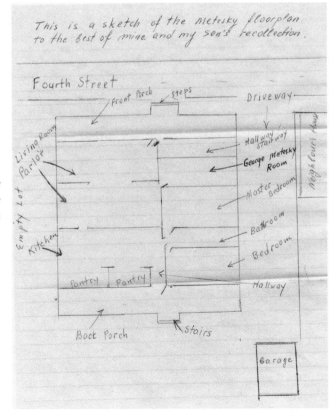

Genevieve Valiulis's sketch of the Metesky house floor plan

The first thing she and her husband were told when they moved in was not to use the front door: "the front door is just for the doctor or the priest." The sisters "never wanted us to have company. My husband said, 'we are not in church we have to have a guest once in a while.' The Meteskys were afraid our boy would make noise, but we were quiet people, and we never used the front door."

Once, Mae came upstairs to complain about friends the Valiulises had over for a visit, and Vytautas pushed Mae out, saying, "Go back to your home!"

"Mae was a monster," Genevieve said. "Anna was afraid of her."

Around the time he had begun to plant his pipe bombs in New York City, Metesky entered into a dispute with another tenant family. He felt the tenants had somehow mistreated his father, George Milauskas, who was then also living in the house, and wanted them to move out. He ultimately wrote to Connecticut governor Robert A. Hurley as well as various officials of the Office of Price Administration, a federal agency established during World War II to control rents and prices. On June 30, 1942, according to the *Waterbury American,* he typed a letter to a local OPA representative named George McDuff: "Due to the CRIMINAL NEG-LIGENCES of Constituted Authority, I have been robbed of my earning capacity and put through a lifetime of misery and suffering . . . Now through this monstrosity of the OPA a landlord is supposed 'to do it or else . . .' They [the tenants] are still here, due to the fact that Constituted Authority is too YELLOW to assume its full responsibilities."

Metesky referred to his workplace injury and denial of compensation, but the recipient would have had no idea what he was talking about. The *Waterbury American* article doesn't specify exactly how many letters he wrote about this matter, but he appears to have written many over a period of five weeks or more. On May 26, 1942, he wrote a two-page letter to George H. Fittz, the "regional rent executive of the OPA" in Boston:

> In the fixing of rents, there has been a lot said about what the Landlord MUST do. As long as this family stays here the raise in rent remains. If further trouble is caused, the rent will go up. The OPA will have to look at both sides of a question. There is no room for a DICTATOR in this country. There should be a ceiling on prices, but there should also be a basement of official brains . . . I have been on three expeditions [with the Marine Corps] and now I have two nephews in the South Pacific.

I am part of this country and this country is a part of me. During the depression this property owner helped to keep this Government going. This house at times had an empty tenement for five months at a stretch. The rent was as low as $17 per month. We could not hide this house and get on relief. Our taxes remained at their highest level, and as everybody knows, the City Government was stealing the taxpayers' money out of the treasury [a scandal that first erupted in 1938].

Here he sounds like many an indignant but patriotic middle-class property owner with tenants.

The bomber was a writer. By his own admission to police he had written eleven to twelve hundred pages of letters on a noiseless Remington portable typewriter belonging to one of his sisters. The letters were sent to churches, newspapers, lawyers—people, he told *Rolling Stone,* from "all walks of life." This tally does not include the anonymous threatening notes, and may not include the two to three hundred letters he sent to Con Ed. Like a parody of the eagle on the masthead of the *J-A,* Metesky held not arrows and an olive branch but pipe bombs and a typewriter.

Metesky's typewriter, radio set visible at right. Photo courtesy of the Waterbury Republican-American.

George Valiulis, like his mother and other people, often saw Metesky walking to or from the gray garage with smoked glass windows where he made his bombs. But did anyone see him writing? His sisters, Mae and Anna? If he produced thousands of pages over the same period he produced forty or fifty pipe bombs, did he spend as much time at his sister's noiseless Remington or with a pencil in his hand as he did at his lathe?

As quoted earlier, Metesky said, "People pay more attention to the noise of a bomb than to the written word, I used the bombs merely to draw attention." If his words had been taken seriously, the tiny Fourth Street bomb factory would have closed.

As for his paranoia and delusions of grandeur, at a sanity hearing in Kings County Court, Dr. Albert LaVerne read a transcript of remarks by George Metesky comparing his own actions to those of nations at war:

> When two nations have a dispute they write notes to each other. When the notes are ineffective then they have to use force. They send over bombers, blow up cities, kill and maim many innocent women and children and then the bombers return from their mission, society pins a medal upon their breast for their good deeds and for services rendered.

Because of his paranoia, Metesky apparently believed that many of those to whom he had written anonymous notes actually knew his identity. In a letter he wrote to a newspaper in 1956, he said, "I have let loose enough information in my letters it seems to isolate a grain of sand in a bucket." And yet, paranoid as he was, he was likely right that Con Edison had isolated that grain of sand. Nonetheless, the extreme nature of his paranoia was one of the things I did not fully fathom until I had read the transcripts of the Kings County sanity hearings, during which he said the judge, his lawyer, and the newspapers were secretly in league with the Consolidated Edison Company.

"George gets very excited when he goes out," his sister Anna told the *J-A*. "He's not calm and happy like people say, but very sad and nervous." He told Dr. LaVerne he smiled a lot because he had heard that smiling prolongs life. George Milauskas, Metesky's father, the night watchman at JE Smith lumber company, "laughed all the time," Steele Smith, one of the company's owners, told me. "But he wasn't really very funny as far as I can tell. He chuckled all the time, but it was sort of just to be friendly, it wasn't in answer to something really humorous usually." Metesky's father was also a great one for handwritten notes, like the one excerpted here, left for his boss, J. Francis Smith:

> Mr. J. Francis Smith 11/6. 1933
> Mr. Smith I Laick [like] moor money.
> And every year 2 Wicks [weeks] Wenisisin [vacation].
> And pay for Wenisisin.
> Seem laick nuder [other] companis Dun [do].

The Smith family was impressed with watchman George's quips and his elegant handwriting, and they kept a file, "Gems by George." True to the story of my research, the best examples had been pilfered.

* * *

Meyer Berger and others reported that, as Metesky was escorted off to jail, reporters called out a question: "You sorry you hurt people, George?"

"And he said, 'Yes I'm sorry I hurt people' and then, as afterthought, 'but I'm not sorry I did.'"

A topic for another essay might be the identification of the writer with his subject. Am I sorry I spent so much time chasing the history of the Mad Bomber? Yes, I'm sorry I did it, but then again, I'm not sorry I did.

ACKNOWLEDGMENTS

Thank you Franklin and Mary Dennis for welcoming me into your home in Westchester. From there I easily drove to Waterbury for my research visits. Thanks to Franklin Dennis, a tireless bookman, talented editor, and history maven, whose valuable advice about my Mad Bomber research, had I heeded it, would have saved me a great deal of time and heartache.

For essential information about the Mad Bomber investigation I would like to belatedly thank a number of people, citizens, journalists, detectives, and police officials, some no longer living.

I must single out John Furey, who was in 1989 the retirees' representative at the Detective Endowment Association. He immediately treated me like a colleague, and helped me contact many retired detectives. The following people and many others were a pleasure to interview:

Marilyn Bender, Frank Creveling, James Falihee, John Justy, Eddie Lehane, James Martin, Joe McNally, Al Melia, Roy Metcalf, John Norris, John O'Brien, Gabe Pressman, Harry Reasoner, Hugh Sang, Bill Schmitt, Marty Steadman, Wes Summerville, George Valiulis and his mother Gene, and Ann Zemaitis. McNally, Sang, and Schmitt were at the heart of the police investigation to capture George Metesky.

Thanks also to the *Waterbury Republican-American,* the Harry Ransom Center, and the Columbia Center for Oral History for the rights to reprint some material. Thanks also to the Mattatuck Museum for material about labor strife in Waterbury, Connecticut. Thanks to the many reference librarians I had the pleasure of meeting.

And thanks also to Jay Feldman, author of the books *When the Mississippi Ran Backwards* and *Manufacturing Hysteria* and the play "A Loud Noise in a Public Place: An Epic Vaudeville Based Upon the Life and Times of George Metesky, the Mad Bomber of New York City." Jay was kind enough to allow me to copy his transcript of the sanity hearings held in Brooklyn County Court under the Hon. Samuel S. Leibowitz.

Quote page 224: The Reminiscences of Frances Perkins (volume 2), p. 23, in the Columbia Center for Oral History Collection (CCOHC).

Quote page 226–27: The Reminiscences of Frances Perkins (volume 2), p. 187 (paragraphs 1–2), 187–89 (paragraph 3), CCOHC.

Quote page 228–29: The Reminiscences of Frances Perkins (volume 3), p. 234–35 (paragraphs 1–2), 236 (paragraphs 3–4), CCOHC.

BRUCE JOSHUA MILLER has edited two books and written for public radio, the *Chicago Tribune,* and other publications. He has worked in the book industry for thirty-five years.

PILGRIM VOICES

Puritans, Immigrants, and Historical Research

One shouldn't begin writing history until you can hear their voices.
SALMAN RUSHDIE, *Joseph Anton: A Memoir*

*I*n the early spring of 1977, I visited an old high school classmate who was pursuing a PhD at an elite midwestern university. Late in the evening he told me that the next morning he had an
appointment with a reference librarian with whom he had met earlier
in the week to discuss his newly approved dissertation topic. The subject matter and key words had been duly noted; following a database
search he would receive a computer printout of the sources he needed
to consult for his research and writing. Aware that dissertation work
would of course involve more than he described, I was nevertheless astonished by this technology, instinctively taken aback that such a simple and painless (and seemingly less intriguing and thorough) path
to research was now available and perhaps deemed sufficient. Who if
anyone was being cheated in the hunt, I wondered, in this changing
world of technology?

EARLY RESEARCH EXPERIENCES
I knew something of the hunt. My wife and I were living in England
at the time, and I too was pursuing my doctoral degree, at Oxford,
with its many vestiges and traditions of an ancient past. We were in
the states for a family wedding, and I had spent a week in various research libraries out East, my subject being Puritanism during the Civil
War and Interregnum period of English history (1640–62), as well as in
colonial New England. At Yale's impressive Beinecke Rare Book and
Manuscript Library I was restricted to blank sheets of paper and a pen-

cil in the reading room and bodily patted down on my exit. By contrast, at the Bodleian in Oxford I had become accustomed to a curt nod of greeting from the elderly porter manning the desk as I entered carrying a stuffed briefcase, only occasionally showing my reader's ticket, which included, among other things, a promise "not to bring into the library or kindle therein any fire or flame, and not to smoke in the library"— an oath I had taken in gown and white-tie *sub fusc* with raised right hand about the time of my matriculation (in Latin) at the Sheldonian Theatre, designed by Christopher Wren. Upon my departure, there was a similar acknowledgment, and sometimes even a quick glance inside the briefcase. I read that this genial sense of trust came to an end not long after, in part the consequence of an Italian research student involved in a bicycle accident in the City Centre where a number of old manuscripts spewed onto the pavement. A subsequent search of his flat revealed quite a stash of pilfered Renaissance treasures.

I could not imagine then that the nature of my research could be managed by a computer search or without tactile and very human contact with sources and networks of real people and places. It seemed to me that the academic guild I aspired to enter was a community of learning impossible to encapsulate within a virtual medium. I certainly never mastered all the ways one located an item in the maze of millions of books and manuscripts at the Bodley. In the Upper Reading Room, one wrestled with folio-size volumes to search their handwritten or typed and pasted entries with call numbers that seemed to defy any rhyme or reason. Of course, there was no subject index, so if you did not know the author's name or, if "anonymous," the book's title, digging was required even to know of its existence. Yet it all seemed so efficient and anything but antiquated.

Scouring footnotes and bibliographies in printed material for primary and secondary sources, for example, made the scholarly trails of the conversation within the guild (often contentious) come alive. A career could be made or broken it seemed on whether one thought the gentry was rising or falling in post-Reformation England! One learned where to find the printed catalogs and subject bibliographies on the reference shelves; such valuable guides as Pollard & Redgrave's *Short-Title Catalogue (1475–1640)* and Wing's corresponding volume of early English books (1640–61) led not only to expanding the number of works one needed to know but to which libraries around the world held copies. And, wonderfully, there are many college and faculty libraries in Oxford (the Bodleian alone has fifty-six within it). Over a period of two years I had been constructing a bibliography of hundreds of sources handwritten on 3x5 index cards, and I knew the task was far from done (and never would be; one simply needed to stop and write at some point). No wonder I was wondering about who might be cheated by the quick and convenient promise of technology.

I was writing on the ecclesiological theories and practices of more moderate Independent and Presbyterian Puritans. They were busy reforming (read: dismantling) the Church of England, engaging in civil war (or a Revolution or a Great Rebellion, depending on whether a Roundhead or Cavalier), lopping off the heads of an archbishop and a king, and endeavoring futilely to reconstruct everything (political, social, religious, and economic) in a single, truly biblical pattern—since most were Calvinists and thought that clearly possible. Censorship laws had been lifted, Puritans were fragmented from radical sectarians on the left to the most conservative establishment preservers on the right, and anyone who had anything to say often did so in print.

My most valuable source was the *Thomason Tracts*, a printed catalog of 22,000 individual books, pamphlets, and tracts, along with an additional 400 periodicals, England's early newspapers. On November 3, 1640, a bookseller, George Thomason, began to notice that something significant and unprecedented was happening, so over the next two decades he made daily rounds to the London bookstalls and acquired hot-off-the-press books and pamphlets, noting the date of purchase along with his signature on the title page. Since many of the controversies I was following were protracted, with at least two and usually several more writers, it was the only way to unravel the sometimes convoluted chronologies and arguments. Though Oxford libraries held many if not most of these items, I frequently went to the British Library in London, where I could fill any gaps by reading the Thomason originals in their beautiful red leather and gild bindings, purchased, bound, and presented to the museum by King George III in 1761.

A microfilming project of these materials has been underway for many years, thus restricting the originals, and is nearing completion. The project "Early English Books Online" will eventually digitize from these microfilms Pollard & Redgrave, Wing, and the *Thomason Tracts*, making items available simply by downloading. The Internet is an amazing tool and not to be ignored for its accessibility to the sources—this is one small but significant example. But for me at least, the hunt and the handling were intangible benefits to learning the craft. And along the way I certainly came to understand Samuel Johnson's saying, "When you are tired of London you are tired of life."

London also had small gems of libraries in my research area, providing some enduring memories. In Gordon Square, Dr. Williams's Library is an eighteenth-century treasure trove of books and sources in nonconformist history. It occasionally had books and manuscripts I required; I discovered somewhat to my surprise that I was free to check out seventeenth-century volumes, take them with me to Oxford, and return them by mail. Because of cost-saving measures, in the winter months the library operated without lights and with minimal heat: I would work wearing coat, hat, and fingerless gloves. Most memorable was studying the original minute books of the Westminster Assembly, which met in the abbey from August 1643 to March 1652. "Minutes" is a bit of a misnomer, however. Its unnamed scribe did not begin recording until the forty-fifth session and had a curious practice of often taking notes in his own shorthand, hastily it seemed, and leaving large gaps, presumably to fill in later and insert official documents. While A. F. Mitchell cracked the code for his three-volume published transcription and edition in 1874, from a research perspective working with the originals could not be matched entirely by a printed or downloaded version, especially when on one page I discovered the clear thumbprint of the anonymous scribe, who apparently had spilled the ink. While unfortunately he cannot be traced in any database of fingerprints, history became especially contemporary to me that day.

On a visit to the Congregational Library I unexpectedly found myself in another position of trust with an unwritten honor code. I was the only researcher, and the volunteer on duty at the desk (the library struggled in those days) was a retired military officer. A genial and proper gentleman, perhaps glad to be of service, he engaged me in friendly conversation. He then led me on a guided tour of the library's treasures—quite a few as I recall. I was especially intrigued by the comprehensive first-edition imprints of John Milton, who early in his career as an Independent published a number of radical political and ecclesial pamphlets. Later in the morning, as I was reading and taking notes, the volunteer tapped me on the shoulder with a request:

"I need to pop out to the post for a few minutes, and I was wondering if you would look after things while I am away?" "Of course," I replied. Perhaps he thought I was indeed trustworthy, but I also sensed a context and culture of civility and trust that came naturally.

I found this quality too, for example, rummaging through old file cabinets in the basement of a church in East London that had survived the bombing, searching for an elusive manuscript minute book of a gathered church of early Congregationalists in the 1650s—or in my own college in Oxford, for that matter, which had a fine library of rare dissenting literature. It had no formal librarian, only on occasion a delightful retired solicitor who had volunteered to catalog (on a manual typewriter) for the first time its holdings—on the condition that he would be allowed to smoke his pipe, thus kindling many flames therein. The resulting aroma of pipe tobacco and old books was most congenial. Research can have its aesthetic benefits, inseparable from people and time and place, all special. The ability to roam freely through these collections (I had my own skeleton key) was in itself a learning experience.

The small rooms also had only minimal heat. Once when I plugged in a tiny electric fire, my doctoral supervisor (also Principal of the college) happened to stop in. He eyed the single glowing bar and remarked wryly, "Those things eat money, you know," and left. I duly yanked the cord. When I met him in his lodgings periodically to discuss my work, usually later in the day, he rarely turned on the lights, and we peered at each other gloomily across the room, drinking tea and conversing in the waning daylight. To be fair, he did suffer from severe migraines. He was a superb mentor in the medieval apprenticeship model, once beginning a session with the remark, "Philip, I am a little concerned about your lack of use of the pluperfect!" Back in the library, I did on occasion steal a nap on an uncomfortable avocado green sofa. Above it was a plaque: "On this couch William Carey died at sunrise, June 7, 1834." I still feel a certain kinship with this pioneer missionary to India.

All of this is not to suggest that some or perhaps all of the printed material I relied upon should not eventually be made available online, because this process is well on its way, and that is most welcome. The result will be ready, universal access to *content* in word-searchable formats, a marvelous technological advance for readers at all levels, scarcely anticipated even two decades ago. But this content is only partial at best, and manuscript sources will probably remain even more elusive. When depending only on what is available online, the researcher has no clue of what has been missed. Moreover, while a wormhole (literally from a bookworm, not a time-travel device or time lost to online distractions) might be visible on the computer screen, that it is not quite like holding the book and observing the impressive tunnels from front to back, the foxed edges, the rubbed corners, and the musty (or moldy) fragrance of old cotton-fiber paper. Once as I read a seventeenth-century book at the James Ford Bell Library at the University of Minnesota, a live book-worm fell from the pages onto the table. I showed it to Jack Parker, veteran curator, and he said he had never before seen a squirming perpetrator. Value-added research experiences, to be sure.

A necessary and early lesson was that history is the construction of narratives that require extensive sources and adequate time for reflection in order to hear the voices of the past. On one research excursion to London I spent a good part of the day with Geoffrey Nuttall, the retired doyen in my field. Since I was working with so many individual writers and players within this complex drama—many of whom made several baffling ecclesial identity shifts during the 1640s and '50s—he gently encouraged me "not to treat them as marbles" but to give them flesh and blood and voice within the story that is told. This was not only a good caution but one that helped me when Nuttall later served as my external examiner in the thesis defense. Interpretive understanding requires assuming the humble and non-presumptuous role of the tourist, entering a time, place, and culture not one's own. To these historical characters, our ways are beyond imagining. One must be willing to ask the most embarrassing and naïve of questions, without in the least knowing how to do so, in order to achieve a closer approximation of the past by listening to voices and constructing a meaningful narrative that would be recognizable to one's hosts. L. P. Hartley's line has become proverbial: "The past is a foreign country; they do things differently there."

For me, these research interests and experiences as a postgraduate evolved into an abiding fascination with the nature of communities in their social contexts, how they were structured and inhabited, how they developed and changed through deliberative or unintended actions and simply the exigencies of time. My subject matter shifted unexpectedly, however, when in the mid-1980s the premature death of a colleague draped a mantle of responsibility on me, namely studies of immigration and ethnicity, generally the mass migration to North America from Sweden and other Nordic countries from the mid-nineteenth century on, and specifically the role of religion in community life. The immediate need to teach courses in that area subsequently opened many expanding doors of archival holdings and professional relationships with scholars of immigration here and in Scandinavia. My association with the Swedish-American Historical Society, which has involved richly rewarding work in archives, publications, and public programming for the past three decades, has resulted in scores of research stories left untold here.

In recent years a project in researching and writing local community history developed unexpectedly for a variety of personal and professional reasons, leading to a fresh pursuit of old voices through a different set of resources. This interest focuses on the small yet sprawling and isolated hamlet of Hovland, Minnesota, in Cook County on the rugged "North Shore" of Lake Superior near the Canadian border, as well as the old homestead of a Norwegian immigrant fisherman—places where one must necessarily depend less on digitized sources. My initial curiosity continues to expand and deepen, along with the stories that naturally accumulate through the experiences of ongoing exploration.

LANDSCAPE OF A COMMUNITY

It was little more than 125 years ago that Hovland was first settled by two Norwegian immigrant families. Two cabinetmakers in Duluth, Ole Brunes and Nels Ludwig Eliasen, built a twenty-six-foot sailboat and in the late spring of 1888 headed up the shore looking for potential fishing grounds. Captivated by the beauty and prospects of Chicago Bay, they claimed homesteads on either side of the Flutereed River. They first constructed Brunes's small log house on the west side, after which their wives and two children each joined them, so eight persons huddled together that first winter until Eliasen's place got built. Other Norwegians soon arrived, enough so that the following year the fledgling community applied for a post office. The proposed name of Hamar was rejected by Uncle Sam; legend has it that Carrie Brunes then suggested Hovland, the name of her grandfather's farm back in

Norway. Cook County was home to about three hundred Ojibwe people, while in 1880 the federal census listed only sixty-five white persons. By the turn of the century, the white population in the county rose to 810—mostly Scandinavian immigrants—and the 1905 Minnesota census listed 421 Swedes and 408 Norwegians settled largely along the eighty-one miles of county shoreline—at Tofte, Lutsen, Grand Marais, Maple Hill, and Hovland.

The "North Shore" of Lake Superior, the largest freshwater body in the world, begins in Duluth and extends northeast to the border crossing at the Pigeon River on the Grand Portage Indian Reservation, a distance of 150 miles. Today, US Highway 61, with its dramatic landscape of a boreal forest wilderness on one side and a mostly landless horizon on the other, punctuated by historic communities with various degrees of development, is one of the most scenic drives in America. When one gets as far up the shore as Hovland, 128 miles northeast of Duluth and twenty-two miles from Canada, time seems to have stood still. Indeed, apart from highway traffic racing back and forth, Hovland is a far less busy place than it was during the days of native life and immigrant settlement, when it could only be reached by the lake or, in winter, by the primitive John Beargrease dogsled trail, before rough automobile roads punched their way through just before the First World War. Exploring and understanding this history has become a persistent preoccupation for me.

Where my interest in the story began is elusive. I first visited at the age of two, staying in a rustic cabin six miles east of Grand Marais, land originally homesteaded in 1896 by Ole E. Erickson, a Swedish immigrant and my aunt's grandfather (by marriage to my father's oldest brother). Family vacations were followed by many visits while canoeing the Boundary Waters Canoe Area Wilderness and then also our honeymoon. I came to love the area's isolation and beauty, the breathtaking power and moods of Gitchi Gumi, as natives called the lake, and consequently to learn in bits and pieces historical stories of people and community life. Perhaps I eventually became a historian because from childhood on I was always curious about these things, tended to listen and be observant, and asked lots of questions. I also discovered the literature of the area: historical accounts, memoirs, books about its natural history, the resources of a very fine Cook County Historical Society. With its pedigree of fishing, logging, mining, and other wilderness vocations, it has been also a place for writers and artists. History has always been a serious enterprise here, and there have been diligent and responsible stewards through the generations.

My personal interests intensified and began to include a professional angle when in the mid-1980s we set about salvaging and renovating an old house a further ten miles up the shore near Chicago Bay, the center of the old village of Hovland. It was homesteaded in 1915 by Anders Haagensen Solgaard, a widowed commercial fisherman from Norway. That autumn he built his house. Yet within a dozen years it, along with his quarter mile of lakeshore and fifty-two acres, was largely abandoned. With no road into the place, our local volunteer fire department wanted to torch it as a practice exercise. Neglected and forlorn as it appeared, it was nevertheless a surviving piece of the material immigrant fishing culture. In 1920, the 145 miles of bays, coves, and inhospitable stretches from Duluth to Hat Point at Grand Portage were home to 276 commercial fishing families and bachelors, 80 to 90 percent of whom were Norwegian American, along with numerous Swedes and Swede Finns. Much of this culture physically had disappeared. So over two decades of restoration and building we gave new life to the structure. Personally and professionally I pursued the stories the old house might yet have to tell of itself and the landscape it inhabits. I have not been disappointed.

The voices can only be discerned from the sources. While some can be increasingly accessed in digital ways (such as census, genealogical, property, and death records), most of the hunt has taken place on the ground. I have analyzed census data and read reels of microfilmed newspapers in the Grand Marais Public Library and at the Minnesota Historical Society. At the county courthouse I have poured over the registers of warranty and patent deeds, which present a complex puzzle in the effort to reconstruct the crazy patchwork quilt of land ownership by homesteaders, speculators in minerals or real estate, and timber companies. Frequently the land was vacated by the owners, which led to excessive tax delinquencies and loan defaults. By and large, this task is not as straightforward as tracing the 160-acre agricultural tracts of Lincoln's Homestead Act of 1862. The Cook County Historical Society in Grand Marais is rich in photographs, oral histories, official records, and sometimes hidden treasures. I have photographed what survives of the old material culture scattered throughout the eight communities of settlers that comprised early Hovland by 1910, and have conducted oral interviews with old-timers and descendants of pioneer families. How else might one learn about backwoods stills and occasional boot-legging during Prohibition? Still, the ongoing digitized record projects of these historical societies and official agencies are and will be immensely helpful to researchers and deserve generous funding.

My research has been fueled by a deepening appreciation of the importance of *place* and *homemaking* in the human experience and the expansive literature that explores these themes. The language of *landscape* has come to embrace the whole character and experience of a community. Hovland is largely a story of immigrants from Norway, Sweden, and Finland, uprooted and transplanted to new places where the endeavors of home- and community building take on distinctive nuances, a case study of so much of the American experience past and present. The Scandinavian term *landskap* has a narrow and technical meaning of geographical location in a province, somewhat like a state or county in the United States. But it has come to include the land itself, its features and inhabitants through time. Such a "lived territory" combines a group's—and an individual's—sense of place (e.g., home, town, county, state, nation, folk) with its physical features (e.g., landscape, scenery, climate, flora, fauna). The Scandinavian immigrants in Hovland would hardly have voiced their experience in this way, but they surely possessed an innate sense of *landskap,* which helped give substance to a community identity conscious of "the Big Lake" and "the North Shore." Hovland called itself "the Lake Trout Capitol," set in the "Tip of the Arrowhead" and "Canoe Country," with its lakes, rivers and streams, and forests rich in natural resources and wildlife, embedded in a much older living history of American Indian neighbors and the French Canadian voyageurs of the vast fur trade era dominated by English, Scottish, and American enterprises.

As a historian working in larger areas of Scandinavian immigration and interethnic life, I have been drawn to the interaction of the Norwegians, Swedes, and Swedish-speaking Finns in the Hovland communities and have written about this in the book *Norwegians and Swedes in the United States: Friends and Neighbors,* coedited with my colleague from Uppsala University, Dag Blanck. During the first decade in the 1890s Hovland came to comprise four settlements, not just Chicago Bay on the shore, where commercial interests and the transportation hub was located, but in clusters of Norwegians and Swedes northeast along Superior in Horseshoe Bay and Big Bay. The fourth was inland to the north and west following the river, an area known as Flutereed Valley settled by fishermen and their families, hewing subsistence farms out of the rocky and timbered soil.

This was my first major insight as I pursued the settlement patterns of these Scandinavians: Hovland was both singular in its community identity and plural in these various pockets of settlement, each with an even more local self-conscious sense of place. The settlers knew and depended on each other socially, vocationally, and in community development, regardless of where they lived. As Hovland grew slowly with the influx of immigrants, an additional four settlements were added in the first decade of the new century, thus making a total of eight. First was a four-mile stretch between the Brule River and Chicago Bay where John Beargrease, an Ojibwe from Beaver Bay, and other early mail carriers ran their dog teams in winter. An ancient Indian trail, known variously in the records as the "Lake Shore Road," the "Dog Trail Road," and the "Hudson's Bay Trail," became home to a half dozen fishermen,

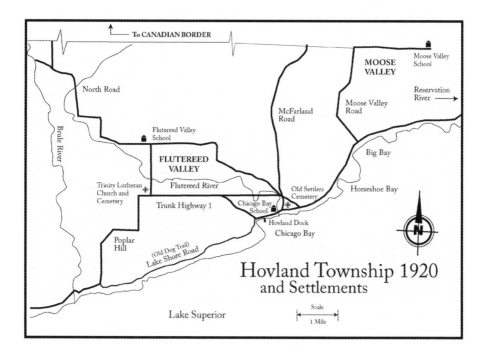

Hovland Township 1920 and Settlements

mostly Norwegian bachelors. This is where my man, Andrew Solgard (now employing his Americanized name), became part of the story in 1915 by homesteading and building his house. The second was Poplar Hill, about four miles north and west of Chicago Bay, settled in 1906 by three Swede Finn families coming from Eveleth on the Iron Range, determined to clear larger tracts for farming. A third was about ten miles due north of the lake on the primitive North Road (on the way to Lost Lake), where two hardy Norwegian families settled in 1907 to farm and trap. The final new settlement was in Moose Valley, about two miles east of Chicago Bay and inland to the north and east for another six miles; an imposing high ridge rising above the valley perhaps added a sense of security and shelter to the two Swedish families that settled there to farm in 1910. Federal census data through 1930 reveals many clues about early Hovland. Enumerators organized their travel and record taking according to the eight settlements, providing information about marriage status, children, age, place of birth and parentage, date

Neighbors gathered at a homestead in Flutereed Valley, c. 1912. Cook County Historical Society

of citizenship, occupation, and whether one knew English. Throughout these years of modest but steady growth, Hovland remained about three-quarters Scandinavian immigrants and their children, with clearly half or more being Norwegian American. Coupled with the patent and warranty deeds in the county courthouse, the pieces of the puzzle of community life begin to come together. Fleshed out further by the *Cook County News-Herald* (where for years the news from Hovland, penned by Newton Bray—teacher, county commissioner, and a Massachusetts native descended from a *Mayflower* family—was the fullest and most interesting), town records, and oral and written reminiscences, the cooperative history of community building can be told.

Elsewhere across America there usually was a long and complex pattern of interethnic tensions, punctuated by times of cooperation, especially true among Norwegians and Swedes. They were uneasy neighbors in most communities (even when intermarrying), but in Hovland the isolation and need for communal life together in often harsh circumstances tells almost unequivocally a story of goodwilled neighborliness. It helped that Scandinavians understood each other's languages, but even more importantly in Hovland the census records reveal that virtually all immigrants knew English. This detail reflects both their relative youth and that Hovland was a secondary and not primary migration for them. Most had lived elsewhere in the United States, at least for a short time.

When Andrew Solgard, a fifty-nine-year-old widower, arrived to claim his homestead and build his small frame house, Hovland had already passed the quarter-century mark in its history. It was a lively and increasingly settled set of pioneer communities forged in the wilderness, complete with commercial and societal networks of relationships and institutional life. In its isolation it was also connected to the wider county and way of life presented by Lake Superior at its front door and the vast forest at its back. But who was Solgard, and what does the old, long-neglected house have to say about him, his times, and the *landskap* that was and is Hovland?

IF THESE WALLS COULD TALK

In Garrison Keillor's Lake Wobegon there is the statue of "The Unknown Norwegian." The vast majority in human history will, of course, descend to such status either immediately or over time. Historians, therefore, are crucial to collective memory and narrative. Anders Haagensen Solgaard most surely would have remained unknown to history had this old house in Hovland not been rescued (like the infant John Wesley, "a brand plucked from the burning") and a search conducted in the county courthouse to prove clear title. A name at the first entry would be the only acknowledgment of an otherwise unknown Norwegian. My first glance at the property abstract introduced me to him and launched the quest to learn just who he was. This pursuit has taken years, and there are admittedly many pieces of the puzzle yet to find and fit.

Homesteaded in 1915, the property was recorded "United States to Andrew H. Solgard" on December 10, 1920, and filed on May 16, 1921. Sadly, Andrew had passed away in another Cook County (Illinois) during the interval, on March 12, 1921. This much I knew from courthouse records, but what about the rest? I began by looking for obituaries in newspapers that might provide personal information. Microfilms of the Grand Marais newspaper, major Chicago dailies, and the Norwegian-language press yielded nothing. Next was a search for his death certificate, and since I lived in Chicago I thought this would be easy. Then I learned that the death record could not be released unless one was a descendent of the deceased. I pleaded that there were no known next of kin and as a historian I needed the record for my research. Request granted. The attending doctor had filled out the certificate, noting that Andrew had provided what little information he had. Date of birth was only noted as 1856; place of birth was only Norway and parents' names unknown; occupation was listed as "Laborer"; he had immigrated ten years earlier and had been in Chicago for only eight days, though a residence was given at 4044 Addison; he died at age sixty-four in the Oak Forest Infirmary (the county poorhouse) of breast cancer, having been attended by his physician, Jacob Mincke, for seven of those days; Andrew was buried three days later in Mount Olive Cemetery.

I found no record of burial at Mount Olive, a largely Scandinavian cemetery on the northwest side of Chicago, so I tried next Mount Olivet, a Catholic cemetery much nearer to the infirmary where he died. No luck there either. I had nearly given up but made one last search at Mount Olive, where I finally found the file card of "Andrew Salgaard" and his burial location—without monument or headstone, only a small round plug in the ground with the number 662. My young daughter cut some roses in our backyard, and we paid our respects. How ironic that after all that searching, Andrew was buried just ten minutes from our home. This was twenty years ago, and Andrew was no longer anonymous or lost.

Solgard had been gone for sixty-five years before I began my research pursuit. Could it be that someone in Hovland might still remember him? After he died intestate, his daughter Jacobine Peterson sold his homestead, the only asset, in August 1924 to two Norwegian brothers, Nels and Jacob Norman, and their half brother, Edwin (listed as "Oven" in the record) Nilson for $850. In his nineties, Nels was still fishing from his place in Big Bay, where he had moved in 1927. I learned from newspapers and cemetery records that he and his wife Gudrun had lost their first two babies, one at seven months and the other stillborn, in the old house in 1925. In his heavily accented English he remembered Andrew fondly and said that he was always singing. Only one other person had a memory of Andrew. Alma Erickson, whose Norwegian family had settled on Poplar Hill, married John Eliasen at age sixteen and homesteaded in 1914 just east of Solgard's in a log cabin, which they sold in 1922 to the nationally famous Swedish vaudeville performer Olle i Skratthult ("Olle from Laughterville"—Hjalmar Peterson being his real name). In and out of memory during her final days in the local nursing home, in a clear moment she recalled her marriage more than seventy-five years before and visiting Andrew often with her infant children. She was so impressed with his fine new frame house and his gentle kind spirit. Moreover, he taught her to bake rye bread, and she recited the recipe. She died soon after. Mere snippets, to be sure, these may well be the last memories to be gleaned after all those years of silence.

More than two decades passed before Andrew's early history began to surface, thanks to the generous help of a friend, Ron Johnson, who is an expert genealogist, and the Norwegian Vesterheim Genealogical Center in Madison, Wisconsin. Here especially the value and accessibility of Internet resources, as well as microfilm records, were most apparent. Andrew was born on September 13, 1856, in Langesund, a port town in southern Telemark on the coast of the North Sea. His parents were Jacob, a sea captain, and Sophie (his middle name Haagensen was her birth name), both in their mid-forties when he was born. A brother, Jamin, was twelve years older, and his sister Jacobine was ahead of him by seven years. The Bramble parish records show him baptized and confirmed. I have visited Langesund once, and it is indeed beautiful. More research in these Norwegian parish and official records may reveal when Andrew emigrated and why. Was it in 1880 as he reported in Hovland to the enumerator for the 1920 US Census, or in 1910 or 1911 as he told Dr. Mincke in Chicago as he lay dying? Shipping registers and exit documents remain elusive thus far. In America he is a widower. Who and when did he marry, how many children did they have, and when and where did his wife pass away? Had he married more than once? Did he emigrate, return, and re-emigrate to America? If so, how many times?

A hint of doubt persisted as to whether this was my Andrew. There was, for example, according to the 1910 federal census an Andrew Solgard—not a common name—living in DeKalb County, Indiana, with his four-year-old daughter Minnie, listed as a railroad worker having immigrated in 1897. But there is an asterisk next to the word "daughter," whose mother is reported to have been born in Norway but her father in the United States, while Andrew is listed as born in Norway. What was this Andrew's relationship to Minnie: perhaps her grandfather? Then who were her parents? A connection seems improbable but perhaps not impossible. Many immigrants returned home only to come back to America. Could this be a third date of immigration of the same Andrew Solgard? And to complicate matters further, there is an Andrew H. Solgard who has a probate court record in Cleveland, Ohio, in 1888 and became a naturalized citizen in Chicago in 1895, as well as an Anden H. Solgard (born in "about 1859") who married Carrie Anderson in Chicago on June 27, 1891.

Andrew's daughter Jacobine (named after his older sister) was born July 18, 1886, in Norway, and she came to Chicago in 1910, about the same time as her father reported his own arrival; an older sister joined her in 1911. She married a Swede, Nestor Peterson, a bread baker who had immigrated in 1908, with whom she had two daughters. Vivian, the oldest, was two when her grandfather, gravely ill, came to Chicago; perhaps she saw him during those eight days before he died. The 1920 US Census states that Jacobine's older sister by two years, also born in Norway, was living with the Petersons. Wilhelmina Bergstrom is listed as single. It remains to be seen how she acquired her surname.

Could she have been widowed or divorced? When gutting the interior lathed walls of the old homestead I discovered a small slat of a shipping crate with a handwritten address on paper tacked to the wood. It reads: "Miss W. Bergstrom c/o Andrew Solgord Chicago Bay Minn <u>via Duluth</u>." Wilhelmina no doubt had been paying her father a visit in Hovland. No longer an unknown Norwegian, Andrew Solgard remains for now something of a mystery man.

The old house, however, had more to reveal about Solgard and its own origins, like a book being opened to reveal its contents—except instead of bookworms, I battled carpenter ants and flushed bats out of the eaves; instead of foxed edges and mold, I replaced rotted wood and removed small animal skeletons from the walls. First of all, the landscape looked very different when Andrew put down roots in 1915. Five years earlier, a devastating forest fire had burned hot and hard to the shore. A lush forest still shows healing rejuvenation from the fire: jack pine, birch, and aspen giving way to spruce and balsam, and abundant blueberries where in patches immense heat scoured the thin soil right down to the rock. In front of the house an ancient yellow birch and a huge white spruce (more than 175 years old) stand as survivors. With rugged and hilly ledge rock on either side, Solgard picked a flat area for his foundation and a short stretch of bouldered beach for his rock-cribbed dock, boat slide, and net house. The unprotected lakeshore must have been a difficult place from which to fish; Nels Norman said that the dock needed to be rebuilt yearly because of powerful storms and winter ice. He also told me that to build the house, Andrew received help (probably paid) from his Swede Finn neighbor Andrew Westerlund, whose own Poplar Hill farmhouse from about 1908 still stands as a testimony to his carpentry skill. They constructed a 16-by-24-foot balloon-framed two-story house with a concrete chimney up the middle for cooking and heat. I found two references in the *Cook County News-Herald*. An entry in Bray's "East End News" for September 16, 1915, reads, "Andrew Solgard has filed on a homestead near Thorson's harbor and is now engaged in building on same." The two Andrews worked fast: by October 28 "Andrew Solgard has moved into his new frame house, recently built on his lakeshore homestead west of 'Agate Beach.'" All these old place names, tied to homesteaders and helpful for lake navigation up and down the shore, are now long forgotten and no longer needed.

Andrew Solgard's homestead as it would have appeared about 1917. Oil painting by Howard Sivertson, 2001.

Andrew's house was indeed a fine one when compared to the many simple log structures and tarpaper shacks of the time. It obviously came as pre-sawn lumber (a true rough cut 2-by-6, for example), flooring, windows, door, and roofing; it would have been brought up by steamer (possibly the *America*), either from Grand Marais and the new Hedstrom lumber mill on Maple Hill or from one of the large lumber companies in Duluth. Dismantling the floor, for example, revealed the occasional "Andrew Solgard, Hovland, Minn." written in blue, signifying bundles unloaded at the Hovland dock, two miles east. Another telltale sign was where the two Andrews ran out of sawn rafters. Uncovered in the southwest corner were hand-hewn poplar poles spliced in, retained but once again hidden in my restoration. Set on a loose stone foundation with impervious tamarack log rim joists (probably hauled in from a few miles away in Big Bay), the house, however neglected, still stood mostly square and true, the exception being that its west end is two inches narrower than its east end—someone had taken a bad measurement, probably with the old cloth tape measure I found sixty years later under the floor on the ground.

The downstairs was open for living, cooking, and eating, and the second floor had two bedrooms, spacious for a Norwegian fisherman living alone. He may have wanted room for visitors, especially his daughters and family. The interior had a fine maple floor, and according to practice and economies of the setting, the stud walls were covered with lathe strips nailed butt to butt, with no thought of plastering. This tedious hammering must have occupied a lot of Andrew's spare time that first winter. He wallpapered it with a colorful floral design. The small house was well lit with six high windows but none on the north side, protection from frigid temperatures and howling winter storms. Whatever his background, Andrew brought with him the means to build a good, solid house.

Inside the walls I discovered Andrew's personal items. Curiously, there was a brass foghorn, shaped like a small megaphone for blowing and carried in the herring skiff to ward off other boats. For insulation he had shoved in remnants of wool pants, shirts, and socks; Norwegian- and English-language newspapers (Andrew subscribed to the *Farmers' Dispatch* in St. Paul and *The Eagle Magazine*, published by the Fraternal Order of Eagles), catalogs, food packages, magazines (some of fashion and domestic advertisements—perhaps signs of Wilhelmina or Jacobine visiting), and many feet of precious gill net, worn past its usefulness. Advertisements included "Tubbs Bilious Man's Friend Removing Sick Headache," with a photograph of the "Chandtedah-Kinnickinnic Campfire Girls, River Falls, Wis. 1915," and stamped with retail information for Ellingsen's store in Chicago Bay. Also in the walls, and out in a small pole-framed storage building (where I subsequently located the original outhouse perch), I found numerous cloth Union Leader tobacco pouches, drawstrings and tax stamps intact. Andrew smoked or chewed or both. Outside we are still discovering a wide assortment of net floats and buried glass bottles, like People's Root Beer from Duluth. Whether Andrew imbibed or was a teetotaler will remain a mystery, though some bottle shapes raise suspicions.

In my research on Hovland, moreover, I have gained a picture of Andrew's neighbors and social life, particularly along the Old Shore Road. There was much more lake traffic in those days of package steamers, gas boats, and herring skiffs. Walking was a common mode of transportation, as many trudged the eighteen miles to Grand Marais or the lesser distances between Hovland's eight settlements. This stretch had the old, well-traveled dog trail, and it ran only 250 feet or so behind Andrew's house. There was much contact with neighbors—homesteaders and seasonal families—and sources reveal late-night campfires and storytelling, food and spirits, and always music, even string quartets on the rocks where the well-known Minneapolis classical musician Henry Woodruff had his tent camp for family and friends. There were many children and young people; at least one youthful courtship and marriage blossomed between a local fisherman and an artist's daughter from Chicago. Despite any sadness in his life or separation from loved ones and homeland, in the midst of Lake Superior's wilderness Andrew was probably not lonely, surrounded by a pioneer community of friends and neighbors, some of whom probably looked in on him as his final illness progressed.

ACCENTED VOICES

This essay has been framed by the research bookends of a historian, focusing first on the voices of Puritans who spoke English with an old-world accent and then on immigrants with a new-world broken lilt. Can I hear Andrew Solgard's voice after all these years of looking for evidences of his life while renovating and living in his old homestead? Despite the absence of any correspondence or memoirs, a photograph or physical description, a personal conversation or contact with any descendants, I believe I do have a certain sense of it. And it is different I admit from the dozens of Puritans I pursued at the beginning of my work as a historian—and with them there was hardly a shortage of words! There I had initially sought to be the unbiased, objective researcher and interpreter of theory and practice espoused and lived by individuals and their respective communities in tumultuous times. I was learning the lesson that historians always bring a point of view and use their imagination in structuring narratives based on available sources. With these seventeenth-century Puritans I had little affinity of place and heritage or personal investment in the issues that so painfully, even violently, divided them. In terms of their theories of church government, power, and authority, it was a theological and intellectual matter for me; in terms of their practices it was an interest in the application of theory and the phenomenology of lived experience. I have been intensely drawn to Puritans as people who were strikingly diverse, defying older general stereotypes, and who put into communal practice their deeply held convictions.

I believe I would have liked Andrew; concerning many of my Puritan subjects, I am not so sure. With the community of Hovland and its 125-year history, I cannot presume to be the detached observer. I may be a small actor in the recent three decades of Hovland's history simply by having been present, but as a historian and ethnographer one becomes in a different way a prime actor in organizing facts into discernible patterns of settlement and life. One becomes sensitive to how the past is interpreted, how the stories are discovered, teased out, and told, imagining a past that is not one's own and seeking to hear the voices for the sake of authenticity.

The historian must also reckon with other questions from Salman Rushdie's memoir, *Joseph Anton:* "Who shall have control over the story? Who has, who should have, the power not only to tell the stories with which, and within which, we all live, but also to say in what manner those stories may be told?" His story, in the face of a fatwa, was quite different in personal magnitude and consequence, but the essential questions still hold true. The world of the Internet and its mostly free access to digitized information is here and part of the work of all historians to their mutual benefit. They will have to work in new ways with archivists and librarians on the cutting edge of innovative information science and delivery systems. It is not an either/or but a both/and, and it is tragic that anyone should be led to believe that digital resources are sufficient in and of themselves for capturing history. The human dimension, the voices, would be lost because the interactive subjectivity is absent, in addition to all the great stories and unexpected finds and rich experiences—the frustration and the enjoyment—gained in no other way. One could never claim a comprehensive approach to research that is strictly of the digital variety.

Despite the amazing resources and potential of the World Wide Web, valuable to the curious researcher, Neil Postman nevertheless feared that culturally we have "transformed information into a form of garbage." Long before the Internet and its glut of unfiltered content, raw material for better or worse, T. S. Eliot wondered in his opening stanza to *The Rock* (1934): "Where is the life we have lost in living? Where is the wisdom we have lost in knowledge? Where is the knowledge we have lost in information?" In this information age, and indeed in any time, the journey to knowledge and wisdom remains fundamentally human and a necessary pursuit. Whether quoting Shakespeare or Sherlock Holmes, "The game is afoot!" and it is an adventure.

PHILIP J. ANDERSON is professor emeritus of church history at North Park University in Chicago, where he has taught since 1979. Since 1989 he has served as president of the Swedish-American Historical Society, also chairing its publications committee. His published writings have included studies in British, American, and Swedish American religious history and culture. He lives with his wife, Karna, in Hovland and Marine on St. Croix, Minnesota.

Ned Stuckey-French

An Essayist's Guide to Research and Family Life

*W*hen you have two writers in the house, research becomes a family project, a way of life. It seeps into everything the family does—the whole family. Family vacations, dinner parties, birthdays are all bound up with our research. My wife and I give each other old books for Christmas. In the summers we have taken our kids to see Elvis tribute artists and the childhood homes of our favorite writers. Research is what we do even if sometimes we don't recognize it as research (though the IRS guidelines for tax deductions help remind us that it needs to be identified and labeled as such). Even our friends— most of whom are writers too—are pulled into this vortex of research. They throw us book parties featuring our obsessions: mermaids, Memphis, rockabilly, and Montaigne. They give me collections of essays and a history of Greenwich Village for my birthday. Our friend Bob Butler, who knows and shares our Elvis obsession, gave us an authenticated lock of Elvis's hair and a portrait of the King made from candy wrappers. At our house it's all research all the time.

Elizabeth is a fiction writer; I write personal essays and cultural criticism. She publishes with New York trade houses; I publish with university presses; we both collaborate with our friend Janet Burroway on a writing textbook published by Pearson. We both teach in the Department of English at Florida State University. Every day we write and talk about writing. Every day we do some kind of research.

We are also both the children of writers. Elizabeth's father published poetry, short stories, and literary criticism; her mother wrote plays and children's books. My dad was an agricultural economist and academic who also wrote for popular magazines. Elizabeth's parents even gave her the middle name of Caroline, after Caroline Gordon, a friend of the family and the subject of a biography Elizabeth's dad published in 1972. Now we have two teenage daughters of our own—Flannery and Phoebe. Can you hear the literary allusions in their names?

Soon after Phoebe was born and about the time Flannery turned three, Elizabeth and I landed our first full-time university teaching jobs. The academic life, especially because we teach at a research university, means we are expected to write books, stories, essays, and articles. It also means we have a lot of freedom to pick our projects and we get to work at home a lot. This is mostly to the good, of course. We have generous vacations, and there's no need to use a sick day if one of the girls gets sick. It's easy to schedule parent-teacher conferences or doctor's appointments. It's a good gig. If there is a downside it has to do mainly with finding the time, the quiet, and the space within one's own home to do one's work. Research and writing don't always look like work, and sometimes we have to remind ourselves and our daughters that what we do is real work and should be treated as such even if we don't head to the office each morning like other parents do. At our house there is a lot of "I can't help you with that right now. I've got to finish this book review. You'll have to talk to your mother." Our house is small, and the only real study we have is a converted garage in the basement, which we use sparingly. As a consequence, the wall we must build to establish our working space is largely virtual. Elizabeth and I have to both pitch in to keep this wall from crumbling.

Take, for example, the fall of 2001. About the middle of August, Elizabeth's editor at Doubleday told her she had put Elizabeth's as-yet-largely-unwritten first novel in the spring catalog, which meant Elizabeth would need to deliver the manuscript by the end of December. When al Qaeda started crashing planes into buildings, our house had already been in panic mode for a couple of weeks. The girls were three and six at the time. I took them to the park a lot. I took them grocery shopping a lot. I took them to the library a lot. But sooner or later the three of us had to come home where Mom was trying to write. I remember fixing dinner, breaking up sibling spats, and watching the news about anthrax scares and sleeper cells while Elizabeth, exhibiting unbelievable powers of concentration, banged away in the next room. She made her deadline.

The novel she wrote is called *Mermaids on the Moon,* and it's set at Weeki Wachee, a postwar tourist attraction created by a former navy frogman just north of Tampa. Elizabeth had visited Weeki Wachee with her friend Lu Vickers, who was researching an article on this clearwater spring where young girls have been dressing up as mermaids and performing before an underwater amphitheater since 1947. Lu's article was to be a paean to the old Florida and the wonderful kitschy attractions that seem doomed by Disney World and the centralization and corporatization of tourism in the Orlando area. In 1997 Weeki Wachee celebrated its fiftieth anniversary, and several of the mermaids who had performed there as teenagers in the 1950s and '60s came back for the celebration. Some of them found they really missed the place and wanted to put their tails back on and perform again. A few still lived in the area, others subsequently retired to Florida, and before long the Mermaids of Yesteryear, or Merhags as they called themselves, were doing a regular Friday-night show. Elizabeth got to know them, and soon we were driving the three and a half hours from Tallahassee to Weeki Wachee whenever we could. It was, I realize now, our girls' introduction to research and writing.

My writing also took us at one point on a Georgia presidents' tour. We saw Jimmy Carter teach Sunday school in Plains and then traveled north to Warm Springs, the location of Roosevelt's Little White House, where he went for polio treatments and died of a cerebral hemorrhage while having his portrait painted. And lo and behold, the trip seemed to strike a chord with both girls. Flannery did a poster project on Carter, Sadat, and Begin at Camp David. Phoebe and a friend worked FDR into a History Fair skit about Jonas Salk and the polio vaccine. They even used Phoebe's vial of water from Warm Springs as a prop.

Elizabeth and I have also found that every year we each have to have some sustained stretches of uninterrupted, out-of-the-house writing time. Occasionally, again when book deadlines demanded it of us, we've given over parts of our winter or spring breaks to our writing, but our regular plan is to each take a week or two during the summer at a writer's retreat, most often the Lillian E. Smith Center for Creative Arts near Clayton, Georgia, but also at the cabins of generous friends. This has worked out well for both of us. A week or two of single parenting is not too bad, certainly nothing like doing it full time. You end up having conversations with your daughters you might not have otherwise. You treat yourself and the girls to some meals out, even if it's just to Whataburger, figuring the three of you deserve it since Mom or Dad is up at the cabin "writing." (Elizabeth may have a different take on this, as it seems the tropical storms always hit Tallahassee and the basement floods while I'm in Clayton.)

Sometimes we take working vacations and the girls get dragged along. Elizabeth and I occasionally teach at the Iowa Summer Writing Festival, for instance. One of us does two weekend workshops sandwiched around the other one's weeklong workshop. The girls get to hang out with us, see where they lived when they were little, and visit old friends. One year, however, Phoebe got an infection in her hip and spent a couple of nights in the hospital, and then Elizabeth and her publicist got their wires crossed and Elizabeth had to fly to San Francisco and back in the middle of the week to do a reading, and the house the University of Iowa found for us to stay in had no air-conditioning and there was a heat wave and it was ninety-five degrees all week, but other than that we had a good time.

So why force this writing life on your innocent children? Why require them to traipse around the scuzzy ruins of an Indiana health spa that is the setting of a story? Why abandon your wife and kids for a couple of weeks to spend beautiful summer afternoons in Harvard's Houghton Library reading the letters between Alexander Woollcott and Harpo Marx? Why take the whole family to the Big E Festival in Cornelia, Georgia, with lawn chairs and T-shirts and "tribute artist" contest, to the home place in Tupelo, and finally to Memphis—a dozen times or more to Memphis—to see Graceland, the house on Audubon Drive, Sun Studio, Dixie Locke's house, the band shell at Overton Park, and the Presley family apartment in Lauderdale Courts? Why do all this seemingly silly research?

Well, because you're a writer, that's why, and writers have their reasons for doing research. Nine of them by my count:

I. GETTING IT RIGHT

Fact checking alone is reason enough to do research. One misstep and you can lose your reader. And this is true whether you're writing fiction or nonfiction.

The great fiction writer Tobias Wolff has also written two wonderful memoirs—*This Boy's Life* and *In Pharaoh's Army*. In a *Paris Review* interview, he talked about accuracy, honesty, and the different allegiance to reality the two kinds of writing have. He wrote his memoirs, he said,

> with the knowledge that they'd be read by people who lived through those times with me. I couldn't write down things that were simply untrue, that I knew were untrue, because I stood to be ferociously

corrected—and embarrassed—by people who knew better. Now that doesn't mean there weren't differences of interpretation—I'm sure, for example, that my then-fiancée would have a very different take on what happened: He had it coming, he was a selfish brute, I needed to get his attention. She would, I'm sure, have an explanation for why she destroyed my car that night, but she wouldn't dispute that she did it. So, too, with the other book. My mother was very much alive when I wrote *This Boy's Life*, and my brother, and other people who saw those times with me. So I was answerable. It's different from writing fiction.

Which is not to say that fiction doesn't also benefit from and even require fact checking as well. When Elizabeth placed a story in the *Atlantic* the first time, she encountered a different level of copyediting there than she had in the little magazines where she'd published previously. I remember the copyeditor from the *Atlantic* calling with two questions: Was there really a circular public swimming pool in Ottumwa, Iowa? And were there tan Volvos in 1972? To the first, Elizabeth said, "I don't know, but I doubt it. I've never been to Ottumwa. I was thinking of my hometown in Indiana." The copyeditor said they would get a lot of mail from people in Iowa. Soon they'd hammered out a solution. Invent an imaginary town in Iowa (Elizabeth called it Magruder) and put the circular pool there. To resolve the second question, the magazine's intern did some research and found out Volvo didn't make tan cars in 1972, so Aunt Merry's car turned gray.

As Wolff says, differences of interpretation are one thing (e.g., the difference between how he and his then fiancée see her destruction of his car), but even with the seemingly objective there are shades of gray. Or perhaps it would be more accurate to say that some such issues are more important than others. Most readers, for instance, would read right past the Ottumwa swimming pool and the tan Volvo, but a writer's concern—no matter whether he or she is writing fiction or nonfiction—must be with those few who won't, those residents of Ottumwa and those Volvo aficionados. For them and for yourself, you have to get it right.

2. ADDING DETAIL AND SPECIFICITY

Not unrelated to getting it right is making it better, and specificity makes it better. There is, after all, a difference between "a beer" and "a Pabst Blue Ribbon," just as there is a difference between a PBR and a Sam Adams.

Picking the right beer is easy for those of us who drink beer, but what if your characters want to drink champagne? Anne Lamott in her wonderful book on writing, *Bird by Bird: Some Instructions on Writing and Life*, tells the following story:

> . . . when I was writing my second novel, I got to the part where the man comes over for his first date with the woman and brings with him a bottle of champagne. He removes the foil. We get to see his hands, which are beautiful, long and broad with white moons on his big square fingernails, so lovely that they almost make up for the fact that he is wearing a yellow polyester shirt. Also, it is in his favor that he has brought along a nice bottle of champagne; the woman loves to drink. So the man has peeled the foil away, and then he begins to remove that wire thing that covers the champagne cork.
>
> Now, I've always thought of that wire thing—that little helmet—as the wire thing, and that is how everyone I've ever known refers to it: "Honey, will you take the wire thing off the champagne? I just had my nails done." "Oh, look, Skippy's playing with that little wire thing; I hope she doesn't cut her little lips on it . . ."
>
> But it must have a name, right? I mean, boxes of them don't just arrive at wineries—five-hundred-count Wire Things. They have to have a label. So I called the Christian Brothers Winery, whose vineyard is near the Russian River. I got a busy signal. I really did.

Eventually Lamott gets through to the receptionist, who puts her in touch with an older gentleman in back, who, as Lamott tells us, "was so glad I'd called. He actually said so, and he sounded like he was." She explains her predicament, how she doesn't know what "the wire thing" is called, and he says, "Ah . . . that would be the wire hood."

And now we know.

3. TIME TRAVEL

My good friend and collaborator Janet Burroway says this about research in her book *Imaginative Writing: The Elements of Craft*:

> I once had the luck, just as I was starting on a novel set in Mexico and Arizona in 1914, to hear a lecture by the great novelist Mary Lee Settle. She offered three rules for historical fiction research:
>
> • Don't read about the period; read in the period. Read letters, journals, newspapers, magazines, books written at the time. You will in this way learn the cadences, the turn of mind and phrase, the obsessions and quirks of the period.

- Don't take notes. If you save everything that interests you, you'll be tempted to use it whether it fits or not, and your fiction will smell of research. Immerse yourself and trust that what you need will be there.
- Don't research beyond the period you're writing about. If you know too much about the future, your characters will inevitably know it too.

Now, these rules are particular to historical fiction, but I think the spirit of them is applicable to any sort of imaginative research.

I'm not sure I agree with every element of this—I'm an inveterate notetaker—but basically, I think this is the right approach for historical research. I also agree with Janet's suggestion that this kind of immersion works not just for historical novels but also for other kinds of imaginative writing. Take personal essays for example. Joan Didion says that one reason to write personal essays is

> to keep on nodding terms with the people we used to be, whether we find them attractive company or not. Otherwise they turn up unannounced and surprise us, come hammering on the mind's door at 4 A.M. of a bad night and demand to know who deserted them, who betrayed them, who is going to make amends. We forget all too soon the things we thought we could never forget.

What if the former self you must summon up is your fourth-grade self? Fourth grade may not seem that long ago, but trust me, in my case, it is. What candy did I favor then and why? Was it Pez or Milk Duds? Slo Pokes or Atomic Fireballs? Was fourth grade the year you began playing Wiffle ball till the streetlights came on? The year you carried a squirt gun to school, listened to the Lone Ranger on the radio, and began longing for the day when you could be on safety patrol? It may not seem as ancient and exotic as the Mexico and Arizona of 1914 to which Janet traveled, but in its own way it is. Retrieving the deep images of that time will require some research. You'll need to leaf through some old *Highlights* magazines, reread a few volumes of Ramona and Beezus, and watch some episodes of *Captain Kangaroo* (which, thank God, are archived on YouTube).

4. ENLARGING YOUR SUBJECT

When writing essays, I think it's best to start with yourself—your memories, concerns, stories, obsessions, all the images and snippets of dialogue that haunt you even if you aren't sure why they haunt you. I've begun essays by free-writing about that afternoon my parents told me they were going to get divorced, or the moment when I heard my dad cuss for the first time, or the night we were driving back from Minnesota and the fan belt broke in the early morning darkness of the South Side of Chicago. I write down the scene, usually in the present tense the first time because I find it gives me more ready access to the past. Then, I let the pages sit for a while until I can listen to them with new ears and begin to figure out what the piece is about—*really* about.

It is only at that point that I think it's okay to plunge into some reading and generalizing and thinking about what others might have said about the issue that seems to lie at the core of my essay. Only then do I feel ready to do a new kind of research about my Subject. Only then am I ready to read what Betty Friedan says about marriage in the fifties, what linguists say about swearing, what Isabel Wilkerson says about Chicago and the Great Migration.

Aldous Huxley sets up a nice system for thinking about essays in the preface to his *Collected Essays* that speaks to the relationship between memory and research, the personal and the universal:

> Essays belong to a literary species whose extreme variability can be studied most effectively within a three-poled frame of reference. There is the pole of the personal and the autobiographical; there is the pole of the objective, the factual, the concrete-particular; and there is the pole of the abstract-universal. Most essayists are at home and at their best in the neighborhood of only one of the essay's three poles, or at the most only in the neighborhood of two of them.

Here, however, is the hitch. Just as Huxley tells us that most of us are good at only one or maybe two of these modes of writing, he then lets us know that the real goal is to become accomplished at all three:

> The most richly satisfying essays are those which make the best not of one, not of two, but of all the three worlds in which it is possible for the essay to exist. Freely, effortlessly, thought and feeling move in these consummate works of art, hither and thither between the essay's three poles—from the personal to the universal, from the abstract back to the concrete, from the objective datum to the inner experience.

Paradoxically, an essay is most universal when it is most individual. Readers can see themselves in your work when you are giving yourself to them with the fullest honesty, particularity, and specificity possible. This is because what you're trying to do is lift your essay above your own life while never leaving that life behind. But lift it you must, for while we love you, we really don't want to hear you drone on about yourself unless there's a payoff and the piece has something to tell us. After all, we're as egotistical as you.

If all I'm telling you are anecdotes, then I'm probably stuck at the level of bar stories and not moving deeply into myself and out into something larger, something universal. Montaigne is good on this phenomenon: "Each man bears the entire form of the human condition."

5. SERENDIPITY

Another great thing about research is that it can surprise you. You never know where you'll end up. One thing leads to another and then that thing leads to yet another, and pretty soon you're someplace you didn't plan to go but are meant to be.

I think this is especially true for the essay, a form that has always been digressive. For the last twenty-two years of his life, Montaigne worked continuously on his *Essais,* which were published originally in three editions (1580, 1588, 1595). He revised constantly and yet never took anything out. He only added, and he didn't just add new essays: he also added a word or a sentence here or there, or dropped a new passage, sometimes several pages long, into an existing essay. He did this even if the new bit seemed to contradict what he'd written earlier. As he put it (long before Whitman bragged about contradicting himself), "I cannot keep my subject still. It goes along befuddled and staggering, with a natural drunkenness. I take it in this condition, just as it is at the moment I give my attention to it. I do not portray being: I portray passing."

You know the experience. You're in the stacks looking for a book, but along the way your eyes fall on another title that looks interesting, and then another. Eventually, you circle back to the one you were looking for in the first place—the note card in your hand with that book's call number on it reminds you why you're there—and you find it and check it out. But you'll also end up checking out some of those other books—wonderful, intriguing, beautiful books that will take you into some new direction, books that you weren't looking for but that seem to have been looking for you.

Of course, it's not just serendipity. As a friend of mine once said, his tongue firmly in his cheek, "Yeah, that Jack Nicklaus—luckiest golfer I've ever seen." Probably it's a little bit of both: skill and luck, preparation and opportunity. Probably it's a little bit like love. You've got to be alert, keep your eyes open, and be ready for that wonderful book to find you, though once it does, make sure to take it out for coffee so you can really get to know each other.

Serendipity doesn't happen only in libraries (though I think it happens in libraries more often than on the Internet, where the frenzy of the search seems to induce ADHD and we're required to put ourselves at the mercy of what Google hands us and narrow our search to this or that keyword, our eyes glued to a single screen). Serendipity also happens when you're out in the world doing fieldwork. Remember Anne Lamott and the wire hood on the champagne bottle? Well, there's more to that story. While she was on hold, waiting for the receptionist at the Christian Brothers Winery, she says she "sat there staring off into space." But she didn't just sit:

> I watched the movie in my mind of the many times I'd passed those vineyards and remembered how, especially in the early fall, a vineyard is about as voluptuous a place as you can find on earth: the sense of lushness and abundance; the fullness of the clumps of grapes that hang, mammarian, and give off an ancient autumnal smell, semiprotected from the sun by their leaves. The grapes are so incredibly beautiful that you can't help but be thrilled. If you aren't—if you only see someone's profit or that in another month there will be rotten fruit all over the ground—someone has gotten inside your brain and really fucked you up. And you need to get well so you can see again, see that the grapes almost seem to glow, with a light dusting of some sort of powdery residue, like an incredibly light snowfall, almost as if they're covered with their own confectioners' sugar.
>
> I wrote all this down and then called the winery again.

Serendipity? Sure, if she had got right through the first time she might not have daydreamed about the fields and the grapes, but she also made smart, efficient use of her time on hold and created some damn fine writing.

6. ADULT EDUCATION

One reason I like to read essays is that I learn something new by reading them. One reason I like to write essays is that I learn something new by writing them.

Reading and writing exist in a kind of dialectical relationship, a Möbius strip of influence. When you read an essay you learn a little about this or that, and soon you're at the library looking to learn more, then you bring that knowledge back to a rereading of the essay and the essay is the richer for it, revealing itself to you in new ways, and so on and so on. It's akin to that phenomenon we've all experienced when we look up a new word and then see it three times in print during the next week.

There's an excitement to such discovery. It's like the excitement you felt back in school when your teacher read *Tom Sawyer* aloud during afternoon rest time and you actually began to hear Tom and Huck talking, or when the cocoon your second-grade class had kept all winter finally opened and a monarch came out, or when your small group presented its project on the Dred Scott decision and as you finished the class burst into applause. The only difference is now you are a grown-up and you are your own teacher.

Essayists are teachers too. I think the genre is especially geared to introduce us to knowledge (which is not to say that essays don't do lots of other things as well). An essay, according to Scott Russell Sanders, "is an amateur's raid in a world of specialists. Feeling overwhelmed by data, random information, and the flotsam and jetsam of mass culture, we relish the spectacle of a single consciousness making sense of a portion of the chaos." I agree, though I don't think either Sanders or I mean to suggest that creative nonfiction is the only genre that teaches us something, but I do think nonfiction is often more explicitly about the imparting of information and so has a special relationship to research. When we read essays we often hope to learn something. We're likely, for instance, to pick up an essay on mountain lions (I'm thinking here of Edward Hoagland's great "Hailing the Elusory Mountain Lion") at least in part because we think it might tell us something new about mountain lions; we're much less likely to pick up Willa Cather's *Death Comes to the Archbishop* because we know it's set in the Southwest and might by chance include some mountain lion information.

7. CONNECTING

It's a cliché to say so, but it's true: writing is a lonely business. It consists of long hours of facing a computer screen or scribbling on a legal pad, long hours alone with your imagination, and as a consequence, a writer can become a hermit.

Research, on the other hand, puts you in touch with people. This is less true of research on the Internet, though even there one can find ways to connect. Increasingly, I see writers on Facebook crowdsourcing. They ask the hive to suggest a good book about this or that subject, answer a question that has them stumped, or help them find the right word. But research can also help connect you to the material world. It can get you out of your study and down the street to talk face-to-face with a butcher about meat, a farmer about tractors, a research librarian about a special collection, or a wine master about the "wire thing" on the top of a champagne bottle (I know, I know, Anne Lamott called him on the phone, but you get the point). These conversations don't just yield information; they also introduce you to new people, help you build new relationships, initiate new projects, knit the culture together, and even promote your book.

8. HAVING FUN

This getting out into the world can even be fun. There's no reason research has to be a dry and boring province populated by eggheads and geeks.

Above I said that Elizabeth and I drag our two daughters along with us on our research trips. Actually I don't think we really have to drag them, not usually. I think the girls enjoyed their several visits to Graceland, Sun Studio, Beale Street, and the Civil Rights Museum when Elizabeth was researching her last novel and I was working on an essay about Elvis.

It's even gotten to the point where it's not just the research of the parents that determines our family vacations. The girls make their preferences known too. When we went to New York, we took them to the Algonquin and the Strand and the dinosaur room at the Museum of Natural History, but they also put in their own requests. They wanted to have tea at the Plaza just like Eloise did, and take a hansom cab ride through Central Park to celebrate one of their favorite *Seinfeld* episodes, the one in which Kramer stupidly feeds Beano to the horse.

Later, in our Times Square hotel, they rode the elevator up and down, taking notes as if they were Nancy Drew or Harriet the Spy:

"Young couple in room 714 may be on honeymoon."

"Old man alone in 651 seems sad."

"Family at end of the hall has left for the Empire State Building."

Our family also reads out loud a fair amount together, and on road trips we listen to books on tape. To me such reading and listening is also a kind of research. We've pretty much memorized our favorite Nancy Drew tapes (which, by the way, are read wonderfully by Laura Linney). Just as certain *Seinfeld* episodes have become touchstones for us (as they have for everyone), so have favorite moments from our favorite books. There is, for instance, always a point near the end of a Nancy Drew book when the semi-bad guy who is basically good but who fell in with the wrong crowd comes clean to Nancy and helps her solve the crime. For us, the line "Honest, Miss Drew" marks any kind of repentance or overeager earnestness.

Just as their parents did, our girls are growing up around writers, which I think is a good thing because maybe then they'll be less likely to romanticize writers, mystify the writing process, or see research as an onerous task. Elizabeth's father organized the visiting writers series at Purdue University for several years, and he and her mom hosted many writers. Some of them . . . well, most of them . . . were pretty self-involved and felt they were above the cow town they'd found themselves in (the poet May Swenson was the notable exception). Elizabeth saw lots of writers off duty—drinking, cussing, and wearing out their welcome. She didn't know it at the time but it was research. It gave her some great and wicked lines for a story she wrote years later titled "Famous Poets."

Our own writer friends, of course, are much better behaved than those famous poets and, in any case, shall remain nameless here, but the girls have seen them all off duty and so they don't think being a writer is a big a deal at all. It's just what Mom and Dad and their friends do. Both girls, for instance, are Facebook friends with a friend of ours who has called on them to critique chapters of a young adult book she's writing. And Phoebe and Flannery were once profiled themselves in *The Believer*. They still like to get out that issue and read it aloud from time to time so they can cackle about the antics of their younger selves.

9. BEING ALERT TO LIFE

As you can tell, I define research broadly. For me it includes watching old Elvis movies, going to blues clubs in Memphis till four in the morning, and visiting Willa Cather's house in Red Cloud, Nebraska, as well as putting on cotton gloves to handle old manuscripts in the Beinecke Rare Book Library at Yale.

In fact, I'd go further. As I've already suggested, I think research often occurs when you don't even think you're doing research. When a draft is really cooking I find I'm alert to the world in a way that I'm not otherwise. I don't mean to suggest that writing leads me into some sort of schizophrenic state in which I begin to see correspondences and messages everywhere, writing on the wall as it were. What I mean is that writing makes me feel like maybe, just maybe, I am, at least now and again, the kind of artist Henry James described in "The Art of Fiction"—"one of the people on whom nothing is lost." When I feel like that kind of person, everything is research.

In her essay "On Keeping a Notebook," Joan Didion talks about how she tries to systematize this process, admitting all the while that such systematization is difficult. She opens her essay by sharing with us an entry from one of her notebooks: "'That woman Estelle is partly the reason why George Sharp and I are separated today.' *Dirty crepe-de-Chine wrapper, hotel bar, Wilmington RR, 9:45 A.M. August Monday morning.*" Then Didion goes on to try to make some sense of the entry:

> Since the note is in my notebook, it presumably has some meaning to me. I study it for a long while. At first I have only the most general notion of what I was doing on an August Monday morning in the bar of the hotel across from the Pennsylvania Railroad station in Wilmington, Delaware (waiting for a train? missing one? 1960? 1961? why Wilmington?), but I do remember being there. The woman in the dirty crepe-de-Chine wrapper had come down from her room for a beer, and the bartender had heard before the reason why George Sharp and she were separated today. "Sure," he said, and went on mopping the floor. "You told me." At the other end of the bar is a girl. She is talking, pointedly, not to the man beside her but to a cat lying in the triangle of sunlight cast through the open door. She is wearing a plaid silk dress from Peck & Peck, and the hem is coming down.

The function of the notebook is both to preserve and to prompt. It is a way to hold onto a moment she suspects has meaning even though she has not yet figured out what that meaning might be:

Why did I write it down? In order to remember, of course, but exactly what was it I wanted to remember? How much of it actually happened? Did any of it? Why do I keep a notebook at all? It is easy to deceive oneself on all those scores. The impulse to write things down is a peculiarly compulsive one, inexplicable to those who do not share it, useful only accidentally, only secondarily, in the way that any compulsion tries to justify itself.

Writers are people who notice things even when they aren't exactly sure what they're noticing. They are collectors. Unfortunately, they have to collect much more than they'll ever use because they don't know in advance what will be useful. Maybe *pack rat* is a more precise and honest term than *collector.* There are lots of ways to collect. Elizabeth keeps a journal that is not unlike Didion's notebook; I've got a gazillion folders on my computer.

Right now I'm living on New York's Upper West Side and teaching at Columbia. I'm going to be here only for a few months so I'm trying to make good use of the time, but again I'm not always sure what "good use" might mean. Earlier this week I read a piece by Jonathan Lethem about the Upper West Side. Lethem grew up in Brooklyn, but as a child he often visited his great-grandmother "Omi," a refugee from Germany, who had "landed in a residence hotel on Broadway and Eighty-something, in a small apartment full of lace and Meissen china." As Lethem explains it, "She spoke barely any English and expressed her affection for me by running her fingers through my hair while calling me 'Yonatan'—so, for me, a drive to the Upper West Side might as well have been a voyage to Europe." At the end of the piece he confides that he "still can't cross Broadway on foot, passing those traffic-island benches, little tulip beds stranded in taxi smog, and not be reminded of the Holocaust."

Lethem's essay, especially that closing line, caught my attention because most mornings I run in Riverside Park and to get there I have to cross Broadway. I run past just such a bench. Now and then there seems to be an Omi or two among the people who sit there, but more often the old friends are African American. Last week, as I ran by, one woman shouted to her fellow bench-sitters, "My sugar was 69 this morning! Coulda died, went into a coma!" When I got home, I wrote down that line, not knowing if it would work its way into an essay I've considered writing about being a member of the sandwich generation, those boomers with responsibilities to both their young kids and aging parents, or an essay about my time on the Upper West Side, or an essay about how to use research in writing.

So, research is wonderful. It enriches your writing, brings your family together, and makes you alert to the world you live in. Great! How wonderful!

Well, yeah, but as with anything, it's also got a downside. You can also overdo it, and so I feel compelled to sound a note of caution.

For one thing, research, while necessary to writing, is also easier than writing. Reading, taking notes, searching the stacks, going through family photos, and doing interviews are all easier than facing a blank page or empty screen. Research can become a way of procrastinating.

A related problem is that it's also easy to drop a piece of research indiscriminately into a draft rather than writing your way toward the moment where such a detail is really needed. In other words, you can add too much research. You can end up with too much of a good thing.

How do you avoid doing this? I'm not sure. I'm still working on it, though I do think experience helps. I've tried playing games with myself—working in some other part of the house so that I can't get at my books and my filing cabinets quite so easily, but to be honest that doesn't work too well. If I want to get at my research, I do. Such games sure as hell don't work with the research that I've put on my computer—all those files of notes, all those bookmarked sites, all that stuff Google makes so available. It's all just too easy to get at. I've heard of these applications that block you from the Internet for a set period of time, but they sound gimmicky too. I try instead to exert some self-discipline and just write, remembering that the goal is significant detail, not detail for detail's sake.

Let me close with one more story about me and my kids. Once, when they were with me at the DMV and I was waiting in line, Phoebe, who was then about two, toddled over with a big three-ring binder in which the motor vehicles people had put a waiting-room magazine so no one would walk off with it. She held the notebook up and announced, "Look, Daddy, it's my manuscript." The clerks and the people in line laughed in astonishment, and I had to explain that both her parents are writers.

Who knows, maybe Phoebe will write a manuscript one day. It wouldn't surprise me. But whether she does or not, I think the ironic distance she displayed that day is a good thing. Many of my own students either paralyze themselves thinking they've got to write a masterpiece the first time out of the gate, or alternatively think they can just put on a beret, get multiply pierced and tattooed, and declare they are a writer. Whether you end up being a writer or not, I think it's good to put the whole process in perspective. In the middle of June 1969, when I was nineteen years old, I still hadn't found a job for the summer. My lollygagging was driving my dad crazy. Finally he hired me himself. Every year for maybe a decade he had written the *World Book Yearbook* entry on Agriculture, and he was getting tired of it. "Here is last year's entry," he said. "You can use this data from the USDA and these articles to do an update. I need a draft in two weeks."

As I mentioned, my dad was an academic, one of those GI Bill of Rights intellectuals that America created after World War II. He loved teaching and scholarship, he loved his family, and he felt there was something to learn everywhere. Our summer vacations took us to Old Ironsides, the Smithsonian, and Mark Twain's house in Hannibal. Sometimes, however, the lesson ended up being different than the one that was planned. I vividly remember spending several minutes opening a can of beans with that funny little hook on a Swiss Army knife while sitting on the tailgate of our Plymouth station wagon in the campground at Valley Forge while my mom held an umbrella over me in the pouring rain. I suppose that moment taught me to appreciate about how rough the winter must have been for Washington and the troops, but what I remember most is how patient and careful I had to be with that knife and how on the next camping trip it would probably make sense to bring a real can opener. That time the lesson was not what Dad had intended, but often he came up with some pretty innovative lesson plans himself. He knew well that there was plenty to be learned outside museums, libraries, and national monuments. His own field of agricultural economics, for instance, was for him much more than data and statistics. It was really about food and where it came from and how it was distributed, marketed, and sold. In ice cream parlors, for instance, he liked to meet the owner, blind taste the product, and guess the butterfat content. When we visited my mom's parents in Florida, he always wanted to go to the docks in the evening to see the fishing boats come in and talk to the captains about the day's catch. I remember him talking excitedly about an early-morning trip to the produce market in Rio. He could even get wound up about a grain elevator or a new kind of silo.

So I felt a little pressure writing his *World Book* entry, though actually I was ghostwriting it. He had been contracted to do it. They'd bought his byline, not mine, and that was part of the pressure. But if I didn't get the byline, I did get some money. I don't remember how much now. It wasn't a lot, but it was the first time I'd gotten paid for a piece of writing, and that was a big deal to me. Still is. More than that, my dad had trusted me to write the piece, and then when I did, he took my draft seriously. He liked it, but he gave me some criticism and asked for some changes. It was going out over his name, after all. He wanted it to be good, and I did too. We collaborated, and when it came out, he sent me a copy. I've still got it. Doing the assignment showed me writing was not something to be afraid of and that I could produce something publishable on deadline. It also showed me to not put too much trust in encyclopedias, or at least to recognize that they aren't as exhaustive and authoritative as their publishers want you to think they are. The articles are one person's take, one person's snapshot, but that year the snapshot was mine.

NED STUCKEY-FRENCH teaches at Florida State University and is the author of *The American Essay in the American Century*, coeditor of *Essayists on the Essay: Montaigne to Our Time*, coauthor of *Writing Fiction: A Guide to Narrative Craft*, and book review editor of *Fourth Genre*. His essays have appeared in magazines such as *In These Times, The Normal School, Tri-Quarterly, culturefront, Guernica*, and *middlebrow* and have been listed five times among the notable essays of the year in *Best American Essays*.

YOUR RESEARCH—OR YOUR LIFE!

*et me tell you about a research project that literally saved my life. This would be going back, oh, quite a few decades, when I was fresh out of Columbia University with a useless master's degree in comparative literature, granted in those days by the philosophy department, further guaranteeing its utter irrelevance.

It had not been my intention, let me hasten to say, to face the harsh glare of postgraduate reality with a worthless degree in my hand. Far from it. When I came to New York to take up my studies, I never doubted for a minute that I would be in it for the long haul. I envisioned a swift, brilliant master's degree, followed by a long and grueling (but profoundly rewarding) program of study in the PhD program, from which I expected to emerge with an even more brilliant degree and a lifetime of (need it be said? brilliant) scholarship ahead of me at some prestigious academic haven. Preferably on the East Coast.

Well, that didn't work out, did it? Although I'd sailed through (well, passed) the language requirements, I can still taste the bilious juices of horror and humiliation that filled my mouth when I took up the qualifying exam and realized that I hadn't a prayer of passing it. (What were all those damned dates? I didn't do *dates!*)

Being expelled so summarily from my Edenic dreamworld would probably qualify as a bona fide trauma. (Thinking back, I do have a vague recollection of momentarily blacking out in the bathroom.)

But did I accept the verdict and return home with my insignificant degree to take up a less lofty, but more appropriate career in retail sales? Not a bit of it. I moved into a small apartment house in Spanish Harlem where a jolly crowd of Columbia postgrads and academic castoffs had taken up cheap communal residence. Once installed in my cheerless walk-up apartment on the third floor, I promptly embarked on an ambitious research project that would surely result in a ground-breaking (and needless to say, brilliant) piece of scholarship that would restore me to my proper place in the hierarchy of academe.

The drawback to this plan was that the boisterous community in which I had pitched my tent was not conducive to study—or even, at times, to sleep. The building superintendent was a third-year philosophy student at Columbia who had recruited all his friends as tenants, so all it took to initiate a house party was for someone to throw open their apartment door and put on some music. But while my housemates may have resembled those giddy young friends you see on television sitcoms, they were nowhere near as vapid.

I remember two battle-weary social workers who were doing their thesis work on street gangs and often thrilled me by bringing their dangerous work home with them. Another tenant, who told everyone she was descended from one of those fifteenth-century Florentine banking families, also attracted interesting people to the house, but she never shared them with the rest of us. And then there was the mysterious long-legged beauty who lived above me and did a lot of shopping in high-end stores like Saks and Bergdorf's. No matter how many times she woke me up in the middle of the night, giggling with whoever was helping her up the stairs, it never dawned on me that she might have been a call girl.

Although it was almost impossible to get any real work done in this environment, I did manage to produce something that made me proud. It was a literary essay that I wrote as a favor to my friend, the philosophy student, who was so panicked about the course assignment he couldn't put his mind to it. With the help of a diet pill, I worked all night and turned over the piece in the morning. The weight of my crime didn't register until a few days later, when my friend the philosopher came pounding on my door with the terrible news that his professor had liked the essay so much he wanted to submit it to a professional journal. I honestly don't remember what action my co-conspirator took, or what he did with his copy of the essay, but I tore mine up into little pieces and flushed it down the toilet.

Clearly, I needed to get out of this house to work on my project. Since my field of study had a medical component, I chose to do my research at the New York Academy of Medicine, which maintains an incomparable library on my research topic and was within walking distance of my seedy neighborhood.

Let me tell you a little something about the New York Academy of Medicine. Founded in 1847, this renowned institution is one of the largest medical libraries in the United States. Its contemporary holdings are rich in esoteric materials not published through conventional channels, and its (gasp!) rare books and special collections are comparable to those of the National Library of Medicine. Most of these treasures go back a ways, some to the fifteenth century, with the lion's share (85 percent) of the books, manuscripts, pamphlets, periodicals, and broadsides in its Americana collection printed between the late sixteenth and early nineteenth centuries.

But that's not really what drew me to the library of the NYAM. It was the mansion on

Upper Fifth Avenue

in which it's housed. Snugly positioned between Mount Sinai Hospital and the Museum of the City of New York, this impressive edifice went up in 1926, designed by the architectural firm of York and Sawyer with all the frills and flounces of the early Romanesque style. That means rounded arches, fluted colonnettes, and carved capitals adorning the facade of the stone palazzo, and interior spaces consisting of large, imposing rooms with coffered ceilings, carved wood paneling, marble staircases, and intricately patterned parquet floors.

Each morning I would strike out for this temple of learning in the crisp autumn air (later, in the cold blast of a New York winter) with a sense of purpose and the conviction that this was where I belonged. Once I was settled in at one of the long wooden tables in the main reading room, under the warmth of a leaded-glass table lamp, I always felt a great sense of peace. And if I should happen to close my eyes, the hushed sounds of pages turning and pencils scratching and wooden chairs scraping on a hardwood floor transported me back to Butler Library and the Widener and even my beloved public library in Boston.

I had always been a meticulous notetaker, so I would arrive early each morning with a fresh notebook that I would proceed to fill with page after page after page of carefully composed, precisely detailed notes written in what I have to admit was a very schoolgirlish script. At some point around midday I would slouch off to the cafeteria at Mount Sinai Hospital (how's that for a depressing luncheon spot?)

and eat a student meal of hot soup and a free roll, and then slouch back to my cocoon for the rest of the day.

Was I happy? Outside library hours and on dark Sundays, I wouldn't go that far. But so long as I was under a reading lamp or flipping through the card files, I was as happy as could be. Given the germ phobia that now rules our lives, I can't imagine any modern-day student tearing himself away from a computer screen and handling those ancient pieces of cardboard without wearing surgical gloves and a mask. But to me, those musty wooden drawers, packed with dirty, thumb-worn cards covered in the handwritten citations of long-dead librarians, smelled more delicious than mountain air.

At some point over that long winter, don't ask me when, my daily library visits began tapering off. The notebooks weren't piling up at the same frantic pace. Some days, I didn't even come back after lunch. And by the time I got used to my new job at a neighborhood newspaper in Brooklyn (a job that was only supposed to tide me over until I got a grant), I seemed to have lost interest in my research project.

It would be nice to say that I recently came across those old notebooks and discovered that my thesis was, indeed, brilliant. Didn't happen. Like the essay I wrote for my friend, that research work is well and truly lost. But thinking about those months I spent in the reading

The Library Reading Room at the New York Academy of Medicine. Courtesy of The New York Academy of Medicine

room of the New York Academy of Medicine library made me wonder if that kind of research was even possible anymore.

A visit to the website assured me that, while the bulk of its treasures are digitally accessible, the physical library of the NYAM had not moved from its stately digs on

Upper Fifth Avenue.

So, if you desperately needed to get a look at Zabdiel Boylston's actual 1730 "Historical Account of the Small-Pox Inoculated in New England," it could be arranged. Of course, you couldn't gain access just by waving a student ID under somebody's nose the way I did, but the library is still open to the public and the need to make an appointment hardly seems like an onerous condition.

Having met that condition, I recently returned to the very place where I had spent so many months working on a research project that I would never finish.

The first hint that this might not be a happy stroll down memory lane was the fact that the entrance to the library was not on

Fifth Avenue,

as I'd remembered it, but around the corner on a side street. There was also the sobering statement that "our resources are housed in closed stacks and cannot be browsed." But that was always the deal, and besides, you can't hardly browse anything in the actual world these days.

There happened to be actual librarians on the premises of the NYAM, and one of them allowed me into the original library reading room—which wasn't there. That is to say, the room itself was where it was supposed to be. So were certain important markers, like the antique tapestry hanging on the back wall, the wall-to-wall bookcases that held leather-bound medical journals, the marble busts of pioneers in the medical field. Even the old patron call-board—where your number popped up when the books you requested were delivered from the stacks to the front desk—was still up. (For some reason, that killed me.) But the reading room as such was no more.

The vast room had been stripped to the walls and was currently being rented out for private events. On the day of my visit, there were two bare twenty-four-foot-long library tables in the middle of the floor. A dais had been set up at the far end, along with a lectern and, behind it,

The Drs. Barry and Bobbi Coller Rare Book Reading Room at the New York Academy of Medicine. Courtesy of the New York Academy of Medicine

a screen for PowerPoint presentations. So the upcoming event scheduled for these palatial quarters could have been anything from a wedding reception to a medical event hosted by Mount Sinai.

No damage had been done to the room, but along with everything
else I remembered, the familiar library aroma was gone.

I must have looked stricken, because my guide gently led me to the
Drs. Barry and Bobbi Coller Rare Book Reading Room, which houses
a significant part of the rare book collection. And there they were, the
touchstones of my academic life: the richly aged library tables . . . the
heavy old chairs with the spindle backs and broad-bottomed seats . . .
the inlaid cork floors . . . the warm table lamps . . . even those wonderful hardwood library steps they don't make anymore.

But no card files. Well, what did I expect? The NYAM went over
to computers in 1986, and digital archiving of the library was almost
complete. Almost. The librarians may answer some fifteen hundred
queries a year electronically, but in the hallway there were some lone
survivors—old-fashioned, upright cabinets made of heavy oak, stacked
from top to bottom with little drawers of alphabetized card files and
sliding panels to hold them steady while your fingers searched.

It was a long shot, but maybe they hadn't gotten to "S" yet. I
skimmed the brass-edged windows of the numbered drawers, looking
for . . . yes! There it was, Drawer Number 728, "SUB—SUMMERLY." That
was my very drawer, and within that drawer were the very files I pored
over for so many months, obsessively researching a subject that seemed
terribly important to me at the time, but faded away before I managed
to do anything definitive about it: "SUICIDE."

MARILYN STASIO is the Broadway theater critic for *Variety*, a columnist
with the *New York Times Book Review*, and the author of several books.